JUST ALGORITHMS

Statistically-derived algorithms, adopted by many jurisdictions in an effort to identify the risk of reoffending posed by criminal defendants, have been lambasted as racist, de-humanizing, and antithetical to the foundational tenets of criminal justice. *Just Algorithms* argues that these attacks are misguided and that, properly regulated, risk assessment tools can be a crucial means of safely and humanely dismantling our massive jail and prison complex. The book explains how risk algorithms work, the types of legal questions they should answer, and the criteria for judging whether they do so in a way that minimizes bias and respects human dignity. It also shows how risk assessment instruments can provide leverage for curtailing draconian prison sentences and the plea-bargaining system that produces them. The ultimate goal of Christopher Slobogin's insightful analysis is to develop the principles that should govern, in both the pretrial and sentencing settings, the criminal justice system's consideration of risk.

Christopher Slobogin holds the Milton Underwood Chair at Vanderbilt University Law School. He has authored or co-authored eight books and over 150 articles on criminal justice issues. He is one of the most heavily cited law professors in the criminal justice field and is the only law professor to have received Distinguished Scholar awards from both the American Psychology-Law Society and the American Board of Forensic Psychology.

Just Algorithms

USING SCIENCE TO REDUCE INCARCERATION AND INFORM A JURISPRUDENCE OF RISK

CHRISTOPHER SLOBOGIN
Vanderbilt University Law School

CAMBRIDGE
UNIVERSITY PRESS

CAMBRIDGE
UNIVERSITY PRESS

University Printing House, Cambridge CB2 8BS, United Kingdom

One Liberty Plaza, 20th Floor, New York, NY 10006, USA

477 Williamstown Road, Port Melbourne, VIC 3207, Australia

314–321, 3rd Floor, Plot 3, Splendor Forum, Jasola District Centre, New Delhi – 110025, India

79 Anson Road, #06–04/06, Singapore 079906

Cambridge University Press is part of the University of Cambridge.

It furthers the University's mission by disseminating knowledge in the pursuit of education, learning, and research at the highest international levels of excellence.

www.cambridge.org
Information on this title: www.cambridge.org/9781108833974
DOI: 10.1017/9781108988025

First published 2021

A catalogue record for this publication is available from the British Library.

ISBN 978-1-108-83397-4 Hardback
ISBN 978-1-108-98434-8 Paperback

Contents

Preface: The Point of This Book

In today's world, algorithms are everywhere. Algorithms—a shorthand way of describing statistical and computer driven decision-making processes—are crucial to our commercial and social life. Insurance companies use them to set premiums, credit card companies rely on them to detect fraud, and investors depend on them to figure out market trends. Algorithms permeate the Internet, smart phones, marketing, and the forecasting of virtually everything, from weather to sports outcomes to pandemics.

Not surprisingly, government agencies rely on algorithms as well, to conduct tax audits, welfare checks, police investigations, and DNA and other forensic analysis.[1] Of most significance to this book, for at least a decade virtually every state has authorized the use of algorithms that purport to determine the recidivism risk posed by people who have been charged or convicted of crime.[2] Commonly called *risk assessment instruments*, or RAIs, these algorithms help judges figure out whether arrested individuals should be released pending trial and whether convicted offenders should receive prison time or an enhanced sentence; they assist parole boards in determining whether to release a prisoner; and they aid correctional officials in deciding

[1] See David Freedman Engstrom et al., Government by Algorithm: Artificial Intelligence in Federal Administrative Agencies, at https://ssrn.com/abstract=3551505; Susan Miller, How Law Enforcement Uses Forensic Algorithms, GCN, May 12, 2020, at https://gcn.com/articles/2020/05/12/gao-forensic-algorithms.aspx.

[2] Memorandum from the Vera Inst. of Justice, Ctr. on Sentencing & Corr. to Del. Justice Reinvestment Task Force 4 (Oct. 12, 2011), at http://www.ma4jr.org/wp-content/uploads/2014/10/vera-institute-memo-on-risk-assessment-for-delaware-2011.pdf ("almost every state uses an assessment tool at one or more points in the criminal justice system to assist in the better management of offenders in institutions and in the community. Overall, over 60 community supervision agencies in 41 states reported using an actuarial assessment tool, suggesting that an overwhelming majority of corrections agencies nationwide routinely utilize assessment tools to some degree.").

how offenders should be handled in prison. Most of these algorithms consist of from five to twenty *risk factors* associated with criminal history, age, and diagnosis, although an increasing number incorporate other demographic traits and psychological factors as well. Each of these risk factors correlates with a certain number of points that are usually added to compute a person's risk score; the higher the score, the higher the risk. Some tools may also aim at identifying *needs*, such as substance abuse treatment and vocational training, thought to be relevant to rehabilitative interventions that might reduce recidivism. This book will provide examples of a number of these instruments so that the reader can get a sense of their diversity and nuances.

One purpose of this book is to explain how risk algorithms might improve the criminal justice system. If developed and used properly, RAIs could become a major tool of reform. Most importantly, they can help reduce the use of pretrial detention and prison, as well as the length of prison sentences, without appreciably increasing the peril to the public (goals that are particularly pressing as COVID-19 ravages our penal facilities). In doing so, they can mitigate the excessively punitive bail and sentencing regimes that currently exist in most states. They can also allocate correctional resources more efficiently and consistently. And they can provide the springboard for evidence-based rehabilitative programs aimed at reducing recidivism. More broadly, by making criminal justice decision-making more transparent, these tools could force long overdue reexamination of the purposes of the criminal justice system and of the outcomes it should be trying to achieve.

Despite their potential advantages, the risk algorithms used in the criminal justice system today are highly controversial. A common claim is that they are not good at what they purport to do, which is to identify who will offend and who will not, who will be responsive to rehabilitative efforts and who will not be. But the tools are also maligned as racially biased, dehumanizing, and, for good measure, antithetical to the foundational principles of criminal justice. A sampling of recent article and book titles makes the point: "Impoverished Algorithms: Misguided Governments, Flawed Technologies, and Social Control,"[3] "Risk as a Proxy for Race: The Dangers of Risk Assessment,"[4] and "Automating Inequality: How High-Tech Tools Profile, Police, and Punish the Poor."[5] In 2019, over 110 civil rights groups signed a statement calling for an

3 Sarah Valentine, Impoverished Algorithms: Misguided Governments, Flawed Technologies, and Social Control, 44 Fordham Urb. L. 364 (2019).

4 Bernard Harcourt, Risk as a Proxy for Race: The Dangers of Risk Assessment, 27 Fed. Sent. Rep. 237 (2015).

5 Virginia Eubanks, Automating Inequality: How High-Tech Tools Profile, Police, and Punish the Poor (2018).

end to pretrial risk assessment instruments.[6] That same year twenty-seven Ivy League and MIT academics stated that "technical problems" with risk assessment instruments "cannot be resolved."[7] And in 2020 another group of 2435 scholars from a wide range of disciplines "demanded" that Springer publishing company, one of the largest purveyors of healthcare and behavioral science books and journals, "issue a statement condemning the use of criminal justice statistics to predict criminality" because of their unscientific nature.[8]

A second purpose of this book is to explore these claims. All of them have some basis in fact. But they can easily be overblown. And if the impact of these criticisms is to prevent the criminal justice system from using algorithms, a potentially valuable means of reform will be lost. A key argument in favor of algorithms is comparative in nature. While algorithms can be associated with a number of problems, alternative predictive techniques may well be much worse in each of these respects. Unstructured decision-making by judges, parole officers, and mental health professionals is notoriously bad, biased, and reflexive, and often relies on stereotypes and generalizations that ignore the goals of the system. Algorithms can do better, at least if subject to certain constraints.

Surfacing those constraints is a third purpose of this book. Although algorithms, on average, are superior to unstructured judgment when it comes to prediction, many are seriously defective in a number of respects. This book provides a set of principles meant to govern the risk assessment enterprise. Influenced by insights gleaned from the algorithms themselves, it advances, in short, a much-needed "jurisprudence of risk" analogous to the jurisprudence of criminal liability that has long governed the definition of crimes and the scope of punishment.

Without a jurisprudence of risk, judges and other legal decision-makers have very little guidance concerning which RAIs, if any, are worthy of consideration, how to evaluate their results, and how much weight to give those results. Social scientists and other researchers who develop these instruments do not have a clear idea of the outcome measures that the law considers relevant, the types of risk factors they may or may not consider, or the

6 The Use of Pretrial "Risk Assessment" Instruments: A Shared Statement of Civil Rights Concerns (Jan. 2019), at https://www.supremecourt.ohio.gov/JCS/casemng/PJRSummit/materials/pretrialRiskAssessInstruments.pdf.

7 Chelsea Barabas, Karthik Dinakar & Colin Doyle, The Problems with Risk Assessment Tools, N.Y. Times (July 17, 2019), at https://dam-prod.media.mit.edu/x/2019/07/16/TechnicalFlawsOfPretrial_ML%20site.pdf.

8 Coalition for Critical Technology, Abolish the #TechtoPrison pipeline (Dec. 30, 2020), at https://medium.com/@CoalitionForCriticalTechnology/abolish-the-techtoprisonpipeline-9b5b14366b16.

psychometric properties that ensure courts will rely on the instrument they develop. In the meantime, to the extent risk assessment influences the pretrial or postconviction process, the fate of offenders, the safety of the public, and even the pace of incarceration rates are subject to a hodgepodge of inchoate views about the impact risk should have on disposition.

The first part of the book's title points to one important aspect of this jurisprudence of risk. If the recommendations in this book are followed, the usual approach taken by legal decision-makers—which is to treat the algorithmic forecast as simply one factor relevant to risk assessment—would generally be impermissible. "Adjusting" the results of a well-validated RAI, based on instincts and experience, defeats the purpose of using an RAI, especially when the decision-maker's intuition about risk is based on factors that have already been considered in the tool. Incorporating human judgment into the risk assessment will usually make matters worse when the RAI meets the basic requirements outlined in this book. This notion is one meaning—the literal one—of "Just Algorithms."

The second meaning of that title is even more important. Properly cabined, predictive algorithms can be just. Numerous writers have argued to the contrary, pointing in particular to racial disparities among those who are identified as high risk. But even if such disparities do exist, they do not necessarily make risk algorithms unjust. This book takes the position that the fairest approach to evaluating risk is to treat people who are of equal risk equally. The primary goal of an RAI should be to identify accurately those who are high risk and those who are low risk, regardless of color, even if that means that a greater percentage of people of color are identified as high risk. At the same time, it must be recognized that assessments of risk may be inaccurate if the influence of racialized policing and prosecutorial practices on the validity of assessment instruments is not taken into account.

Another, related complaint about predictive algorithms—one that has special salience at sentencing and other post-conviction settings—is that punishment should never be based on conduct that has not yet occurred, both given the uncertainty of prediction and its insult to human dignity and autonomy. The point this book makes on this score is, again, a comparative one. The primary competitor to sentencing that considers risk is a purely retributive system—one that relies solely on backward-looking assessments of criminal conduct and the mental states that accompany it. But such a system is rife with speculative claims about just desert, and can be remarkably inattentive to the impact of mitigating human foibles. Properly regulated algorithmic risk assessments, in contrast, can differentiate high and low risk offenders at least as reliably as judges and juries can calibrate culpability, and can do so without abandoning condemnation based on blame, especially if sentence ranges are still based on retributive principles. The needs part of the assessment can also facilitate the identification of autonomy-affirming and dignity-enhancing treatment programs that help offenders help themselves.

To take full advantage of risk assessment's potential for curbing incarceration and rationalizing sentencing, however, we must also rethink our current punishment regime, which is a fourth goal of this book. In the past fifty years, a large number of states have moved away from indeterminate sentences controlled by parole boards toward determinate sentencing, which shifts power to prosecutors who can now essentially dictate the sentence received after trial through the charging decision. Most of the states that have not adopted determinate sentencing have effectively gone in the same direction by significantly circumscribing the authority of parole boards to make release decisions. These changes were understandable, given the dispositional disparities that occurred with indeterminate sentencing, the checkered history of parole boards, and the difficulty of assessing risk and rehabilitative potential.

With the advent of more accurate and objective predictive algorithms, however, indeterminate sentencing should be given a second chance. More specifically, while judges should still impose a sentence range that is determined by desert, risk-needs algorithms should be instrumental in determining whether offenders who are imprisoned stay there beyond the minimum term of that sentence. Sentencing would no longer be based on convoluted front-end calculations which attempt to divine the precise culpability of the offender, tempered or enhanced by the prosecutor's or the judge's speculative intuitions about deterrence, risk, or rehabilitative goals. Rather, after the judge imposes the retributively defined sentence range based on the charge of conviction, offenders would serve the minimum sentence (which for misdemeanors and lower level felonies might not involve prison), and only be subject to prolonged restraint if they are determined to be high risk via a validated risk assessment instrument. In this form of limiting retributivism, desert would set the range of the sentence, risk its nature and duration.

With this type of sentencing system, not only will the arbitrariness of the old parole-driven scheme be reduced, but the power structure within the criminal justice system will be profitably reoriented. Today, the plea bargaining process allows prosecutors to threaten draconian sentences that bludgeon defendants, even innocent ones, into accepting convictions without trial. If, instead, post-trial dispositions within the sentence range depend on a parole board's determination of risks and needs, the ultimate disposition after a trial will be unknowable, and prosecutorial bargaining power inevitably would be reduced. Defendants can turn down prosecutorial offers with virtual impunity if they are considered low risk. And even high risk defendants might want to roll the dice with the parole board. Innocent people would be much less likely to plead guilty, and guilty people would be much less likely to acquiesce to harshly punitive bargains. The prosecutor's main leverage will come from offers of reduced charges or alternatives to prison, because with parole boards controlling release, threats to recommend the maximum sentence to the judge will be meaningless.

These proposals may appear to be radical. But in fact they merely reinstate a version of the sentencing regimes that existed in much of this country before the middle of the twentieth century, when dispositions were more flexible and plea bargaining and guilty pleas were less dominant. At the same time, a key difference in these proposals, and the primary reason rejuvenating indeterminate sentencing is justifiable, is the reliance on risk assessment algorithms. Without them, judges and parole boards are simply guessing about dangerousness, and their default judgment—absent heroic efforts to resist public pressure and normal human risk-averseness—will be to find that offenders pose a high risk of reoffending. With them—and assuming their results are treated as presumptive—judges who refuse to imprison an offender and parole boards that make a release decision can point to known base rates (which, in the case of violent crime, are very low) and can blame the algorithm if things go awry.

The overarching hypothesis of this book is this: whether implemented prior to trial in lieu of the bail system, or post-conviction in lieu of unstructured predictive decision-making, just algorithms can be a central component of any effort to reduce the human and financial cost of incarceration, without sacrificing public safety. That hypothesis may be wrong, but it is worth a fair test. Because when developed and used in a manner consistent with a coherent jurisprudence of risk, algorithms could be the single most potent mechanism we have for bringing about real reform of the American criminal justice system.

***

I would like to thank the Charles Koch Foundation for supporting the research that went into this book, as well as the following experts who provided useful feedback: Sarah Desmarais, Melissa Hamilton, Rhys Hester, Cecelia Klingele, John Monahan, Sandra Mayson, Michael O'Hear, Kevin Reitz, Ed Rubin, Jennifer Skeem, and Megan Stevenson. Much of this book derives from my previous work: *How Changes in American Culture Triggered Hyper-Incarceration: Variations on the Tazian View*, 58 Howard L. J. 305 (2015); *Principles of Risk Assessment: Sentencing and Policing*, 15 Ohio St. J Crim.

L. 583 (2018); *Preventive Justice: How Algorithms, Parole Boards and Limiting Retributivism Could End Mass Incarceration*, 56 Wake Forest L. Rev. 97 (2021); *A Defence of Modern Risk-Based Sentencing*, in Predictive Sentencing: Normative and Empirical Perspectives 107 (J. de Keijser et al., eds., 2019) (Hart Publishing); *Limiting Retributivism and Individual Prevention*, in The Routledge Handbook on the Philosophy and Science of Punishment 49 (Farah Focquaert, ed., 2021) (Routledge Press), and *Plea Bargaining and the Substantive and Procedural Goals of Criminal Justice: From Retribution and Adversarialism to Preventive Justice and Hybrid-Inquisitorialism*, 57 Wm. & Mary L. Rev. 1505 (2016).

For those with a legal background, I would also like to direct attention to a shorter publication of mine, Primer on Risk Assessment Instruments for Legal Decisionmakers, which can be found at https://law.vanderbilt.edu/academics/academic-programs/criminal-justice-program/Primer_on_Risk_Assessment.pdf. This 32-page document provides an overview of the debates about risk assessment, and provides legal decisionmakers with a series of principles and questions that can inform decisions about whether and when to use a risk assessment instrument.

1

Rationale

What Risk Algorithms Can Do for the Criminal Justice System

Risk algorithms can help mitigate three of the most pressing problems associated with the criminal justice system today: high incarceration rates, racial disproportionality, and the soaring costs of prisons and jails. All three problems are driven by the uniquely American phenomenon known as mass incarceration. Some understanding of that phenomenon helps highlight the ways risk algorithms can be useful.

1.1 THE PLAGUE OF MASS INCARCERATION

The incarceration rate in the United States has skyrocketed since the late 1960s—from the neighborhood of 100 people per 100,000 to somewhere between 500 to 700 people per 100,000—so that now prisons and jails house well over two million individuals.[1] A huge proportion of that number are people who have not even been convicted. Back in 1982, we only booked about 50 percent of the people police arrested; over three decades later we are jailing 95 percent of arrestees and either demanding that they forfeit bail (usually according to preset schedules), or explicitly detaining them as flight or recidivism risks under the federal Bail Reform Act of 1984

[1] Compare Roy Walmsley, Institute for Criminal Policy Research, World Prison Population List 6 tbl.2 (12th ed. 2018), available at https://www.prisonstudies.org/sites/default/files/resources/downloads/wppl_12.pdf (listing the U.S. rate as 655 per 100,000) with E. Ann Carson, U.S. Dep't. of Justice, NCJ 253516 Prisoners in 2018, at 9 tbl.5 & 10 tbl.6 (2020), available at https://www.bjs.gov/content/pub/pdf/p18.pdf (listing the U.S. rate of those sentenced to *a year or longer* as 431 per 100,000 for residents of all ages and 555 per 100,000 for residents age 18 or older, despite also including individuals in "boot camps, halfway houses, treatment facilities, hospitals, local jails, or another state's facilities").

and its state counterparts.[2] At a cost of over $20 billion a year,[3] jails annually log over twelve million admissions, some of which involve misdemeanants who have been sentenced, but over 60 percent of whom are poor people arrested for minor offenses, including traffic offenses, who cannot post bail.[4] Many of these people are incarcerated for the entire time needed to resolve their cases, meaning they may spend months in jail, even when they end up being acquitted or having their charges dropped.[5] In the meantime, their families suffer, their jobs disappear, and they are subject to the degradations of incarceration.[6] In felony cases, pretrial detention can be even more prolonged. For instance, in federal cases the average time from arrest to resolution averages over six months for felony cases, despite statutory speedy trial rules that attempt to limit that period to 100 days.[7]

When people *are* convicted and sentenced today, they too are incarcerated more often and for longer periods of time than ever before. For instance, the average time spent in prison for noncapital murder before the 1970s was never over twenty-five years; now, the mean duration of such sentences is upwards of sixty years.[8] One in nine prisoners are serving life sentences and a third of these, or well over 50,000, are saddled with life

2 Ram Subramanian et al., Vera Inst. of Justice, Incarceration's Front Door: The Misuse of Jails in America 22 (Patricia Connelly, ed., 2015), available at https://www.vera.org/downloads/publications/incarcerations-front-door-report_02.pdf.

3 Christian Henrichson, Joshua Rinaldi & Ruth Delaney, Vera Inst. of Justice, The Price of Jails: Measuring the Taxpayer Cost of Local Incarceration 4 (Jules Verdone & Patricia Connelly, eds., 2015), available at https://www.vera.org/downloads/publications/price-of-jails.pdf.

4 Subramanian et al., supra note 2, at 5, available at separate site https://www.vera.org/ending-mass-incarceration/reducing-the-use-of-jails ("nearly 75 percent of the population of both sentenced offenders and pretrial detainees are in jail for nonviolent traffic, property, drug, or public order offenses").

5 Eli Rosenberg, Judge in Houston Strikes Down Harris County's Bail System, N.Y. Times (Apr. 29, 2017), https://www.nytimes.com/2017/04/29/us/judge-strikes-down-harris-county-bail-system.html?mcubz=1.

6 *See* Nick Pinto, The Bail Trap, N.Y. Times Mag. (Aug. 13, 2015), available at http://www.nytimes.com/2015/08/16/magazine/the-bail-trap.html?_r=1 (describing the consequences of pretrial detention on poor defendants in New York's criminal justice system, including lost wages, homes, child custody, and opportunity to meaningfully assist in the defense).

7 See Christopher Slobogin, The Case for a Federal Criminal Court (and Sentencing Reform), 108 Cal. L. Rev. 941, 946–47 (2020) (reporting data compiled by Ryan Vacca indicating that the median processing time for criminal cases was 92 days for the 5 years from 1972 to 1976 and 219 days for the 5 years from 2013 to 2017).

8 William J. Stuntz, *The Collapse of American Criminal Justice* 237 (2011) (chart). See also N. Mullane, *Life after Murder: Five Men in Search of Redemption* 147 (2012) (stating that "a person serving a life sentence with the possibility of parole in California has a greater chance of dying in prison than of ever getting out of prison on parole").

without parole.[9] Only about half of the prisoners serving life sentences were convicted of homicide; about 10,000, or about 5 percent of the total, committed nonviolent offenses, predominantly drug- and property-related offenses.[10] Further, well over one hundred thousand individuals are imprisoned each year on "technical violations" of probation and parole for routine behavior such as drinking, missing appointments, or leaving the jurisdiction;[11] in twenty states more than half of all yearly admissions are for such supervision violations.[12] Overall, about 70 percent of those who are convicted are sent to prison, for an average sentence of three years.[13]

Particularly troubling is the fact that this hyper-incarceration does not appear to have had a significant impact on crime rates. Those rates *have* gone down in the last decade or so. But, as one report summarized the findings of several studies, "[r]igorous social science research based on decades of data shows that increased incarceration played an extremely limited role in the crime decline."[14] Another study similarly concluded that America's "severe punishment" regime has had little to do with the crime drop, given analogous drops in many European countries.[15] Perhaps most importantly, the

9 The Sentencing Project, Life Goes On: The Historic Rise in Life Sentences in America 1, 8 (2016), available at https://www.sentencingproject.org/wp-content/uploads/2016/01/Trends-in-US-Corrections.pdf.

10 Id.

11 Council of State Governments, Confined and Costly: How Supervision Violations are Filling Prisons and Burdening Budgets 1 (2019), available at https://csgjusticecenter.org/wp-content/uploads/2020/01/confined-and-costly.pdf (showing that 25 percent of the 590,234 admissions to state prisons in 2017 were for technical violations).

12 Id. at 2.

13 Ram Subramanian & Alison Shames, Vera Inst. of Justice, Sentencing and Prison Practices in Germany and the Netherlands: Implications for the United States 10 (Patricia Connelly & Mary Crowley, eds., 2013), available at https://www.vera.org/downloads/Publications/sentencing-and-prison-practices-in-germany-and-the-netherlands-implications-for-the-united-states/legacy_downloads/european-american-prison-report-v3.pdf. See also, Mark Motivans, U.S. Dep't. of Justice, NCJ 251770 Federal Justice Statistics, 2015–2016, at 10 tbl.7 (2019), available at https://www.bjs.gov/content/pub/pdf/fjs1516.pdf (median federal sentence is thirty months).

14 James Austin & Lauren-Brooke Eisen with James Cullen & Jonathan Frank, Brennan Ctr. for Justice, How Many Americans Are Unnecessarily Incarcerated?, at 21 (2016), available at https://www.brennancenter.org/sites/default/files/publications/Unnecessarily_Incarcerated_0.pdf. See also Holgar Spamann, The U.S. Crime Puzzle: A Comparative Perspective on U.S. Crime and Punishment, available at http://ssrn.com/abstract=2463720 (2014) (concluding, based on regression analysis, that "either residual US punishment is not working, or some omitted factor, such as segregation, pushes up the latent US crime rate"); Justin McCrary & Sarath Sanga, General Equilibrium Effects of Prison on Crime: Evidence from International Comparisons, 13 Cato Papers on Public Policy 165 (2012) (concluding that the five-fold increase in incarceration since the 1970s has had, at best, a modest impact on crime).

15 Andromachi Tseloni et al., Exploring the International Decline in Crime Rates, 7 Eur. J. Criminol. 375, 389 (2010).

data show that twenty-seven states have managed to reduce *both* imprisonment and crime.[16]

As this last statistic suggests, prison growth has moderated somewhat in the past several years[17]. But, as Nazgol Ghandnoosh notes, while the decarceration trend in the United States began in 2010, "the pace of contraction has been slow: a total decline of 3% by 2014"; she concludes that, at that rate, it will take until 2101 for the prison population to return to its 1980 level.[18] Furthermore, state-by-state prison growth rates vary tremendously. Despite declining crime rates since 2000, including a drop of more than 50 percent in violent crime from its peak in the early 1990s,[19] twenty-five states have seen an *increase* in their prison populations over the past decade.[20] And while eight states have managed to reduce their prison populations by more than 20 percent since 2000, that has not put much of a dent in the 600 percent increase in the national prison population since the 1970s.[21]

As these numbers indicate, sentencing severity is not a trend that has come and gone. Since 2008, the number of convicted criminals serving life sentences has increased by nearly 12 percent, and the number serving life sentences without the option of parole by over 32 percent.[22] In 1984 an inmate

16 Austin & Eisen, supra note 14, at 21.

17 Jacob Kang-Brown et al., Vera Inst. of Justice, People in Prison in 2018, at 1–2 (Léon Digard, ed., 2019), available at https://www.vera.org/downloads/publications/people-in-prison-in-2018-updated.pdf (noting a 1.8 percent drop in prisoners but also noting the drop is largely attributable to reductions in four states and federal prisons, while "[t]he number of people in prison increased in 19 states").

18 Nazgol Ghandnoosh, Minimizing the Maximum: The Case for Shortening All Prison Sentences, in Smart Decarceration: Achieving Criminal Justice Transformation in the 21st Century 137, 139 (Matthew W. Epperson & Carrie Pettus-Davis, eds., 2017). See also Malcom C. Young, Why "Tweaking Around the Edges" Won't Reduce Mass Incarceration, The Crime Report (May 2, 2019), available at https://thecrimereport.org/2019/05/02/why-tweaking-around-the-edges-wont-reduce-mass-incarceration/.

19 Federal Bureau of Investigation, Estimated Violent Crime Total, Uniform Crime Reporting Statistics, available at https://ucrdatatool.gov/Search/Crime/State/TrendsInOneVar.cfm (select "United States-Total" in the dropdown menu labeled "a."; click "Get Table") (showing that violent crimes peaked in 1992 at 1,932,274 and was at its lowest in 2014 (the last year for which data is available) at 1,197,987).

20 Jennifer Bronson & E. Ann Carson, U.S. Dep't of Justice, Prisoners in 2017, tbl. 2 (2019) with Heather C. West & William J. Sabol, U.S. Dep't of Justice, Prisoners in 2007, tbl. 2 (2009).

21 Id.

22 Ashley Nellis, The Sentencing Project, Still Life: America's Increasing Use of Life and Long-Term Sentences 7 fig.1, 9 (2017), available at https://www.sentencingproject.org/publications/still-life-americas-increasing-use-life-long-term-sentences/ (showing that 142,727 people were serving life sentences in 2008 while 161,957 people were serving life sentences in 2016, and stating that 53,290 people were serving life sentences without parole in 2016); Ashley Nellis, The Sentencing Project, Life Goes On: The Historic Rise in Life Sentences in America 1 (2013), available at https://www.sentencingproject.org/wp-content/uploads/2015/12/Life-Goes-

convicted of manslaughter or murder served, on average, 9.2 years; by 2004, that figure had increased to 14.27 years.[23] During that same period, time served for rape increased from 5 to 8 years, for robbery from 3.5 to 5 years,[24] and for drug offenders from 22 months to 62 months; by 2017 there were nearly 11 times as many drug offenders in prison as there were in 1980.[25]

Compare these figures to what has been going on in Western Europe, which demographically and politically is the polity most comparable to the United States. The number of people detained prior to trial in the twenty-seven member states of the European Union is roughly one-third the number of pretrial detainees in the U.S., despite the fact that the EU has a population 150 million greater than ours; in Germany, for instance, only 3 to 5 percent of arrested individuals are remanded to custody.[26] And our overall *post-conviction* imprisonment rate is at least *six* times that of Western Europe's:[27] the rate per 100,000 of countries like Germany, France, and the Netherlands is below 100, and in the United Kingdom in the low one-hundreds.[28] Even the rates of most eastern European countries are less than half of ours.[29] To get our pace of imprisonment anywhere near that of Western Europe's, we'd have to release 1.8 million inmates.[30]

Our penalty structure is also much harsher than that of most Western European countries. We have the death penalty in twenty-eight states,[31] while European countries have banned capital punishment.[32] While the practice has recently been curbed, we still allow life sentences for juveniles.[33] Europe does

On.pdf (stating that in 2008 there were 40,174 individuals serving life sentences without parole).

23 Steven Raphael & Michael A. Stoll, Why Are So Many Americans in Prison? 50–51 (2013).

24 Allen J. Beck & Alfred Blumstein, Trends in U.S. Incarceration Rates: 1980–2010 28 (2012).

25 The Sentencing Project, Trends in U.S. Corrections 3 (2017), available at http://sentencingproject.org/doc/publications/inc_Trends_in_Corrections_Fact_sheet.pdf.

26 Christine Morgenstern, Alternatives to Pre-trial Detention (Gerben Bruinsma & David Weisburd, eds., 2014), available at https://research-paper.essayempire.com/examples/alternatives-to-pre-trial-detention-research-paper/.

27 Walmsley, supra note 1, at 12–13 tbl.4.

28 Id.

29 Id. at 14.

30 Kevin Reitz, American Exceptionalism in Crime and Punishment—Broadly Defined, in American Exceptionalism in Crime and Punishment 1, 4 (2018).

31 States With and Without the Death Penalty, Death Penalty Information Center (January, 2021), available at https://deathpenaltyinfo.org/state-and-federal-info/state-by-state.

32 Charter of Fundamental Rights of the European Union, art. 2, available at www.europarl.europa.eu/charter/pdf/text_en.pdf (banning the death penalty in member states).

33 Graham v. Florida, 130 S.Ct. 2011, 2015 (2010) (stating that seven jurisdictions permit life without parole for juvenile offenders for homicide crimes and thirty-seven states, the District of Columbia, and the Federal Government permit sentences of life without parole for

not.[34] While 10 percent of our adult prisoners are serving life sentences (representing more than the entire American prison population in 1970),[35] a few European countries—Portugal, Spain, and Norway—do not allow life sentences even for adults.[36] In most other European countries the percentage of life sentences is much lower than 10 percent—in France, for instance, it is about 0.8 percent, in Germany 3 percent, and in Italy 5 percent.[37] Moreover, in those European countries that have life sentences, virtually none recognizes life without parole (LWOP). In contrast to our prolific use of LWOP, judicial reconsideration of a life sentence is usually required after a relatively "short" period of time—ten years in Belgium, fifteen years in Austria, Germany, Luxembourg, and Switzerland, and eighteen years in France, although in most of these countries judges individualize the minimum sentence, so it varies from case to case.[38] In practice, most prisoners are released well ahead of the full life sentence. In Austria for instance, 75 percent are released at fifteen years;[39] similarly, in Ireland a "mandatory" life sentence usually amounts to fifteen years.[40]

That pattern is followed for lesser sentences as well. In countries like Germany and the Netherlands, only about 30 percent of convicted offenders receive a prison sentence, compared to 70 percent in the U.S. And the average

a juvenile non-homicide offender in some circumstances). Miller v. Alabama, 467 U.S. 460 (2012), declared *mandatory* life without parole sentences unconstitutional, but life sentences with parole for that group are still permissible, and ten years ago roughly 7000 juveniles were serving such sentences. Ashley Nellis & Ryan S. King, No Exit: The Expanding Use of Life Sentences in America 3, 17–25 (2009), available at www.sentencingproject.org/doc/publications/publications/inc_ noexitseptember2009.pdf.

34 Connie de la Vega & Michelle Leighton, Sentencing our Children to Die in Prison: Global Law and Practice, 42 U. San Fran. L. Rev. 983, 989 (2008) (reporting that 135 countries, including every country in Europe, has expressly rejected life sentences for juveniles).

35 See The Sentencing Project, People Serving Life in Prison Exceeds Entire Prison Population of 1970 (Feb. 20, 2020), available at https://www.sentencingproject.org/publications/people-serving-life-exceeds-entire-prison-population-1970/.

36 Frieder Dünkel, Dirk van Zyl Smit & Nicola Padfield, Concluding Thoughts, in Release from Prison: European Policy and Practice 395, 420 (Nicola Padfield, Dirk van Zyl Smit & Frider Dünkel, eds., 2010) (hereafter European Policy and Practice).

37 Kim Reuflet, France, in European Policy and Practice, supra note 36, at 177 (indicating that "about 500 prisoners are serving life sentences" out of a prison population of 62,700) and Frieder Dünkel & Ineke Pruin, Germany, in European Policy and Practice, supra note 36, at 192–93 (1,973 prisoners serving a life sentence in a prison population of approximately 74,000) and Alessandra Gualazzi & Chiara Mancuso, Italy, in European Policy and Practice, supra note 36, at 266, 275 Table 11.2 (1,408 serving a life sentence out of a population of 26,587).

38 Dünkel, Zyl Smit & Padfield, supra note 36, at 408.

39 Karin Brickmüller & Veronika Hofinger, Austria, in European Policy and Practice, supra note 36, at 69 (Table 3.1.).

40 Thomas O'Malley, Ireland, in European Policy and Practice, supra note 36, at 238, 258.

sentence in those countries is less than twelve months, compared to three years in the U.S.[41]

1.2 WHY? CRIME, CULTURE, AND CODES

The gap between United States and European incarceration rates is astonishing. One explanation for these differences is our heightened crime rate. But it is a weak one. As Nora Deimleitner has pointed out, "a number of sophisticated statistical studies have shattered the myth that the United States and European countries have dramatically different crime rates," especially with respect to property crime.[42] Further, we are barely in the upper third of the pack in terms of simple assaults and burglaries.[43] In any event, our crime rate is nowhere near six times that of European countries, the current differential in imprisonment rates.

A more plausible theory is that, compared to European countries, we suffer proportionately more very-serious crimes than other types of crimes, which might justify a greater proportion of longer sentences. For instance, if one compares U.S. rates to those in EU nations, our homicide rate is nearly 30 percent higher than that of the nearest country and five times higher than the average European rate.[44] Even so, our homicide rate expressed as a fraction of all violent crimes is still less than 1 percent,[45] far below the 10 percent-plus life-sentence rate. As Tapio Lappa-Sepala concluded after an exhaustive statistical analysis, "in global comparison, the extraordinarily high U.S. incarceration rate cannot be explained by a higher victimization rate or by a higher homicide rate."[46]

So crime rates are not the only, or even the main reason, for our gargantuan incarceration numbers compared to Europe's.[47] Rather, it is highly likely that

41 Subramanian & Shames, supra note 13, at 9–10.

42 Nora V. Deimleitner, Is There a Future for Leniency in the United States Criminal Justice System? 103 U. Mich. L. Rev. 1231, 1264 (2005).

43 Nick Cowen, Civitas: Inst. for the Study of Civil Soc'y, Comparisons of Crime in OECD Countries 7–8 (2010), available at http://www.civitas.org.uk/content/files/crime_stats_oecd jan2012.pdf; Office on Drugs and Crime, Burglary, United Nations, available at https://datau nodc.un.org/data/crime/burglary.

44 Cowen, supra note 43, at 7–8.

45 For instance, in 2014, there were 11,961 homicides out of 1,197,987 violent crimes. Federal Bureau of Investigation Uniform Crime Reports, available at https://ucr.fbi.gov/crime-in-the-u .s/2014/crime-in-the-u.s.-2014/tables/expanded-homicide-data/expanded_homicide_data_table_8_ murder_victims_by_weapon_2010-2014.xls. See supra note 19 for method for accessing this cite.

46 Tapio Lappa-Sepala, American Exceptionalism in Comparative Perspective, in Reitz, supra note 30, at 256.

47 National Research Council et al., The Growth of Incarceration in the United States: Exploring Causes and Consequences 3 (2014). ("The best single proximate explanation of the rise in incarceration is not rising crime rates, but the policy choices made by legislators to greatly increase the use of imprisonment as a response to crime.")

distinctive American sociocultural factors—the nature of our democracy, our individualist self-image, our religious and economic institutions, and our history of racism—are the main culprits behind the incarceration plague.[48] These aspects of American society—many of which have served us well in some domains—have, in the criminal justice sphere, created a perfect storm of punitiveness in the United States of the late twentieth and early twenty-first centuries.

Perhaps first and foremost, there is our long history of populist democracy, which differs in important respects from European democracy. Comparativists contrast "liberal market economies," of which the U.S. is a prime example, and "coordinated market economies," which predominate in Europe. As developed by Michael Cavadino and James Dignan[49] and elaborated on by Nicola Lacey,[50] a liberal market economy aims at a free-market "characterized by vibrant economic and political competition in a relatively regulatory-free world," and thus tends to generate a distrust of government intervention and produce adversarial and polarized legislatures and bureaucracies.[51] A coordinated market economy, in contrast, is more heavily regulated, in an effort to please a wide array of groups; it tends to be associated with proportional representation and multiparty governance.[52] The cacophony of parties in the latter type of system requires significant compromise and consensus building, and usually results in center-left governments with generous welfare policies, because the center is controlled by a middle class interested in robust social services.[53]

Following Lacey, Andrew Taslitz has argued that the impact of a European-style coordinated economy and more diffuse democratic process on criminal justice policies is at least threefold.[54] First, "[t]he broad-based, coalitional nature of the electoral system [in Europe] ... makes it harder for any one social group to use criminal justice as a way to wage war on another such

48 See Christopher Slobogin, How Changes in American Culture Triggered Hyper-Incarceration: Variations on the Tazian View, 58 Howard L. J. 305, 317–31 (2015).

49 Michael Cavadino & James Dignan, Penal Systems: A Comparative Approach (2006).

50 Nicola Lacey, The Prisoner's Dilemma: Political Economy and Punishment in Contemporary Democracies (2008).

51 Andrew E. Taslitz, The Criminal Republic: Democratic Breakdown as a Cause of Mass Incarceration, 9 Ohio St. J. Crim. L. 133, 157–58 & 160 (2011) (noting that a "winner-take-all attitude leads the winning party to seek to dominate all level of policymaking while it has control," including the appointment of bureaucrats, who are "seen as less an independent stable, professional source of policy input than servants of the governing party's will").

52 Id. at 153–54. ("Even right-leaning [coordinated market economy] governments are more likely to be left of what constitutes the center in the United States.")

53 Id.

54 Id. at 156.

group." Second, the same coalition-seeking reduces the ability of any given party to control policymaking, which, together with a greater trust in government generally, increases deference to relatively lenient criminal justice experts. Third, "[t]he more generous welfare state ... reduces poverty, social isolation, and other arguably criminogenic social situations," reducing the necessity of harsh punishment policies. The result, borne out by data comparing criminal justice systems in liberal market and coordinated market economies, is less severe punishment.[55]

A nay-sayer might note that we had a two-party, highly populist system before 1970, and yet our incarceration rates at that time were European-like. What changed? Here crime rates do play a role, but not in the direct fashion some surmise. Due to the huge influx of baby boomers, the expansion of drug markets, and various other factors, the number of index crimes in the United States more than doubled between 1960 and 1972.[56] Not surprisingly, crime became more salient to the American public during that time.[57] The media added fuel to the fire, reporting not only increases in crime but also exaggerating its impact.[58] Even today, with crime rates receding, Americans perceive offending to be on the upswing because of what they see and hear on TV, radio, newspapers, and the Internet,[59] most recently as amplified through a presidential emphasis on "law and order." The way in which our political

55 Id. (citing Lacey, supra note 50, and Michael Tonry, Punishment Policies and Patterns in Western Countries, in Sentencing and Sanctions in Western Countries 3, 3–28 (Michael Tonry & Richard S. Frase, eds., 2001)).

56 In 1960, the FBI reported 2,019,600 index crimes; by 1972 the number was 5,891,924. FBI, U.S. Dep't of Justice, Crime in the United States 1972: Uniform Crime Reports 61 tbl.1 (1973). See also Satoshi Kanasawa, When Crime Rates Go Down, Recidivism Rates Go Up, Psychology Today (August 24, 2008), available at www.psychologytoday.com/blog/the-scientific-fundamentalist/200808 ("Crime rates increased in the 1970s ... as the baby boomers became young adults"); Lawrence Rosenthal, Pragmatism, Originalism, Race and the Case against Terry v. Ohio, 43 Tex. Tech. L. Rev. 299, 304 (2010). ("There is something approaching a consensus among criminologists that the crime spike of the late 1980s and early 1990s was a function of the introduction of crack cocaine into major cities.")

57 Search of Gallup Poll Public Opinion Database, Scholarly Resources, Wilmington, Del. (accessed August 12, 2014), available at http://brain.gallup.com/home.aspx (noting that in October 1951 1 percent of respondents thought crime was the most important issue facing the United States, while in January 1994, 49 percent of respondents ranked crime the most important noneconomic problem facing the United States).

58 Crime on the Rise?: Public Perception of Crime Out of Sync with Reality, The Crime Report, Nov. 10, 2008, available at www.utexas.edu/features/2008/11/10/crime/ (noting that, while today "crime is a staple topic of media coverage and political campaigns," prior to the 1960s it was not, and quoting a criminologist to the effect that "mass media" was a principal, and misleading, source of the public's information about crime).

59 Gallup, American Concerns about National Crime Abating, Nov. 17, 2018, available at https://news.gallup.com/poll/244394/americans-concerns-national-crime-abating.aspx (noting that,

system parlays this state of affairs into higher incarceration rates is well-known. In the United States at both the federal and state levels, tough-on-crime rhetoric is seen as an electoral no-brainer, with candidates from both parties trying to outdo one another in convincing the public how outraged they are by criminal conduct.[60]

But it is in comparing our experience with Europe's reaction to influxes of crime that the impact of our unique political culture becomes apparent. Crime rates during the 1960s and 70s increased even more rapidly in Europe than they did in the U.S.[61] And Europeans too are assaulted by media reports about crime, reports that leave them feeling as insecure as Americans.[62] Yet crime has not become the political football it did in the United States, where it was a central theme in the 1968 elections that presaged hyper-incarceration and has often figured prominently in subsequent federal and state campaigns as well.[63] In Europe, as James Whitman has observed, politicians are as likely to engage in debates about prison reform and the rights and dignity of convicts as they are to inveigh against the criminal element.[64] I had a similar experience; I took a class of American students I taught in

between 2017 and 2018, there was a decrease from 60 percent to 50 percent in those who believe that the crime problem is "very serious" or "extremely serious" but that, over the past twenty years, a majority of Americans have consistently said that crime is worse than the year before, in contrast to the actual decrease in crime rates over that period).

60 Katherine Beckett & Theodore Sasson, The Origins of the Current Conservative Discourse on Law and Order 44, 50, in Defending Justice, The Rise of the Modern "Tough on Crime" Movement (2005), available at www.publiceye.org/defendingjustice/pdfs/chapters/tough crime.pdf (arguing that, beginning in the 1960s, conservative politicians have "worked ... to alter popular perceptions of crime ... and to promote policies that involve 'getting tough" and 'cracking down,'" as part of a larger effort to increase votes, and documenting how, observing the success of this move, Democrats jumped on "the law-and-order bandwagon"); David Garland, The Culture of Control: Crime and Social Order in Contemporary Society 133 (2001). ("Many of the laws passed in the 1990s—Megan's law, Three Strikes, sexual predator statutes, the reintroduction of children's prisons, paedophile registers, and mandatory sentences – ... are designed to be expressive, cathartic actions, undertaken to denounce the crime and reassure the public.")

61 Michael Tonry, Sentencing in America, 1975–2025, 42 Crim. & Just. 141, 184–85 (2013) ("All wealthy developed countries except Japan experienced steep rises in crime rates, including homicide rates, from the 1960s to the 1990s, but only a handful adopted harshly punitive criminal justice policies: the United States during the tough on crime period, England and Wales after 1993, and New Zealand since the late 1990s") (citations omitted).

62 See generally, Goradz Meško et al., Crime, Media and Fear of Crime (2009), available at www.academia.edu/1470327/Crime_media_and_fear_of_crime (discussing media coverage of crime in several European countries and noting, inter alia, that reporting on crime in Germany doubled between the early 1950s and the mid-1990s).

63 See Beckett & Sasson, supra note 60.

64 See James Q. Whitman, Harsh Justice: Criminal Punishment and the Widening Divide between America and Europe 76 (2003) (recounting the French response to a prison scandal,

Dublin, Ireland in 2000 on a field trip to the national Parliament, where the leader of the "conservative" party expressed amazement that the United States still had the death penalty and three-strikes laws, and emphasized that his party favored rehabilitative programs for prisoners ("otherwise, what's the point?").

The differences between the relatively adversarial nature of our system and the more coalitional, inclusive nature of European governments helps explain these different political repercussions of rising crime. In part because of Europe's less populist background, politicians are less likely to have a knee-jerk reaction to the latest crime or crime wave, whether or not manufactured by the media.[65] Furthermore, coordinated economies are more likely to rely on experts in criminal justice matters.[66] Indeed, in some European countries criminal statutes are drafted not by legislators or their aides but by unelected scholars, who are less likely to be influenced by the public's moods.[67] In contrast to all of this, our political system feeds punitive attitudes, a tendency in full flower during the recent Trump administration with respect to immigrants, inner city crime, and protesters.

Excessive punitiveness is also likely to accompany a second aspect of American-style democracy. Most states have carried populism to its logical end by requiring the election of judges and prosecutors,[68] a phenomenon that is unheard of in Western Europe.[69] Unfortunately, considerable research shows that both judges and prosecutors change their behavior, in a more

in which "French politicians of all major tendencies, and in every branch of French government, vied with each other over the issue of prison reform [and] entered into a contest to show who had the deeper commitment to making punishment more *humane*") (emphasis in original).

65 Id. at 15 ("For the most part, . . . American-style politics has failed to exert an American-style influence on German or French criminal justice," in large part because of the "success of bureaucratic control").

66 Taslitz, supra note 51, at 186–87.

67 Markus Dirk Dubber, The Promise of German Criminal Law: A Science of Crime and Punishment, 6 German L. J. 1049, 1051 (2005) (noting that the German system of criminal law has been "assembled by generations of scholars and their stables of assistants").

68 David E. Pozen, The Irony of Judicial Elections, 108 Colum L. Rev. 265, 266 (2008) ("roughly 90 percent of state general jurisdiction judges are currently selected or retained" through an election process); Robert L. Misner, Recasting Prosecutorial Discretion, 86 J. Crim. L. & Crimin. 717, 734 (1996) (95 percent of state prosecutors are elected).

69 Mary L. Vulcansek, Appointing Judges the European Way, 34 Ford. Urb. L. J. 363, 368 (2007) (noting that "continental Europe" has "three models for naming judges: civil service, shared appointment, and shared appointment with partisan quotas"); Micah S. Myers, Prosecuting Human Rights Violations in Europe and America: How Legal Structure Affects Compliance International Obligations, 25 Mich. J. Int'l L. 211, 238 (2003). ("European prosecutors are selected largely on the basis of competitive examinations, which helps 'insulate [them] from political influence'").

punitive direction, near election time.[70] In Europe, in contrast, professional bureaucracies are insulated from retributive demands from the public because they are not subject to the beck and call of the populace, which may be uninformed or reacting to the most recent media-driven crisis.[71] Prosecutors in Europe are also professionalized in a way that has no counterpart in the United States.[72]

Of course, we have been electing judges and prosecutors for some time, well before the punitive upsurge. But again, our willingness to subject the justice system to popular vote has grown appreciably in the last quarter-century. As Matthew Streib noted in 2007, since the mid-1980s,

> Judicial elections have changed immensely, perhaps more so than elections for any other office. Once compared to playing a game of checkers by mail, many of today's judicial races are as rough and tumble as any congressional election. As one observer famously remarked, judicial elections are getting "noisier, nastier, and costlier." Candidate spending in judicial elections, both at the supreme court and intermediate appellate levels, has skyrocketed. Interest groups and political parties, recognizing the extreme importance of electing judges who support their views, are becoming more active.[73]

The pace described by Streib has accelerated in the past decade and a half. In 2000, contested campaigns figured in only four of eighteen state supreme court

[70] Gregory A. Huber & Sanford C. Gordon, Accountability and Coercion: Is Justice Blind When It Runs for Office?, 48 Am. J. Pol. Sci. 247 (2004) (documenting a 30 percent increase in expected sentence length from the first to the last day of a judge's term in Pennsylvania, at which time they stand in noncompetitive retention elections); Jason J. Czarnezki, Voting and Electoral Politics in the Wisconsin Supreme Court, 87 Marq. L. Rev. 323 (2003) (finding that justices are less likely to protect defendant and prisoner rights once they have experienced elective politics); Melissa Bann Hall, Justices As Representatives: Elections and Judicial Politics in the American States, 23 Am. Pol. Q. 485, 495–97 (1995) (finding that state judges are more likely to uphold death sentences in last two years of their term); Siddhartha Bandyopadhyay & Bryan C. McCannon, The Effect of the Election of Prosecutors on Criminal Trials 161 Public Choice 141, 155 (2014) (finding that "when reelection pressures are strong, prosecutors increase the number of cases taken to trial and plea bargain less").

[71] See Myers, supra note 69. Cf. Joel D. Aberbach, Robert D. Putnam & Bert A. Rockman, Bureaucrats and Politicians in Western Democracies 94–95 (1981) (noting the "startling" difference between American bureaucrats, who see their role as furthering political aims, and European bureaucrats, who do not).

[72] Mirjan Damaška, Structures of Authority and Comparative Criminal Procedure, 84 Yale L. J. 480, 512 (1975). ("In most American states, public prosecutors are locally elected officials with surprisingly great and virtually uncontrolled authority .... [H]ierarchical subordination is negligible by continental [European] standards.")

[73] Matthew J. Streib, The Study of Judicial Elections, in Running for Judge: The Rising Political, Financial, and Legal Stakes of Judicial Elections 2 (Matthew J. Streib, ed., 2007).

elections; by 2006, they occurred in ten out of eleven.[74] Negative campaign ads and attacks on candidates by opposing candidates increased significantly during that period.[75] The Supreme Court's 2010 decision in *Citizens United v. Federal Election Commission*[76] undoubtedly stoked the flames, as evidenced by the fact that spending on state judicial elections more than doubled between 2007–08 and 2011–12,[77] and has continued unabated since.[78] Prosecutorial elections are not likely to be as fiery, but they too hardly reflect deliberative democracy. According to Ronald Wright, "when it comes to the prosecutor, one of the most ubiquitous and powerful figures to appear regularly on the ballot, we rely mostly on anecdotes."[79] Progressive prosecutors have been able to win elections in recent times, but they are few and far between and have to fight an uphill battle against a variety of interest groups.[80]

A related but separate phenomenon is the common American attitude toward the causes of human behavior. We pride ourselves on our individualism, which posits that people, not situations, are responsible for criminal acts. This again can be attributed in part to our "liberal market economy" — another way of describing relatively uncabined capitalism. Compared to coordinated economies, where there is a widely held view that the criminal system is in many ways simply an extension of the welfare system, aimed at those who act out antisocially,[81] a regime driven by a market economy is epitomized by lower welfare levels and a lack of effort to ensure economic

74 James Sample et al., The New Politics of Judicial Elections vi (2006), available at www.followthemoney.org/press/Reports/200705171.pdf.

75 Id.

76 558 U.S. 310 (2010) (holding that a federal statute barring independent corporate expenditures for electioneering violated the First Amendment).

77 Brennan Center for Justice, New Politics of Judicial Elections, 2011–2012 (Oct. 23, 2013), available at www.brennancenter.org/publication/new-politics-judicial-elections-2011-12.

78 Douglas Keith, Patrick Berry & Eric Velasco (Brennan Center for Justice), The Politics of Judicial Elections, 2017–2018 (Dec. 11, 2019), available at https://www.brennancenter.org/our-work/research-reports/politics-judicial-elections/2017-18. ("While elections during this period broke few of the spending and other records set in recent years, many of the worst features of modern judicial elections appear here to stay.")

79 Ronald F. Wright, How Prosecutor Elections Fail Us, 6 Ohio St. J. Crim. L. 581, 590 (2009).

80 Rashad Robinson, The People Who Undermine Progressive Prosecutors, N.Y. Times (June 11, 2020) ("police departments and unions, as well as … judges, lawmakers and even some corporations … have used their power to prevent these [progressive] prosecutors from doing their jobs").

81 Richard Wike, PEW Research: Five Ways Americans and Europeans are Different (April 29, 2016), available at https://www.pewresearch.org/fact-tank/2016/04/19/5-ways-americans-and-europeans-are-different/ (survey indicating that Americans are much less likely than Europeans to want the government to "play an active role in society to guarantee that nobody is in need").

equality.[82] It also tends to be associated with a dog-eat-dog, laissez-faire, winner-or-loser ethos.[83] Translated to the criminal justice context, one can imagine how people immersed in our political economy are more likely to attribute crime and its close associate—poverty—to individual choice rather than to mitigating circumstance;[84] likewise, they are more likely to see a person who offends as an "outsider" not worthy of empathy.[85] Retributivism—the idea that offenders should get what they deserve—is a perfect fit in such a society, as are determinate sentences based on just desert.[86]

Again, however, this homo economicus mindset would seem to describe the United States throughout its history. It must also be noted that retributivist dispositions do not have to be harsh; deserved punishment can be short.[87] Before drawing a connection between our individualist tendencies and hyper-incarceration, some explanation of why it blossomed only after the 1960s is needed.

That something else was the resurgence of conservatism in the 1970s, a movement that parlayed a number of traditional American values into a concerted campaign against the "criminal element." The adversarial American political system was the perfect vehicle for bringing this campaign to fruition. As Thomas and Mary Edsall demonstrate, "[c]onservatives, mostly Republicans, recognized in the 1960s that 'tough on crime' policies could be used as 'wedge issues' to separate white and working class Americans from

82 Taslitz, supra note 51, at 159 (stating that liberal market economics tend to be associated with "a relatively weaker welfare state and a less coordinated state commitment to maintain worker skills," as well as "more poverty and life-course economic instability").

83 Id. at 160 (describing "winner-take-all attitude").

84 Id. at 312 (reporting survey results showing that Europeans are much more likely than Americans to believe that "success is determined by forces outside their control").

85 Incheol Choi & Richard E. Nisbett, Situational Salience and Cultural Differences in the Correspondence Bias and Actor-Observer Bias, 24 Personality & Soc. Psychol. Bull. 949 (1998) (describing a cognitive bias known as "fundamental attribution error" or "observer bias" that attributes behavior to internal rather than external causes and finding that this bias is more likely to be found among Americans); Whitman, supra note 64, at 20 (arguing that using punishment to degrade others to make them feel "inferior, lessened (and) lowered," is a key difference between American and European approaches to criminal punishment).

86 For a description of retributivism and determinate sentencing, see Robert Pugsley, Retributivism: A Just Basis for Determinate Sentences, 7 Hofstra L. Rev. 379, 398 (1979). ("Retributivism affirmatively supports determinate sentencing schemes because articulable, narrowly drawn sentencing ranges can be derived from ascertaining what an offender deserves for committing a particular type of offense.")

87 For instance, Andrew Von Hirsch, one of the progenitors of modern retributivism, proposed a maximum sentence of five years for first offense homicide and a maximum of three years for all other serious crimes. Andrew Von Hirsch, Censure and Sanctions 36–46 (1993).

their traditional support of liberal politicians."[88] A key avenue for creating this wedge was the rejuvenation of American individualism. For instance, one 2003 poll indicated that the percentage of Americans who believed that success is determined by forces outside their control had fallen from 41 percent in 1988 to 32 percent by the time of the poll, whereas the opposite trend was found in Germany.[89]

Religious attitudes—in particular, those held by sects with a strong individualist orientation—were another phenomenon the conservative movement exploited. There is no doubt that the United States is more religious than Europe. In most European countries, even heavily Catholic ones like Spain and Italy, less than 25 percent of the population says that religion is important to them.[90] Fewer than 10 percent of citizens in Germany, the Netherlands, Sweden and Denmark attend church services once a month or more.[91] In the U.S., in contrast, more than half say a belief in God is important to them and more than half attend church.[92] Although Christianity certainly has its forgiving elements, many American Christians, especially those of the evangelical stripe, believe strongly in the concept of evil, the need to exact vengeance, and the importance of expressing moral outrage at criminals.[93] Fundamentalist Christians "equate criminal behavior with sinful behavior," leading them to endorse "the view that crime results from the defendant's character and not from unfortunate or unjust circumstances."[94] Rather than an attitude of "there but for the Grace of God go I," their reaction to crime, especially if they see

88 Thomas Edsall & Mary Edsall, Chain Reaction: The Impact of Race, Rights and Taxes on American Politics (1991). See also, Beckett & Sasson, supra note 60, at 49–51.

89 John Mickelthwait & Adrian Wooldridge, The Right Nation 312 (2004). Since the 2008 economic crash, Americans' willingness to attribute poverty to moral fault rather than devastating events has lessened considerably. Patrick O'Connor, Attitudes toward Poverty Show Dramatic Change, Wall St. J. (June 24, 2014) (description of poll showing that 46 percent of Americans today attribute poverty to circumstances rather than attitude, and that the increase occurs among Republicans and independents as well as Democrats), available at http://blogs.wsj.com/washwire/2014/06/20/attitudes-toward-poverty-show-dramatic-change-wsjnbc-poll/. Perhaps that change in attitude, which might be accelerated by the economic crisis precipitated by the pandemic, presages a more lenient attitude toward crime.

90 Pew Research Report, The American-Western European Values, Feb. 29, 2012, available at http://www.pewglobal.org/2011/11/17/the-american-western-european-values-gap/.

91 Noelle Knox, Religion Takes a Back Seat in Western Europe, USA Today, Aug. 8, 2005 (chart), available at http://usatoday30.usatoday.com/news/world/2005-08-10-europe-religion-cover_x.htm.

92 Id.; see also, Wike, supra note 81 (indicating that "religion is significantly less important to Europeans than to Americans").

93 Mickelthwait & Wooldridge, supra note 89, at 326. ("America's religiosity has encouraged Americans to see problems in terms of individual virtues and vices.")

94 James D. Unnever & Frances T. Cullen, Christian Fundamentalism and Support for Capital Punishment, 43 J. Res. Crime & Delinq. 169, 171 (2006).

God as angry or judgmental, is an "eye for an eye."[95] This view is consonant with both the adversarialism of American populism and the individualistic aspects of a liberal market economy.

Most important to the thesis developed here, this conservative brand of religion has mushroomed over the past four decades, precisely the period of hyper-incarceration. With the advent of the New Religious Right, the United States is more religiously conservative now than it was in the 1960s, by a large margin.[96] These conservative religious groups have been extremely effective at raising money, using the media and lobbying elected officials.[97] There is no analogously strong political force in largely secular Europe.

Before leaving the liberal market economy theme, there is another, more prosaic way capitalism may lead to harsher punishments. Because the U.S. is a bastion of free enterprise, many Americans prefer private solutions to government-initiated ones, even in arenas, like health care and education, that are seen as quintessentially governmental endeavors in Europe. It has only been in the past several decades, however, that we've begun privatizing prison and jails, with imprisonment-enhancing consequences. Companies like CoreCivic (formally the Corrections Corporation of America) are taking over state prison systems, with the aim of expanding them.[98] As one spokesperson for the company said in explaining its construction of three, at the time unnecessary, prisons in California: "If you build it in the right place, the prisoners will come."[99] One stunning consequence of this development is that states like Florida and Tennessee have agreed to produce a certain number of prisoners per year or pay the private facility for the empty beds, a surefire method of encouraging unnecessary

[95] Christopher D. Bader et al., Divine Justice: The Relationship between Images of God and Attitudes Toward Criminal Punishment, 35 Crim. J. Rev. 90 (2012).

[96] Michael Hout, Andrew Greeley & Melissa Wilde, The Demographic Imperative in Religious Change in the United States, 107 Am. J. Sociology 468, 468 (2001). ("The decline of the 'mainline' religious denominations and concomitant growth of more conservative denominations and sects has been among the major U.S. religious trends of the past 60 years or so.")

[97] See generally, William Martin, With God on Our Side: The Rise of the Religious Right (2004) (describing the increasing power of evangelical Christians, particularly from the 1960s through 2004). That power has increased in the past decade. See, e.g., Clyde Haberman, Religion and Right-Wing Politics: How Evangelicals Reshaped Elections, N.Y. Times (Oct. 28, 2018).

[98] The Sentencing Project, Private Prisons in the United States (Oct. 24, 2019), available at https://www.sentencingproject.org/publications/private-prisons-united-states/ ("Since 2000, the number of people in private prisons has increased 39.3%, compared to an overall rise in the prison population of 7.8%"); Center for Law and Global Justice, U.S. Sentencing Practices in Global Context 16 (2012) (noting that "[t]he rise of private prisons [has] contributed to the increase in lengthy prison terms," in part because their owners fund "campaigns and policies seeking longer criminal sentences and mandatory sentences").

[99] James A. Morone, Hellfire Nation: The Politics of Sin in American History 460 (2003).

incarceration.[100] Again, this relatively recent development could explain some of the American-European divergence in punishment, because relatively socialist Europe has for the most part maintained prisons as public entities.[101]

Another aspect of American individualism is our strong commitment to criminal procedure rights, including the right to jury trial, the right to confront accusers, and the privilege against self-incrimination. William Stuntz has made the counterintuitive argument that one cause of our increased imprisonment rate and longer sentences has been our commitment to these strong procedural protections for criminal defendants.[102] According to Stuntz, the rights to a jury and to confront one's accusers in particular make trial so time-consuming that, given their increasing caseloads, prosecutors have had to resort to plea bargaining and guilty pleas as the main method of adjudicating criminal cases.[103] Needing bargaining leverage to sustain this system, Stuntz continued, prosecutors have lobbied for easy to prove crimes and heavy penalties, which legislators, for reasons already alluded to, have been only too happy to enact.[104]

As a result, modern criminal codes have become bloated. For instance, in many states proof that the defendant is anywhere near illicit drugs can result in a very stiff sentence.[105] These drug possession laws can also be used to prosecute

100 Andy Kroll, This is How Private Prison Companies Make Money Even When Crime Rates Fall, Mother Jones, Sept. 19, 2013), available at http://www.motherjones.com/mojo/2013/09/private-prisons-occupancy-quota-cca-crime ("In the Public Interest found that 41 of [contracts with private prison companies] included occupancy requirements mandating that local or state government keep those facilities between 80 and 100 percent full. In other words, whether crime is rising or falling, the state must keep those beds full.")

101 Cody Mason, International Growth Trends in Prison Privatization 2 (2013), available at http://www.sentencing project.org/doc/publications/inc_International%20Growth%20Trends%20in%20Prison%20Privatization.pdf (noting that most private prison growth has taken place in English-speaking countries).

102 Stuntz, supra note 8, at 257–74.

103 Id. at 235–36 (noting the huge decrease in criminal trials in the 1970s and stating that the Warren Court's "law of criminal procedure raised the cost of policing and prosecution when that cost was already too high").

104 Id. at 264–67 (describing how "criminal liability rules grew broader, the number of overlapping criminal offenses mushroomed, and the definition of crimes grew more specific" (and thus easier to prove), in part because these moves allowed legislators to look tough on crime and in part because "broader and more specific substantive law was a means of inducing guilty pleas"). See also William J. Stuntz, The Pathological Politics of Criminal Law, 100 Mich. L. Rev. 505, 533–39 (2001) (explaining why prosecutors lobby legislators for more and easier-to-prove crimes and stating that the "single most important feature of the existing system for defining criminal law" is that "legislators have good reason to listen when prosecutors urge some statutory change").

105 Stuntz, supra note 8, at 267–68 (providing examples, including a case holding that conviction for possession with intent to distribute and conspiracy to do the same is proven simply by "some nexus between the defendant and the drugs").

people for suspected, but harder to prove, more serious crimes like robbery and homicide.[106] The reach of rape, theft, and fraud law has also expanded.[107]

If Stuntz's diagnosis about the pathology of American crime definition and prosecutorial-legislative interaction is correct,[108] then our commitment to defendant-oriented procedural protections as a method of ensuring fair punishment has backfired. In most European countries, there are no all-lay juries, making rules of evidence minimal, and the right to silence and prevent disclosure of information to the court is much reduced.[109] As a result, trials are a much cheaper proposition and take place in virtually all serious cases, the most importance consequence of which, for purposes of this book, is that judges have much more control over the adjudication and sentencing process.[110] While some sort of plea bargaining system exists in most European countries,[111] it does not create the up-ratcheting of punishment that Stuntz describes in the United States because judges, not prosecutors, are the primary power-brokers.[112]

106 Id. at 269.

107 Id. at 263–64.

108 For an article providing empirical support for Stuntz's position, see Daniel P. Kessler & Anne Morrison Piehl, The Role of Discretion in the Criminal Justice System, 14 J. L. Econ. & Org. 256 (1998) (finding, based on a study of prosecutorial behavior after the passage of California's three-strikes laws, that prosecutors not only sought longer sentences for those charged with a third strike but also sought longer sentences for those charged with "similar crimes," in a process the authors call "prosecutorial maximization"). See also Paul J. Hofer, Has Booker Restored Balance? A Look at Data on Plea Bargaining and Sentencing, 23 Fed. Sent'g Rep. 326, 329 (2011) ("stating that the Department of Justice 'has sought more and harsher mandatory sentencing laws 'not because the enhancements are inherently just or required for adequate deterrence, but precisely because higher sentences provide increased plea bargaining leverage'").

109 For a description of European models of criminal justice and recent trends toward "convergence" of the inquisitorial/inquest and adversarial/contest traditions, see John D. Jackson, The Effect of Human Rights on Criminal Evidentiary Processes: Towards Convergence, Divergence or Realignment?, 68 Mod. L. Rev. 737, 740–43 (2005).

110 Mar Jimeno-Bulnes, American Criminal Procedure in a European Context, 21 Cardozo J. Int'l & Comp. L. 409, 453 (2013) (noting that "a common aspect" of the plea bargaining process that occurs in France, Germany, Italy, and Spain is that judges control the process, and that such control "usually takes place at the appropriate hearing").

111 See Maximo Langer, From Legal Transplants to Legal Translations: The Globalization of Plea Bargaining and the Americanization Thesis in Criminal Procedure, 45 Harv. Int'l. L. J. 1, 27, 63 (2004) (noting that numerous countries now allow plea bargaining, but concluding, based on a survey of four continental and Latin American criminal justice systems, that criminal procedure is "still overwhelmingly conceptualized around the model of the official investigation," which eschews guilty pleas and requires trial in most cases).

112 Jenia Iontcheva Turner, Judicial Participation in Plea Negotiations: A Comparative View, 54 Am. J. Comp. L. 199, 215–17 (2006) (describing the high degree of control German judges have over charging, adjudication and sentencing decisions, and noting that the German approach is representative of the "civil-law, inquisitorial criminal justice system" prevalent in Europe).

One potential counter to Stuntz's thesis that heightened procedure causes heightened punishment is that, from its inception, our Constitution has provided for an adversarial rather than inquisitorial process. But the obvious rejoinder is that those adversarial rights were not applied to the states, where most criminal cases are tried, until the 1960s. That is when the Warren Court's incorporation of the guarantees found in the Fourth, Fifth, and Sixth amendments changed the face of American criminal trials.[113] That is when plea bargaining took off.[114] And, of course, that is when hyper-incarceration began.

Finally, a very important contributor to mass incarceration is America's disturbing attitude about race, a phenomenon that has deservedly received much more attention since the death of George Floyd in May 2020 and the resulting rejuvenation of the Movement for Black Lives. The percentage of African-Americans in prison far outpaces their representation in the general population, and that percentage has increased significantly since the 1960s.[115] Compared to their proportion in the population, people of color are more likely than whites to be stopped by police, arrested, convicted, and sentenced to long terms. Not all of this can be attributed to racism of course. African-Americans migrated to urban areas in huge numbers after War World II, and their resulting ghettoization and poverty inflated their crime rate.[116] As even Paul Butler—long a critic of racialized policing, as well as an advocate for abolishing prisons because of their impact on black people—has conceded, "African American men commit a disproportionate share of . . . serious crimes, including homicide, assault, and robbery . . . ."[117] But, as Butler also reminds

113 See Charles H. Whitebread & Christopher Slobogin, Criminal Procedure: An Analysis of Cases and Concepts 2 (7th ed. 2020) (noting that the Warren Court found "virtually every Bill of Rights guarantee pertaining to the criminal process. . . to be inherent in the due process of law and . . . thus imposed on the states through incorporation into the Fourteenth Amendment").

114 Albert W. Alschuler, Plea Bargaining and Its History, 79 Colum. L. Rev. 1, 38–39 (1979) (noting that, while guilty pleas have been a predominant aspect of the American system for decades, "[a] major effect of the 'due process revolution' was to augment the pressures for plea negotiation" and produce "more intense plea negotiation," with the result that guilty pleas increased significantly).

115 Michael Tonry, Malign Neglect: Race, Crime, and Punishment in America vii (1995). ("[B]y 1990 a quarter of young black males were in jail or prison, on probation or parole [and t]he chance that a black male was in jail or prison was seven times that of a white male.")

116 Stuntz, supra note 8, at 20–21 (noting, inter alia, that murder rates went up as the urban black population increased).

117 Paul Butler, Chokehold: Policing Black Men 121 (2018). According to the Department of Justice, blacks are arrested for violent crime (defined as homicide, robbery, and aggravated assault) far more often than whites, relative to their proportion in the population. In 2018, whites, who comprised about 60 percent of the population, committed approximately 288,620 violent crimes, while blacks, comprising about 13 percent of the population, committed approximately 187,000 violent crimes. Department of Justice, Estimated Numbers of

us, structural disadvantages for people of color, including outright racism, help explain this difference.

More importantly, a tempered response to black crime that recognizes these disadvantages and prejudices is usually a political non-starter in the United States. As Taslitz noted, compared to coalitional societies, liberal market economies tend to shut out minority groups that do not "play by the rules," at the same time those societies demonize them as prime causes of most social ills, including crime.[118] Further, urban minority groups have a hard time exerting their influence on criminal law matters at the state or federal levels, where "legislators from farm country, small towns, and white middle-class neighborhoods" predominate.[119]

Of course, our country has been afflicted by racism since its birth, and the political attributes described by Taslitz have also been with us for some time. What racialized practices changed in a way that can help explain the hyper-incarceration of the past fifty years? Here the work of Michelle Alexander comes to the fore. Professor Alexander notes that the rise in black incarceration rates from the late 1970s through the 1980s parallels the hyper-criminalization of conduct associated with drug possession, and that most of our drug crime policies came during the Nixon and Reagan presidencies when Republicans were developing their Southern strategy.[120] From these types of observations, she argues that our so-called "war on drugs" was, and still is, a cover for a continuation of the racially tinged criminal justice practices of yesteryear, when blacks suspected of crime used to be lynched or beaten rather than prosecuted in court. In other words, she argues, incarceration for drug crimes has taken the place of Jim Crow.[121]

The story of race and hyper-incarceration is undoubtedly more complicated than simple unalloyed racism. For instance, both progressives and blacks themselves lobbied for increased drug penalties during the last quintile of the twentieth century, as a way of supporting struggling minority neighborhoods.[122] The important point for present purposes is that, for

Offenses by Offense and Race, 2018, available at https://www.ojjdp.gov/ojstatbb/crime/ucr.asp?table_in=2.

118 Taslitz, supra note 51, at 161–62.

119 Id. at 143–73.

120 Michelle Alexander, The New Jim Crow 43–44 (2010). See also, Tonry, supra note 115, at 31–35 (arguing that the War on Drugs was probably planned, or at least predicted, to be a war on poor racial minorities, particularly African-Americans).

121 Alexander, supra note 120, at 11 ("mass incarceration is, metaphorically, the New Jim Crow").

122 See James Forman, Jr., Racial Critiques of Mass Incarceration: Beyond the New Jim Crow, 87 N.Y.U. L. Rev.21, 36–44 (2012) (describing "black support for punitive crime policy").

a host of reasons, changes in the way racial themes influenced formal policy fed directly into harsh imprisonment policies.[123] Europe, with less of a racial history, simply could not emulate this pattern.

In short, several unique aspects of modern American culture—all of which, with the obvious exception of racism, have their positive elements—have contributed to our incarceration debacle. Their overall impact on criminal justice has several manifestations. For example, in most states today sentence lengths are essentially fixed at the front-end. Prodded by congressional largess designed to encourage states to require that prisoners serve their "just" sentence, in the 1990s almost thirty states adopted some form of "truth-in-sentencing" rule, usually requiring that prisoners serve a minimum of 85 percent of their sentence.[124] Since the 1970s, American legislatures have also eagerly adopted three-strikes laws and mandatory minimum sentencing provisions that leave no discretion to judges, even for relatively minor crimes.[125] Parole has either been abolished or made nondiscretionary in most states.[126] All of these practices have led to longer sentences and more people in prison,[127] and have provided

123 Anders Walker, The New Jim Crow? Recovering the Progressive Origins of Mass Incarceration, 41 Hastings L. Q. 845, 866 (2014) ("the War on Drugs contributed directly to the evil of mass incarceration. However, the origins of that war stemmed not simply from a conservative conspiracy, as Alexander implies, but a complex set of concerns, including a liberal desire to help minorities trapped in high-crime neighborhoods.")

124 Paula M. Ditton & Doris J. Wilson, Truth in Sentencing in State Prisons 3 (1999), available at http://bjs.gov/content/pub/pdf/tssp.pdf (noting that twenty-eight jurisdictions implemented truth-in-sentencing policies partially funded by federal grants).

125 U.S. Dept. of Justice, National Institute of Justice, "Three Strikes and You're Out": A Review of State Legislation 1 (Sept.1997), available at https://ncjrs.gov/pdffiles/165369.pdf (stating that between 1993 and 1995, twenty-four states and the federal Government enacted three strikes laws); Jonathan Simon, Governing through Crime: How the War on Crime Transformed American Democracy and Created a Culture of Fear 101 (2007) (describing the proliferation of mandatory penalties and noting that it was part of a broader shift toward a "zero tolerance" approach that applied to both severe and low-level crimes).

126 Between 1976 and 1999, parole was abolished in one-third of the states and discretionary parole was severely reduced in most of the remaining states, so that more than three-quarters of parole release dates are now essentially set at sentencing, varying only by good time credits. Jeremy Travis & Sarah Lawrence, Urban Inst. Justice Policy Ctr., Beyond the Prison Gates: The State of Parole in America 4–7 (2002).

127 William Spelman, Crime, Cash, and Limited Options: Explaining the Prison Boom, 8 Criminol. & Pub. Pol'y 29, 57 (2009) (study examining over thirty variables in multiple states during the period 1977 to 2005 that found that a truth-in-sentencing policy (e.g., i.e., no discretionary parole) was positively correlated with prison population); Susan Turner et al., The Impact of Truth-in-Sentencing and Three Strikes Legislation: Prison Populations, State Budgets, and Crime rates, 11 Stan. L. & Pol'y Rev. 75, 75–76, 79 (1999) (finding that implementation of the Truth-in-Sentencing and three strikes laws increased correctional spending but did not appear to reduce violent crime); Mark Osier, Amoral Numbers and Narcotics Sentencing, 47 Val. U. L. Rev. 755, 755 (2013). ("[T]he arbitrary mandatory

prosecutors more leverage against criminal defendants during the plea bargaining process.[128]

In Europe, in contrast, indeterminacy reigns. European countries have resisted mandatory sentences except with respect to the most severe crimes, have rejected stringent sentencing guidelines systems, and have retained numerous early release mechanisms.[129] That does not mean that our mid-twentieth century system of indeterminate sentences would have prevented hyper-incarceration. Research suggests that states that have abolished parole and provided sentencing guidelines to judges have, on the whole, seen no more prison growth than states that have maintained more indeterminate regimes.[130] Rather, the point is that in the types of sentencing systems that have existed in the U.S. to date, the dynamics of modern American society have produced policies that are responsible for astronomical prison growth compared to those of other Western democracies.

A growing number of policymakers and commentators think pretrial detention and post-conviction incarceration rates are an acute problem. Those on the left are most concerned about the human cost, not only to suspects and offenders but to their families and their communities. In particular, these critics point to the fact that a huge proportion of people of color are in prison—at a rate roughly six times that of whites[131]—and to the disruption that

minimums and sentencing guidelines that rank-order the severity of crimes . . . have too often created broad and often tragic outcomes in our society.")

128 This dynamic is discussed further in Chapter 5. One diagnosis of mass incarceration is that prosecutorial charging policies—in particular increased felony arrest filings—are the primary "drivers" of incarceration rates. See John Pfaff, Locked In: The True Causes of Mass Incarceration—And How to Achieve Real Reform 206 (2017). However, the data on which that thesis relies have been called into question. Jeffrey Bellin, Reassessing Prosecutorial Power Through the Lens of Mass Incarceration, 116 Mich. L. Rev. 835 (2018).

129 Ely Aharanson, Determinate Sentencing and American Exceptionalism: The Underpinnings and Effects of Cross-National Differences in the Regulation of Sentencing Discretion, 76 L. & Contemp. Probls. 161, 166–175 (2013) (describing differences between the U.S. and Europe in these three areas).

130 See, e.g., Kevin Reitz, Don't Blame Determinancy: Incarceration Growth Has Been Driven by Other Forces, 84 Texas L. Rev. 1787, 1794 (2006). ("The prison explosion in America has occurred during a time period in which indeterminate sentencing remained the structure of choice across the country.") However, as Chapter 5 elaborates, Reitz may overestimate the effect of indeterminate sentencing on prison growth.

131 Alexander, supra note 120, at 7–8, 43–44. The disparity holds true even when socio-economic status is held constant. See National Research Council, supra note 47, at 5. ("Among white male high school dropouts born in the late 1970s, about one-third are estimated to have served time in prison by their mid-30s. Yet incarceration rates have reached even higher levels among young black men with little schooling: among black male high school dropouts, about two-thirds have a prison record by that same age—more than twice the rate for their white counterparts.")

imprisonment causes to the families and neighborhoods from which they came.[132] More generally, they emphasize the research that suggests the imprisonment is itself criminogenic.[133] Those on the right may have these reactions as well,[134] but are probably at least as concerned about the cost of prisons, jails, and correctional staff.[135] The money spent on the carceral state has quadrupled since the 1990s and now is undoubtedly over $70 billion a year;[136] the indirect costs of this prison boom have been estimated at over $500 billion (about one-sixth of the gross domestic product).[137] From a more philosophical

132 Nicole Lewis & Beatrix Lockwood, The Hidden Cost of Incarceration, N.Y. Times, Dec. 17, 2019 (stating that families spend $2.9 billion a year on commissary accounts and phone calls; have to buy basic for prisoners; and pay about $13,000 in fines and fees per prisoner); Frederic G. Reamer, On the Parole Board: Reflections on Crime, Punishment, Redemption, and Justice 257 (2016) ("Incarceration is also strongly correlated with negative social and economic outcomes for former prisoners and their families … Men with a criminal record often experience reduced earnings and employment after prison … Fathers' incarceration and family hardship, including housing insecurity and behavioral problems in children, are strongly related"); National Research Council, supra note 47, at 6. ("The partners and children of prisoners are particularly likely to experience adverse outcomes if the men were positively involved with their families prior to incarceration.")

133 Michael Tonry, Less Imprisonment Is No Doubt a Good Thing, More Policing Is Not, 10 Criminology & Pub. Pol. 137, 137–38 (2011) (explaining that "[t]he effects of imprisonment on individual deterrence are most likely perverse; people sent to prison tend to come out worse and more likely to reoffend than if they had received a lesser punishment," citing "tentative but not yet conclusive" evidence that "imprisonment is criminogenic and increases released inmates' rates of reoffending"); Dan Nagin, Frank Cullen & Cheryl Lero-Jonson, Imprisonment and Reoffending, in 38 Crime and Justice: A Review of Research 115 (Michael Tonry, ed., 2009) (same); William D. Bales & Alex R. Piquero, Assessing the Impact of Imprisonment on Recidivism, 8 J. Experimental Criminol. 71, 98 (2012) (finding, based on a study in Florida, that offenders released from prison committed more crime than matched offenders released from community programs); see generally, Jennifer E. Copp, The Impact of Incarceration on the Risk of Violence Recidivism, 103 Marquette L. Rev. 775, 781–87 (2020) (collecting studies, and concluding that "prison is not a particularly effective intervention, as it has no deterrent effects after release—and may actually increase individuals' propensity of reoffending").

134 See, e.g., Press Release, Law Enforcement Leaders to Reduce Crime & Incarceration, Law Enforcement Leaders Urge President to Back Sentencing Reform, Spurn More Incarceration as Part of Anti-Crime Agenda (Feb. 13, 2017), http://lawenforcementleaders.org/wp-content/uploads/2017/02/LEL-Report-Release.pdf.

135 See David Dagan & Steven Teles, Prison Break: Why Conservatives Turned against Mass Incarceration (2016); Charlie Savage, Trend to Lighten Harsh Sentences Catches on in Conservative Circles, N.Y. Times, Aug. 12, 2011.

136 Christina Henrichson & Ruth Delaney, The Price of Prisons: What Incarceration Costs Taxpayers 2 (July 20, 2012), available at https://www.vera.org/downloads/Publications/price-of-prisons-what-incarceration-costs-taxpayers/legacy_downloads/price-of-prisons-updated-version-021914.pdf ($60 billion); Lewis & Lockwood, supra note 132 ($80 billion).

137 Michael McLaughlin, Carrie Pettus-Davis, Derek Brown, Chris Veeh & Tanya Renn, The Economic Burden of Incarceration in the U.S. 2 & 32 (Concordance Inst. for Advancing Soc.

perspective, both those who believe punishment should focus on just desert and those who are more utilitarian in orientation favor some degree of decarceration.[138] Sentencing reforms in "red states" such as Texas, Georgia, and South Carolina,[139] and the recently enacted First Step Act[140]—a bipartisan bill passed by Congress in 2018 aimed at promoting early release for nonviolent offenders—are further evidence of this trend. Whatever the reason, a consensus has built among policymakers that reducing the number of people in prison is a critical objective, at least if it can be done without increasing the danger to the public.

The public seems to agree. In a 2006 poll, only 38 percent of respondents said that reducing the prison population was "very important" as a stand-alone goal, while 81 percent considered "very important" the goal that "the punishment fits the crime."[141] But by 2016, surveys showed that over 80 percent favored reduction of prison populations as a primary goal of the criminal justice system.[142] And when given more context, the public's attitudes toward incarceration appear to be even more attuned to its negative aspects. In one 2012 PEW poll, 78 percent of respondents stated it would be acceptable to reduce prison time for low-risk, nonviolent offenders to close budget deficits,[143] and over 80 percent believed that more money should be spent on alternatives to prison for such offenders.[144] Well over a majority of respondents in the same poll endorsed the following statement: "It does not matter whether a nonviolent offender is in prison for 18 or 24 [or] 30 months . . . What really matters is that the system does a better job of making sure that when an offender does get out, he is less likely to commit another crime." In two polls of Wisconsin citizens (a "purple" state) in 2012–13, a majority of respondents supported early release for both nonviolent and *violent* offenders—at a point

Justice, Working Paper No. CI072016, 2016), https://joinnia.com/wp-content/uploads/2017/02/The-Economic-Burden-of-Incarceration-in-the-US-2016.pdf.

138 See generally, Tonry, supra note 133.

139 See generally Jessica Kelley & Arthur Rizer, Keep Calm and Carry on with State Criminal Justice Reform, 32 Fed. Sent. Rep. 86 (2017).

140 H.R. 5682, 115th Cong. (2018), https://www.congress.gov/bill/115th-congress/house-bill/568.

141 Princeton Survey Research Associates International. The NCSC Sentencing Attitudes Survey: A Report on the Findings 38 (2006).

142 *See* Holly Harris & Andrew Howard, Ryan's Victory Trumps Justice Reform Opponents, The Hill (Aug. 15, 2016, 4:51 PM), available at http://thehill.com/blogs/pundits-blog/crime/291500-ryans-victory-trumps-justice-reform-opponents; see also Justin McCarthy, Americans' Views Shift on Toughness of Justice System, GALLUP (Oct. 20, 2016), available at http://www.gallup.com/poll/196568/americans-views-shift-tough-ness-justice-system.aspx.

143 PEW Center on the States, Public Opinion on Sentencing and Corrections Policy in America 5 (2012).

144 Id. at 1, 4, 7.

halfway through their sentence no less—if the offender "can demonstrate that he is no longer a threat to society."[145]

Those types of sentiments cry out for some form of risk assessment.

1.3 THE POTENTIAL ROLE OF RISK ALGORITHMS

Several worthy solutions to the mass incarceration problem have been proposed and, in some states, they have been implemented. Prominent initiatives include replacing cash bail with release on recognizance or some sort of nonmonetary condition, shortening sentences either at the front end or through early release, and creating more alternatives to jail and prison. The latter development has been spurred in part through innovative funding initiatives. For instance, California's "realignment" policy of a decade ago prohibited the use of state prisons for the purpose of confining certain categories of offenders, which created an incentive for localities to develop cheaper options.[146] In Minnesota, the state directly subsidized the development of community-based programs and, partly as a result, has a much smaller prison population and a much larger probation population than neighboring Wisconsin, which still functions under vestiges of a truth-in-sentencing regime.[147]

Despite their appeal, however, all of these initiatives have been difficult to pull off. Within a few months of eliminating cash bail, the state of New York passed a bill retracting many of the changes, after a reported spike in crimes.[148] While several states have eliminated mandatory minima and softened other sentencing schemes, judges and correctional officials have exercised their new discretion under the influence of the same dynamics that brought us the tough-on-crime movement at the end of the twentieth century; in the federal system, after judges were freed from abiding by the relatively rigid federal

[145] Michael O'Hear & Darren Wheelock, Imprisonment Inertia and Public Attitudes toward "Truth-in-Sentencing," 2015 BYU L.Rev. 257, 279. See also Colleen M. Berryessa, A Tale of "Second Chances": An Examination of U.S. Public Support for Early Release Mechanisms that Reconsider Long-Term Prison Sentences tbl. 2 (forthcoming, 2021) (finding that a substantial majority of those surveyed were in favor of early release even for violent offenders and that a key reason for this stance is the supposition that the individual "is no longer or unlikely to be a threat to public safety").

[146] For a description of realignment, see Michael O'Hear, *The Failed Promise of Sentencing Reform* 171–91 (2017).

[147] Id. 207–08.

[148] Jamiles Lartey, New York Tried to Get Rid of Bail. Then the Backlash Came, Politico (Apr. 23, 2020), available at https://www.politico.com/news/magazine/2020/04/23/bail-reform-coronavirus-new-york-backlash-148299.

sentencing guidelines, sentences actually increased.[149] While California's realignment policy did dramatically reduce the state prison population by 25 percent over a six-year period, it was the result of a unique set of circumstances, including a desperate economic situation and an extremely unusual Supreme Court command that the state restructure its prisons;[150] further, many of the offenders who would have been sent to prison ended up still being confined in local jail (often in worse conditions than in prison),[151] and over 10,000 more should never have been incarcerated in the first place, since they were there on "technical violations" of parole or probation that did not involve a new crime.[152]

Another popular reform that has had more success focuses on extending leniency to offenders convicted of nonviolent crimes. Prodded by the Justice Reinvestment Initiative (JRI)—a public-private coalition of the Department of Justice, the Pew Charitable Trust, the Center for State Governments, and the Vera Institute for Justice that aims to shift money from prisons to community programs—states like Texas, Georgia, and South Carolina have reduced sanctions, accelerated probation and parole, and increased treatment programs for lower-level offenders such as those charged with drug possession crimes.[153] To attract bipartisan support, however, these efforts aimed solely at the "low-hanging fruit" of minor offenders who ended up in prison, which meant that they had little long-term impact on prison populations.[154] During the period in which these

149 United States Sentencing Commission, Report on the Continuing Impact of *United States v. Booker* on Federal Sentencing (Wash., D.C. USSC, 2012), Part C, 19.

150 The immediate triggering case was the Supreme Court's decision in Brown v. Plata, 563 U.S. 493 (2011), which held prison overcrowding in California and the state's failure to provide treatment for prisoners with mental illness violated the Eighth Amendment.

151 Abbie Vansickle & Manuel Villa, Who Begs to Go to Prison? California Jail Inmates, available at https://www.themarshallproject.org/2019/04/23/who-begs-to-go-to-prison-california-jail-inmates (April 23, 2019) (stating that, as a result of realignment, 175,000 people were sentenced to county jails rather than penitentiaries and that many want to go back to the penitentiaries, given horrific jail conditions, as evidenced in part by an increased death rate in jails, increases in gang warfare, and inadequate funding).

152 Joan Petersilia, California's Correctional Paradox of Excess and Derivation, 37 Crime & J. 207, 265–66 (2008) (stating that 20 percent of the 77 percent of prisoners returned for parole violations were "administrative," not criminal).

153 See James Austin et al., Ending Mass Incarceration: Charting a New Justice Reinvestment 1, 6 (2013), http://sentencingproject.org/doc/publications/sen_Charting%20a%20New%20Justice%20Reinvestment.pdf.

154 William J. Sabol & Miranda L. Baumann, Justice Reinvestment: Vision and Practice, 3 Ann. Rev. Criminol. 317, 334 (2020). ("JRI could not achieve substantial reductions in prison populations or significant cost savings because it did not deal with violent offenders or those with long criminal histories (other than reserve prison space for them). . . . These are not issues around which bipartisan compromise could have been easily forged within the confines of the program.")

initiatives took hold only about 6 percent of state inmates and less than 2 percent of federal inmates qualified as "unambiguously low-level" drug offenders,[155] almost 80 percent of those serving time for a nonviolent offense actually were classified as "serious" offenders and thus rendered ineligible for release,[156] and people convicted of violent crimes accounted for over two-thirds of state prison growth.[157] Expansion of the reforms to a greater number of "nonviolent" offenders, much less violent offenders, has been successfully resisted.

As both the experience of reform states and the poll data indicate, real change in incarceration practices will not occur unless politicians, government officials, and the public have reasonable assurances that most of the individuals who are meant to benefit from these types of reforms will not commit new serious felonies. Even advocates for abolishing prisons always express the important caveat that confinement needs to be retained for the "dangerous few."[158] Those focused on civil liberties have an additional concern. They worry that, to the extent these initiatives depend upon the subjective judgments of judges and parole boards, the move toward unconditional pretrial releases, shorter sentences, and intermediate dispositions will not be evenly distributed, but rather disfavor people of color or others who fit certain stereotypes.[159]

Risk assessment instruments, or RAIs, can play a significant role in assuaging these fears. As subsequent chapters will demonstrate, these instruments are more accurate than unstructured assessments of risk. They permit decision-makers to identify more precisely the risk posed by individuals, and thus can mollify the public's natural fear of decarceration. A comparison of bail reform efforts in the adjoining states of New York and New Jersey makes the point. In New York, as noted above, the legislature's attempt at reform simply ended cash bail for large categories of offenders. Jail populations plummeted, but police reported that crime rates went up.[160] While these crime statistics were probably

155 Eric L. Sevigny & Jonathan P. Caulkins, Kingpins or Mules: An Analysis of Drug Offenders Incarcerated in Federal and State Prisons, 3 Criminol. & Pub. Pol'y 401, 418 (2004).

156 Bert Useem & Anne Morisson Piehl, Prison State: The Challenge of Mass Incarceration 60–61 (2008).

157 Marie Gottschalk, No Way Out? Life Sentences and the Politics of Penal Reform, in Life Without Parole: America's New Death Penalty? 227, 237 (Charles J. Ogletree & Austin Sarat, eds., 2012).

158 Allegra M. McLeod, Prison Abolition and Grounded Justice, 62 UCLA L. Rev. 1156, 1168 (2015). ("Who and how many are the dangerous few? The answer to this question is by no means self-evident but its complete and final resolution ought not to interfere with serious engagement with abolitionist analysis.")

159 Tonja Jacobi, Song Richardson & Gregory Barber, The Attrition of Rights under Parole, 87 U.S.C. L. Rev. 887, 891–92 (2014).

160 Jamiles Lartey, New York Rolled Back Bail Reform. What Will The Rest Of The Country Do?, The Marshall Project (Apr. 23, 2020, 6:00 AM), available at https://www

inflated, the public reaction to them led to a rollback of the reform. In neighboring New Jersey, the virtual elimination of bail occurred two years earlier, and led to a 30 percent decrease in jail populations with virtually no backlash. The key difference between the two reform efforts: New Jersey's law focused on public safety by requiring judges to consult a risk assessment tool and training them on how to do it.[161] Similar instrument-based pretrial programs have been established in numerous other jurisdictions, with similar results.[162] In New York itself, the instrument now used after the aborted reform recommends release without conditions for 83.9 percent of Blacks, 83.5 percent of whites and 85.8 percent of Hispanics.[163]

As this last set of statistics illustrates, RAIs can also reify, in a way that unstructured risk assessment cannot, the fact that most offenders pose only a low risk, particularly of violent reoffending. For instance, one study of the pretrial setting that used an RAI found that only 8 percent of the sample population was at high risk of offending prior to trial,[164] a far cry from the 60 percent who are currently detained without bail or on bail they cannot meet. Another study of pretrial detention practices using New York data concluded that 42 percent more arrestees would be released as low risk if an RAI replaced cash bail with an RAI using machine learning.[165] Numerous other studies indicate that jurisdictions using RAIs can release a greater number of people without raising crime rates.[166]

.themarshallproject.org/2020/04/23/in-new-york-s-bail-reform-backlash-a-cautionary-tale-for-other-states.

161 Id.

162 Tiana Herring, Bail Reform: Reducing Pretrial Populations and Protecting Public Safety, The Crime Report, Nov. 27, 2020, https://thecrimereport.org/2020/11/17/bail-reform-reducing-pretrial-popluations-and-public-safety/ (detailing programs in Kentucky, Washington, D.C., New Orleans, San Francisco, Jefferson County, Colo., Santa Clara County, Calif., Cook County, Ill., and Yakima County, Wash).

163 Corinne Ramey, Algorithm Helps New York Decide Who Goes Free Before Trial, Wall St. J., Sept. 20, 2020, https://www.w.sj.com/articles/algorithm-helps-new-york-decide-who-goes-free -before -trial-11600610400.

164 Shima Baradaran Baughman, The Bail Book 198 (2017) (describing a study in which only 8 percent of arrestees were considered high risk, and arguing that only this group should be confined pretrial).

165 Jon Kleinberg et al., Human Decisions and Machine Predictions, NBER Working Paper Series (February 2017), at https://www.cs.cornell.edu/home/kleinber/w23180.pdf ("[A] policy simulation shows crime can be reduced by up to 24.8% with no change in jailing rates, or jail populations can be reduced by 42.0%with no increase in crime rates").

166 Douglas B. Marlowe et al., Employing Standardized Risk Assessment in Pretrial Release Decisions: Association with Criminal Justice Outcomes and Racial Equity, 44 L. & Hum. Behav. 361 (2020); Evan M. Lowder et al., Effects of Pretrial Risk Assessments on Release Decisions and Misconduct Outcomes Relative to Practice as Usual, J. Crim. Just. (2020),

The story is similar in the post-conviction setting. Researchers with bipartisan credentials who audited the compositions of the prison populations in three states estimated that, if danger to the community were the only justification for continued confinement, roughly half the prisoners would be released.[167] The PATTERN (for Prisoner Assessment Tool Targeting Estimated Risk and Needs), the risk assessment instrument developed in connection with the First Step Act, adopts a very narrow definition of low risk, but nonetheless initially identified 48 percent of its sample population of prisoners as "low" or "minimum" risk and thus eligible for early release from their prison sentences.[168] In Virginia, RAIs designed to recommend to judges who should be sentenced to prison alternatives identified as low risk 63 percent of drug offenders and 43 percent of larceny and fraud offenders, with low risk defined as between a 10–15 percent chance of recidivating with the next three years.[169]

When offender risk and base rates for reoffending are not quantified in this way, the tendency, at least in the United States, is to opt for incarceration. In particular, judges and prosecutors who are subject to election (which describes almost all state court judges and prosecutors), and parole board members who owe their livelihoods to fickle politicians, have good reason to avoid appearing "soft" on crime, given the American cultural proclivities that this chapter has highlighted.[170] As David Ball's parsing of the psychology

available at https://doi.org/10.1016/j.jcrimjus.2020.101754.; Jodi L. Viljoen et al., Impact of Risk Assessment Instruments on Rates of Pretrial Detention, Postconviction Placements, and Release: A Systematic Review and Meta-analysis, 43 L. & Hum. Behav. & L. 397 (2019); Laura & John Arnold Foundation, About the Public Safety Assessment: Research, available at https://advancingpretrial.org/psa/research/ (last visited May 31, 2020) (reporting studies in Cook County, Ill; Bernalillo County, NM; New Jersey; Mecklenberg County, NC; Kentucky; and Yakima County, Wash.; Kenneth Rose, Virginia Pretrial Risk Assessment Instrument (VPRAI) & Praxis Overview 16 (2018)), available at https://www.dcjs.virginia.gov/sites/dcjs.virginia.gov/files/announcements/vpraipraxisoverview6112018.pdf (reporting that judges who used risk assessment instruments released more arrestees than those who did not).

167 Anne Morrison Piehl, Bert Useem & John J. DiIulio, Jr. Right-Sizing Justice: A Cost-Benefit Analysis of Imprisonment in Three States (1999). See also Bert Useem & Anne Morrison Piehl, Prison State: The Challenge of Mass Incarceration ch. 3, text before note 129 (2008) (concluding, based on three economic cost-benefit studies of five state prison systems, that "[a]lthough it clearly pays on incapacitation grounds alone to incarcerate those at the eightieth percentile [of risk] in all five states, it does not appear to 'pay' to incarcerate those below the median").

168 The First Step Act of 2018: Risk and Needs Assessment System 58 (2019), available at https://www.bop.gov/inmates/fsa/docs/the-first-step-act-of-2018-risk-and-needs-assessment-system.pdf.

169 Va. Criminal Sentencing Commission, 2012 Annual Report (2012), www.vcsc.virginia.gov/2012VCSCAnnualReport.pdf.

170 See Jeffrey Rachlinski and Andrew J. Wistrich, Judging the Judiciary by the Numbers: Empirical Research on Judges, 13 Ann. Rev. L. & Soc. Sci. 203 (2017).

literature shows, there is also "the human tendency to desire certainty and simplicity"; Ball suggests that this desire, which he attributes to judges as well as everyone else, "may help explain why our default seems to be to keep someone locked up, 'just in case'—and why this desire is resistant to information and argument."[171]

In contrast, the quantified results of well-validated risk assessment instruments can provide a concrete, rational basis for diversion or release. If, as recommended in this book, adherence to those results is *required* in most circumstances, the human urge to incapacitate those in the law's grasp can be even more effectively resisted, because decision-makers must obey the objective facts. Evidence of such a dynamic comes from Virginia, which found that judges using risk algorithms were willing to reduce sentences even for sex offenders, "when they can point to the low risk-assessment score as a second opinion to support their decision."[172]

For the same reasons, racial and other types of bias in decision-making about pretrial and post-conviction release can be significantly reduced if the relevant cut-points have the force of law.[173] Even if, as some claim, risk assessment instruments are more likely to misclassify blacks than whites as high risk (a claim that Chapter 4 looks at closely), large numbers of blacks will still be classified as low risk. If that categorization creates a presumption against incarceration, more people of color will be eligible for release.[174] In contrast, a regime that is based on intuitive or clinical judgments about who is "dangerous" is too easily manipulated and prone to overly conservative outcomes influenced by conscious or unconscious prejudices. Indeed, the available research indicates that racial disparity becomes pronounced when, contrary to the recommendation of this book, legal decision-makers depart from the risk algorithm.[175]

171 W. David Ball, The Peter Parker Problem, 95 N.Y.U. L. Rev. 879, 879 (2020). Ball suggests, as one antidote, requiring judges to look at cases in "tranches," a form of RAI. Id. at 916.

172 Megan T. Stevenson & Jennifer L. Doleac, IZA Inst. of Labor Econ., Algorithmic Risk Assessment in the Hands of Humans 20 (2019), available at http://ftp.iza.org/dp12853.pdf; see also, Sarah Desmarais & Samantha A . Zottola, Violent Risk Assessment: Current Status and Contemporary Issues, 103 Marquette L. Rev. 793, 804–07 (2020) (reporting research indicating that the majority of studies show that risk assessment instruments, when implemented properly, reduce both use of restrictive conditions and violent recidivism).

173 Stéphane Mechoulan & Nicolas Sahuguet, Assessing Racial Disparities in Parole Release, 44 J. Leg. Studies 49, 70 (2015) (finding that parole boards that use actuarial instruments were not racially biased in their decisions to release blacks and white prisoners).

174 Kevin Reitz, The Compelling Case for Low Violence-risk Preclusion in American Prison Policy, 38 Beh. Sci. & L. 207 (2020).

175 Megan Stevenson, Assessing Risk Assessment in Action, 103 Minn. L. Rev. 303, 373 (2018) ("Kentucky's experience with risk assessment should somewhat assuage concerns about expanded racial disparities, but further research is needed"); Ben Green & Yiling Chen,

Risk algorithms can also help identify ways of ameliorating the risk of arrestees and offenders, whether they are released or confined. The old mantra that "nothing works" in the battle against recidivism has been soundly debunked.[176] As one 2008 review of the research summarized it: "The global question of whether rehabilitation treatment works to reduce recidivism has been answered in the affirmative by every meta-analyst who has conducted a systematic synthesis of a broad sample of the available experimental and quasi-experimental research."[177] Ten years later, another meta-analysis of institutional programs confirmed that the recidivism of treated adults was roughly 35 percent lower than those who are not treated.[178]

In many types of cases, community-based programs are even more effective at curbing violent behavior. This is especially so of rehabilitation efforts that focus on skills rather than discipline, that concentrate on high risk offenders rather than low risk offenders, and that take place in lieu of prison rather than post-release.[179] Numerous books published in the last several years, including *Smart Decarceration*;[180] *From Retribution to Public*

Disparate Interactions: An Algorithm-in-the-Loop Analysis of Fairness in Risk Assessments (2019) (unpublished manuscript), available at https://scholar.harvard.edu/files/19-fat.pdf [https://perma.cc/Q8QA-AHHL] ("while race had a direct role in increasing the risk score's influence on participants, the disparities in influence and deviations also arose due to participants responding to particularly salient features that are unevenly distributed by race (such as number of prior convictions)—essentially double-counting features for which the risk assessment had already accounted"); Jon Kleinberg et al., Human Decisions and Machine Predictions 32 (2020), available at https://papers.ssrn.com/sol3/papers.cfm?abstract_id=2920398 (showing, using an algorithm, that "it is possible to reduce the share of the jail population that is minority – that is, reduce racial disparities within the current criminal justice system – while simultaneously reducing crime rates relative to the judge").

176 See generally Robert Martinson, New Findings, New Views: A Note of Caution Regarding Sentencing Reform, 7 Hofstra L. Rev. 243 (1979) (in which the author essentially repudiates his earlier review of research, which had come to stand for the proposition that "nothing works" in terms of reducing recidivism).

177 Mark W. Lipsey & Francis T. Cullen, The Effectiveness of Correctional Rehabilitation: A Review of Systematic Reviews, 3 Ann. Rev. L & Soc. Sci. 297, 306 (2008).

178 Nina Papalia et al., A Meta-Analytic Review of the Efficiency of Psychological Treatments for Violent Offenders in Correctional and Forensic Mental Health Settings, 26 Clinical Psychology: Science and Practice 1, 15 (2019), available at https://onlinelibrary.wiley.com/doi/epdf/10.1111/cpsp.12282.

179 Lipsey & Cullen, supra note 177; Christopher T. Lowenkamp, Edward J. Latessa & Alexander M. Holsinger, The Risk Principle in Action: What Have We Learned from 13,676 Offenders and 97 Correctional Programs? 52 Crime & Delinq. 77, 89–90 (2006) (meta-review finding that targeting offenders identified as high risk is more effective at reducing risk); Francis T. Cullen & Cheryl Lero Jonson, Rehabilitation and Treatment Programs, in Crime and Public Policy 293, 303 (James Q. Wilson & Joan Petersilia, eds., 2011).

180 Smart Decarceration: Achieving Criminal Justice Transformation in the 21st Century (Matthew Epperson & Carrie Pettus-Davis, eds., 2017).

Safety;[181] *Beyond Recidivism*;[182] and *Juveniles at Risk: A Plea for Preventive Justice*[183] (the latter a book I coauthored with Mark Fondacaro), provide theoretical and empirical support for the proposition that community-based offender rehabilitation and reentry programs for released offenders can be a smart investment. And examples of such programs succeeding in the field are legion.[184]

While these programs are an essential component of any attempt to reduce risk, this book only briefly rehearses the vast literature that already exists on the topic of risk reduction and risk management.[185] Rather, the emphasis here will be on the fact that RAIs can play a very significant role in sorting out which offenders should go in which programs. For instance, numerous authors in *Smart Decarceration* recommend that the decisions about prison entry and release should be aided by actuarial-based risk assessment and risk management tools, if steps are taken to enhance their accuracy and transparency, and if they are used primarily as a mechanism for decreasing sentences and fitting rehabilitation programs to the individual needs of the offender.[186] These types of changes should lessen public fears that shortened prison terms will unleash

181 William R. Kelly et al., From Retribution to Public Safety: Disruptive Innovation of American Criminal Justice (2017).

182 Beyond Recidivism: New Approaches to Research on Prisoner Reentry and Reintegration (Andrea Levenretz, Elsa Y. Chen & Johnna Christian, eds., 2020).

183 Christopher Slobogin & Mark Fondacaro, Juveniles at Risk: A Plea for Preventive Justice 80–93 (2011).

184 For specific risk management programs, see id. at 129–52; HudsonLink.org, "What We Do," available at http://www.hudsonlink.org/what-we-do/; James McGuire, What Works in Correctional Intervention? Evidence and Practical Implications, in Offender Rehabilitation in Practice: Implementing and Evaluating Effective Programs (Gary A. Bernfeld, David P. Farrington & Alan W. Leshied, eds., 2001); What Else Works?: Creative Work with Offenders (Jo Brayford, Francis Cowe & Jon Deering, eds., 2010). As noted in the text, programs that are therapeutic rather than punitive, aim at high-risk offenders, and take place in the community are the most effective at reducing risk. Brandon C. Welsh et al., Promoting Change, Changing lives: Effective Prevention and Intervention to Reduce Serious Offending, in From Juvenile Delinquency to Adult Crime: Criminal Careers, Justice Policy, and Prevention 245 (Rolf Loeber & David P. Farrington, eds., 2012). Programs aimed at reducing recidivism produce especially robust results. See Kansas Juvenile Justice Reforms Slash Number of Youths in Confinement by 63%, The Crime Report (Apr. 19, 2019), available at https://thecrimereport.org/2019/04/29/Kansas-juvenile-justice-reforms-slash-number-of-youths-in-confinement-by-63/; Christina Carmichael, Juvenile Justice and Youth Aids Program 45 (2015) (description of Wisconsin program).

185 See in particular, Chapter 2's discussion of the intervention criterion (section 2.6).

186 Julian Adler, Sarah Picard-Firtshce, Michael Rempel & Jennifer A. Tallon, Empirical Means to Decarcerative Ends? Advancing the Science and Practice of Risk Assessment, in Smart Decarceration, supra note 180, at 210; Faye S. Taxman & Amy Murphy, Community Interventions for Justice-Involved Individuals: Assessing Gaps in Programming to Promote Decarceration, in Smart Decarceration, supra note 180, at 194–95.

hordes of dangerous criminals, at the same time they provide offenders with the best opportunity to succeed.

In theory, then, risk assessment instruments could bring significant benefits. First, fewer people—of all ethnicities—would be put in jail prior to trial and in prison after conviction. Second, for a substantial number of those who are imprisoned, overall sentences would be shorter. Third, treatment resources would be more efficiently allocated. Fourth, for these three reasons, the capital outlays for prisons and jails would be substantially less (although alternatives to prison, including good treatment programs, would cost more). Fifth, the public would continue to be protected, and perhaps would be even better protected, from the most dangerous individuals. Sixth, lower risk individuals would be less subject to the well-documented criminogenic effects of incarceration,[187] and better positioned to build and maintain a life outside of jail or prison that does not involve criminal activity.

For some or all of these reasons, at least fourteen states have adopted pretrial RAIs,[188] about half the states use RAIs in some fashion at the dispositional stage, and almost all rely on them to allocate correctional resources.[189] Despite their increased use, however, the full impact of risk algorithms has yet to be either realized or adequately assessed. That is because—contrary to the position adopted in this book—their use is, in every jurisdiction, entirely discretionary.[190] For instance, even in jurisdictions, such as Kentucky and

187 See supra note 133; David Roodman, The Impacts of Incarceration on Crime, ssrn.com/abstract=363864; Martin H. Pritkin, Is Prison Causing Crime?, 2008 Wisc. L. Rev. 1049, 1082 ("we can tentatively estimate that incarceration causes about 7 percent of total crime: 1 percent because of in-prison crime, 2 percent because of prison-induced recidivism, and 4 percent because of the impact of incarceration on the delinquency of inmates' children"); Thomas H. Cohen, The Supervision of Low-Risk Federal Offenders: How the Low-Risk Policy has Changed Federal Supervision Practices without Compromising Community Safety, 80 FED. PROB. 3, 3 (2016); Marie VanNostrand & Gena Keebler, Pretrial Risk Assessment in the Federal Court, 73 FED. PROB. 3, 6 (2009) (finding that low-risk pretrial defendants have better chance of success if released pending trial with minimal conditions).

188 Amber Widgery, Nat'l Conference of State Legislatures, Trends in Pretrial Release: State Legislation Update (2018), available at https://www.ncsl.org/portals/1/ImageLibrary/WebImages/Criminal%20Justice/pretrialEnactments_2017_v03.pdf.

189 Jodi L. Viljoen et al., Do Risk Assessment Tools Help Manage and Reduce Risk of Violence and Reoffending? A Systematic Review, 42 Law & Hum. Behav. 181, 181 (2018).

190 Generally the statutes say that state officials should "consider" the risk assessment results. See, e.g., Ky. Rev. Stat §532.007(3)1) ("Sentencing judges shall consider... the result of a defendant's risk and needs assessment included in the presentence investigation"); Ohio Rev. Code §5120.114 (the department "shall select a single validated risk assessment tool for adult offenders" to be used by judges at sentencing, corrections officials at the state and local levels, and parole officials); Wash. Rev. Code § 9.94A.500 (2013) ("the [sentencing] court may order the department [of corrections] to complete a risk assessment report," which "the court shall consider" before imposing sentence).

Virginia, where the results of RAIs are supposed to heavily influence judicial determinations, judges often ignore them. In Kentucky, both the initial switch to a pretrial risk assessment regime and the introduction of an RAI two years later led to an increase in releases of arrestees, with no appreciable surge in pretrial criminal activity. But soon after both events, judges reverted to their old methods of evaluating risk, and pretrial releases dropped back to their original level; additionally, judges who ignored the instruments (in about two-thirds of the cases overall) increased the racial disparities in the group that was released.[191] Likewise, in Virginia, a 2016 study found that RAI-based sentencing recommendations were overridden in 40 percent of the cases; judges imprisoned 42 percent of those recommended for alternatives to prison and permitted alternative dispositions for 23 percent of those recommended for imprisonment.[192] Other researchers report similar dynamics.[193]

The little evidence we do have about the impact of taking RAIs seriously, however, is encouraging. The Kentucky experience suggests that an RAI can have the desired effect on incarceration rates, without increasing the danger to the public, *if* judges adhere to the RAI results. Consistent with that finding, in 2015 Charlotte, NC used a risk tool to cut its jail population by about 20 percent with no perceptible increase in the crime rate,[194] and in 2018 New Jersey experienced a 55 percent decline in pretrial detainees after the adoption of its risk assessment tool, with only 20 percent of its arrestees kept in jail prior to trial and no increase in pretrial crime rates.[195] Very likely, the reason risk algorithms had more impact in New Jersey than Kentucky was that, as noted earlier, New Jersey judges were consulted about the introduction of RAIs, and thus bought into a more structured decision-making

191 Stevenson, supra note 175, at 308–09.

192 See Brandon Garrett, Alexander Jakubow & John Monahan, Judicial Reliance in Risk Assessment of Drug and Property Offenders: A Test of the Treatment Resource Hypothesis, 46 Criminal Just. & Beh. 799, 807 (2019).

193 Sarah Brayne & Angele Christin, Technologies of Crime Prediction: The Reception of Algorithms in Policing and Criminal Court, Social Problems 1, 11 (2020), available at doi:10.1093/socpro/spaa004 ("most judges and prosecutors did not typically rely on the risk scores at their disposal").

194 Shaila Dewan, Judges Replacing Conjecture with Formula for Bail, N.Y. Times (June 26, 2015), available at https://www.nytimes.com/2015/06/27/us/turning-the-granting-of-bail-into-a-science.html.

195 Criminal Justice Reform Info. Ctr., Initial Release Decisions for Criminal Justice Reform Eligible Defendants, January 1, 2018–November 30, 2018 (2020), available at https://www.njcourts.gov/courts/assets/criminal/cjrreport2018.pdf?cacheID=i1yaARV; Glenn A. Grant, New Jersey Judiciary, 2018 Report to the Governor and the Legislature, available at https://njcourts.gov/courts/assets/criminal/2018cjrannual.pdf?c=taP&_ga=2.200160302.1876251703.1599063577-1894928735.1599063577

process.[196] At a minimum, these findings call for more research on the effect of treating RAI results presumptively.

More research is also needed on the possible cost-savings that RAIs could produce. Presumably, the significant reduction in pretrial detainees in New Jersey substantially reduced the state's correctional costs (although New Jersey has also established a Pretrial Monitoring Unit that did not previously exist).[197] The Virginia RAI, if given greater influence, could have the same effect, without increasing crime.[198] Consistent with such speculation, the JRI Institute estimated that, even when focused solely on non-violent offenders, evidence-based programs would have reaped about $4.6 billion in savings over a ten-year period in the seventeen states that pursued the initiative, had it been applied with rectitude.[199]

While scanty, the evidence that does exist suggests that, when given presumptive effect, risk algorithms can be instrumental in reducing incarceration rates, jail and prison costs, racial disparities, and threats to public safety, at the same time they can enhance the accuracy and integrity of risk assessments and the consistency of matches between offenders and rehabilitation programs. At the least, legislatures and courts should ignore the negative hyperbole directed at risk algorithms instruments long enough to allow a meaningful evaluation of whether they can help achieve these goals, an evaluation which to date has not occurred.[200] Ideally, policymakers would proactively facilitate efforts to ensure that these tools are given a fair test, through enabling their use and funding empirical analysis. Otherwise, the country may miss out on a powerful method of transforming the criminal justice system.

[196] See Criminal Justice Reform Info. Ctr., Pretrial Release Recommendation Decision Making Framework (DMF) (March 2018), available at https://www.njcourts.gov/courts/assets/criminal/decmakframwork.pdf?cacheID=7mEYXdb.

[197] Stuart Rabner & Glenn A. Grant, Criminal Justice Reform Info. Ctr., Pretrial Services Programs (2017), available at https://www.njcourts.gov/forms/12088_cjr_pretrial_svcs_brochure.pdf.

[198] See Va. Criminal Sentencing Comm'n, 2007 Annual Report (2007), available at http://www.vcsc.virginia.gov/2007VCSCReport.pdf. While Stevenson and Doleac, supra note 172, reach a different conclusion, they in fact find that more low risk offenders are being released, and that the recidivism rate for new felonies (undefined) within a three-year period for nonviolent offenders ranges from 9 to 16 percent. Id. at 13.

[199] Sabol & Bauman, supra note 154, at 330. However, this report also notes that, in fact, cost savings due to JRI in 28 states was closer to only $1.1 billion. Id.

[200] Id. at 334. (criticizing JRI research for its unfocused methodology). One promising report comes from Recidiviz.org, which claims that during the COVID crisis its algorithms were used by 34 states "to safely release 25,000 people," three times the rate of states that did not use its model. Doug Dais, The Missing Data in Criminal Justice Reform, Jan. 21, 2021, available at https://www.freethink.com/shows/catalysts/criminal-justice-technology).

To ensure a fair test of RAIs, legislatures and courts must also make clear the types of information they want the instruments to address, the measures empiricists should use in evaluating whether that information is accurate, and the types of risk factors that are off limits. In other words, to achieve their full legal potential, risk algorithms must meet three requisites. They must address the questions the law wants answered. They must do so as accurately as possible, in a way that allows their error potential to be known. And they must do so without trenching on the values of equality, autonomy and dignity that underlie the American criminal justice system. I call these mandates the fit, validity and fairness principles. They are the subject of the next three chapters, the first of which begins with a more detailed description of what risk assessments instruments are.

2

Fit

Why and When Data about Groups Are Relevant to Individuals

By one count, there are over 400 risk assessment instruments worldwide.[1] They come in all shapes and sizes. Most RAIs consist of five to ten variables, others purport to consider over 100. Some consist entirely of "static" risk factors that do not change over time because they are historical in nature (such as one's criminal record) or are based on immutable characteristics (such as gender or age at the time of one's first offense). Others also include "dynamic" or "variable" factors that are changeable, such as substance abuse, impulsivity, or mental health problems. Some include not only risk factors, but protective or promotive factors—factors that indicate *reduced* risk, such as a strong family structure.[2]

Many of the most prominent RAIs are strictly actuarial—meaning that the risk and protective factors are assigned weights based on statistical analysis and produce a numerical probability of reoffending—while others rely on "structured professional judgment" that gives the evaluator preset variables but allows more discretion as to how much effect those variables have on the ultimate conclusion. Some are focused solely on answering the "front-end" question of whether a person poses a significant risk. Others also aim at identifying ways of reducing risk through assessment of what are often called the person's "needs" (such as substance abuse treatment) and of his or her "responsivity" to intervention.[3]

1 Jay P. Singh et al., International Perspectives on the Practical Application of Violence Risk Assessment: A Global Survey of 44 Countries, 13 Int'l J. Forensic Mental Health 193, 193 (2014).

2 John Monahan & Jennifer Skeem distinguish between promotive factors that reduce risk, such as strong family life, and protective factors that act to reduce risk among high risk individuals, such as treatment for substance abuse. John Monahan & Jennifer Skeem, Risk Assessment in Criminal Sentencing, 12 Ann. Rev. Clinical Psychol. 489, 494 (2016). In this book, the word "protective" will be used to denote both types of factors.

3 The term "needs" is subject to numerous definitions. It is probably best reserved for dynamic factors that, if changed, reduce risk. See generally, Jennifer Skeem & John Monahan, "Risk," "Needs" and "Evidence" in Implementing the First Step Act, 38 Beh. Sci. & L. 287, 290 (2020) (noting that employment status and substance abuse are both dynamic factors but asserting

One often sees the comment that the legal system should use an RAI only for the purpose for which it was designed.[4] That is generally true. But the point emphasized in this chapter is different and, in a sense, the converse: an instrument's design should be structured to meet the law's purposes. Legal policymakers should be dictating the parameters of RAIs, not picking them off the shelf and hoping they meet the law's objectives. In a word (one popularized by the Supreme Court in its case law on scientific evidence),[5] the law should demand that risk algorithms "fit" legal needs.

In doing so, the criteria for assessing risk in the pretrial and post-conviction settings need to be framed just as carefully as elements of culpability are delineated when legislatures and courts seek to create crimes. Typically, a crime is defined in terms of particular conduct that occurs under particular circumstances and produces a particular result, with a particular mental state. These are usually called the conduct, circumstance, result, and mental state elements of crime. Risk can also be said to comprise four elements. At a minimum, for each type of legal setting (pretrial detention, front-end sentencing, back-end release, within-prison disposition), a risk assessment should address: (1) the probability (P), (2) that a particular type of offense outcome (O), (3) will occur within a specified period of time (T), (4) in the absence of a specified intervention (I). While these are all difficult questions to answer empirically, perhaps even more difficult is determining, as a *legal* matter, the values of P, O, T, and I that justify a particular intervention, particularly if that intervention involves a deprivation of liberty. To help think through the relevant considerations, some feel for current RAIs and the types of information they produce is useful.

2.1 RISK ASSESSMENT INSTRUMENTS

John Monahan and Jennifer Skeem have provided a helpful typology of "risk assessment."[6] That term encompasses a number of different practices that

that, to date, only substance abuse has clearly been shown to be a criminogenic need—that is, one that, if successfully treated, reduces risk).

4 See Erin Collins, Punishing Risk, 107 Geo. L.J. 57, 77 (2018) (noting that many RAIs were developed to address "how to administer punishment efficiently and effectively" yet are often used "to serve a different purpose, and one that their creator specifically warned against–to determine how much punishment is due").

5 Daubert v. Dow Chemical Pharmaceutical Co., 509 U.S. 579, 591 (1993) ("'Fit' is not always obvious, and scientific validity for one purpose is not necessarily scientific validity for other, unrelated purposes.").

6 John Monahan & Jennifer Skeem, Clinical and Actuarial Predictions of Violence: Scientific Status, in Modern Scientific Evidence: The Law and Science of Expert Testimony 179–80 § 9.11 (2019–20).

differ in the extent to which they: (1) rely on empirically valid risk and protective factors; (2) use a structured method for measuring these risk and protective factors; (3) establish a procedure for combining scores on the individual risk and protective factors into a total score; and (4) produce a final estimate of risk. *Clinical* risk assessment—the traditional and still typical method used by many judges, parole boards, and mental health professionals—structures none of these components; rather an estimate of risk is based on experience and perhaps intuition, and the factors considered may vary from case-to-case and be applied differently in different cases. *Checklist* risk assessment provides structure on the first component, by listing the factors that should be considered. *Structured professional judgment* (SPJ) risk assessment satisfies the first two components, by providing a list of factors and indicating how they should be measured (e.g., on a scale of 0–2), but avoids combining these measures for a total score, instead counselling that the item ratings be considered merely in arriving at an overall conclusion about risk. *Adjusted actuarial* risk assessment lists the factors, describes how they should be measured, and produces a total score, but allows evaluators to adjust or modify the score based on clinical judgment that is not structured by the instrument. Stand-alone *actuarial* risk assessment does not permit such adjustments, but rather produces a probability estimate that is considered final.

The term "risk assessment instruments" applies only to the last three types of practices. Consider these five examples. The Violence Risk Appraisal Guide-Revised (hereafter, VRAG), is an actuarial RAI relied on extensively in Canada and in several jurisdictions within the United States, mostly in connection with sentencing and criminal commitments.[7] It contains twelve largely static risk factors, having to do with the individual's score on the Psychopathy Checklist (a measure of psychopathy that takes into account criminal history); elementary school misconduct; diagnosis (with personality disorders positively correlated with risk, and—perhaps counterintuitively—schizophrenia negatively correlated with risk); age; presence of parents in home before age sixteen; performance on conditional release; nonviolent offenses; marital status; victim injury; victim gender; and history of alcohol abuse. The evaluator assigns a numerical subscore in connection with each risk factor and then adds the subscores to

7 For a description of the instrument and relevant research, see Grant T. Harris et al., Prospective Replication of the Violence Risk Appraisal Guide in Predicting Violent Recidivism Among Forensic Patients, 26 L. & Hum. Behav. 377 (2002). An updated description is found in N. Zoe Hilton et al., Actuarial Guides for Appraising the Risk of Violent Reoffending Among General Offenders, Sex Offenders and Domestic Assaulters, in Handbook of Violence Risk Assessment 131, 131–36 (Kevin S. Douglas & Randy K. Otto, eds., 2021) (hereafter, Douglas & Otto).

determine a total score that can range from less than –21 to more than 28. Initial research associated the lowest score on the VRAG with a 0 percent chance of violent offending within seven years, and the highest score with a 100 percent chance of violent offending within that period. Seven other "bins" or ranges are associated with recidivism probabilities of 8 percent through 76 percent.

A much slimmer actuarial RAI, called the Non-Violent Risk Assessment (NVRA), is used in Virginia.[8] The NVRA actually consists of several RAIs, with a separate tool for different categories of crime. For instance, if the crime of conviction is fraud, the instrument relies on just five static factors: offender age at the time of the offense (twenty-two points if the offender is younger than twenty-one); offender gender (ten points for males; one point for females); prior adult felony convictions (ten points if more than three); prior adult incarcerations (four points if one to nine; thirty-two points if more than ten); and legal restraints (e.g., probation) at the time of conviction (six points). If an offender receives more than thirty-one points on this instrument, prison is recommended; otherwise, the tool counsels the judge to consider "alternative punishment." Note that on this instrument a young male receives a prison recommendation if he has one prior felony conviction before the offense of conviction.

A third, more complicated instrument is the Correctional Offender Management Profiling for Alternative Sanctions tool (COMPAS).[9] It can be used either as an actuarial RAI or an adjusted actuarial RAI. Originally developed as an aid to corrections departments making decisions about placing, managing, and treating offenders, it has also informed sentencing, parole and pretrial release decisions. The COMPAS is much less transparent than the VRAG or the NVRA. Although the questions canvassed by the COMPAS (over 120) are available, the weight given to particular answers to those questions has not been disclosed, nor is it publicly known whether a given answer is even relevant to the ultimate risk assessment. The company that developed the COMPAS, equivant (formerly Northpointe), has stated that the factors that affect the tool's Violence Recidivism score consist of age at the time of the assessment, age at the time of the offender's first adjudication, the History of Violence Scale, the History of Noncompliance Scale, and the

8 For a description of the original instruments and some data on their implementation, see Richard Kern & Meredith Farrar-Owens, Sentencing Guidelines with Integrated Offender Risk Assessment, 16 Fed. Sent'g Rep. 165, 169 (2004) ("The non-violent risk assessment tool adopted as part of the discretionary sentencing guidelines serves to safely divert a significant share of low risk felons away from expensive prison beds into less costly alternative punishment programs.").

9 For a PDF of one version of the instrument, see www.documentcloud.org/documents/2702103-Sample-Risk-Assessment-COMPAS-CORE.html.

Vocational Educational Scale, but it is not willing to reveal the impact of each factor on the risk score or how the various scales are constructed. Also in contrast to the VRAG and the NVRA, the COMPAS recidivism scores are reported not in terms of probabilities or prison recommendations but in terms of "deciles;" inclusion in the first decile does not mean that the offender poses a 10 percent probability of recidivism but rather that the offender's risk and protective factors are similar to those in the bottom 10 percent of the group on which the COMPAS was validated. An offender is designated "low risk" if he or she fits within the first through fourth deciles, "medium risk" if within the fifth through seventh deciles, and "high risk" if within the eight through tenth deciles.[10]

The first three instruments are usually used to assist in determining whether imprisonment should occur or the types of interventions that might best prevent or reduce reoffending after conviction. In contrast, the Public Safety Assessment (PSA), developed by the Arnold Foundation, is an actuarial instrument used solely in the pretrial context to help determine whether a person should be released prior to trial and, if so, under what conditions.[11] It consists of three scales that evaluate the general risk, violence risk, and risk of failing to appear for trial, after considering factors such as age, convictions, pending charges, and prior failures to appear in court. Evaluations using the instrument generate a score ranging from one to six, with higher scores leading to a recommendation of detention prior to trial.

A final RAI that is sometimes used at sentencing, and often used to help figure out dispositional programs that might reduce risk, is the HCR-20.[12] As the name implies, this RAI, now in version 3, consists of twenty risk factors, ten having to do with historical matters, five relating to clinical symptoms, and five relating to risk management or treatment. The historical factors are previous violence; age at first violent incident; relationship instability; employment problems; substance use problems; major mental illness; psychopathy; early maladjustment; personality disorder; and prior supervision failure. The clinical factors are all dynamic: lack of insight; negative attitudes; active symptoms of major mental illness; impulsivity; and unresponsiveness to treatment. The risk management

10 See Northpointe, Practitioner's Guide to COMPAS 5 (2012), available at http://www.northpointeinc.com/files/technical_documents/FieldGuide2_081412.pdf.

11 For a description of this instrument, see https://www.psapretrial.org/about.

12 For a description of this instrument, see Kevin S. Douglas & Christopher D. Webster, The HCR-20 Violence Risk Assessment Scheme: Concurrent Validity in a Sample of Incarcerated Offenders, 26 Crim. Just. & Behav. 3, 8 (1999). An updated description is found in Kevin S. Douglas & Catherine S. Shaffer, The Science of and Practice with the HCR-20 V3, in Douglas & Otto, supra note 7, at 253–93.

factors are also variable: unfeasibility of plans; exposure to destabilizers; lack of personal support; noncompliance with remediation attempts; and stress. Each of the twenty factors is scored on a scale of 0–2, so that the maximum total score is forty. However, the developers of the HCR-20 strongly recommend that a strictly mathematical assessment should be avoided and that, instead, individuals should simply be characterized by the evaluator as "high," "medium," or "low" risk. Thus, the HCR-20 is generally considered a structured professional judgement (SPJ) tool, as distinguished from instruments like the VRAG, NVRA, COMPAS, and PSA, which are actuarial in nature.

All of these instruments but the HCR-20 rely on regression models, a relatively simple form of machine learning that involves humans inputting data and then relies on computers to calculate which variables correlate most strongly with the outcome variable of interest. Developers of these instruments must make several decisions during the RAI construction process.[13] They must decide where to get their data (e.g., government records, self-reports), what data to obtain with respect to reoffending (arrest, convictions, probation revocations, institutional incidents), what counts as a risk or protective factor, and the weight the risk and protective factors will be assigned in the algorithm. More sophisticated versions of RAIs involve computers setting their own rules about how much weight to assign variables, based on large amounts of "training" data.[14] The inner workings of this type of machine-learning tool are much less transparent to human observers than the RAIs described above. While such RAIs are not currently widely used in the criminal justice system,[15] they may become more available in the near future.

Their developers claim these instruments can validly estimate risk. But even if an RAI does what it purports to do (as defined in the next chapter), the important predicate question is whether its results are relevant to the legal system. That is the question addressed here.

2.2 G2I-USING INFORMATION ABOUT GROUPS TO RESOLVE INDIVIDUAL CASES

The most fundamental fit objection voiced about risk assessment instruments—at least those, like the VRAG, the NVRA, and the PSA, that are

13 Jessica Eaglin, Constructing Recidivism Risk, 67 Emory L.J. 59, 67–88 (2017).

14 For a description of machine learning and risk assessment, see Richard Berk, Machine Learning of Risk to Inform Sentencing Decisions, 27 Fed. Sent. Rep. 222 (2015).

15 Turgut Ozkan, Predicting Recidivism through Machine Learning 17 (2017) available at https://utd-ir.tdl.org/bitstream/handle/10735.1/ ("criminology … is lagging … when it comes to incorporating novel algorithmic decision-making tools").

actuarial in nature—is the allegation that they cannot provide information that is useful in deciding an individual case. One of the reasons the developers of SPJ instruments like the HCR-20 avoid a more quantitative approach is the belief that associating probabilities with an individual offender misrepresents the risk assessment enterprise to the extent it suggests that research about groups can predict whether a given individual will reoffend. The point was put most strongly by Stephen Hart, a developer of another SPJ instrument, who stated that "[i]t is impossible to directly measure (using some technology) or calculate (using some natural law) the specific probability or absolute likelihood that a particular offender will commit . . . violence, and even impossible to estimate this risk with any reasonable degree of scientific or professional certainty."[16] David Cooke and Christine Michie have chimed in, stating—and purporting to demonstrate statistically—that "it is clear that predictions of future offending cannot be achieved, with any degree of confidence, in the individual case."[17] If that is true, the numerical conclusions reached by the VRAG and the other actuarial instruments described above are meaningless. Rather, all that can be said is that, given a person's constellation of risk and protective factors, he or she is more or less likely to offend if certain interventions do not take place.

The view that nomothetic (group-based) information is irrelevant to a decision about an individual is not new with Hart, Cooke and Michie. In 1942, Gordon Allport, a psychologist, said "A fatal nonsequitur occurs in the reasoning that if 80% of the delinquents who come from broken homes are recidivists, then this delinquent from a broken home has an 80% chance of becoming a recidivist. The truth of the matter is that this delinquent has either 100% certainty of becoming a repeater or 100% certainty of going straight."[18] Some lawyers take the same view. In 1994, Justice Coyne of the Minnesota Supreme Court wrote "Not only are . . . statistics concerning the violent behavior of others irrelevant, but it seems to me wrong to confine any person on the basis not of that persons' own prior conduct but on the basis of statistical evidence regarding the behavior of other people."[19] Consistent with these views, courts have frequently excluded "statistical speculation"

[16] Stephen Hart, Evidence-Based Assessment of Risk for Sexual Violence, 1 Chapman J. Crim. Just. 143, 164 (2009).

[17] See David J. Cooke & Christine Michie, Limitations of Diagnostic Precision and Predictive Utility in the Individual Case: A Challenge for Forensic Practice, 34 Law & Hum. Behav. 259, 272 (2010).

[18] Gordon Allport, The Use of Personal Documents in Psychological Science, 49 S.S.R.C. Bulletin 156 (1942), quoted in Paul Meehl, Clinical versus Statistical Prediction 19 (1954).

[19] In re Linehan, 518 N.W2d 609, 616 (Minn. 1999) (Coyne, J., dissenting).

about risk on the ground that it is not "individualized" or "particularized" – more often than not, it is interesting to note, when the party introducing it is the defense.[20]

David Faigman, John Monahan, and I have called the issue raised by these types of comments the "G2i" problem, the translation of general information to individual cases.[21] While we agree that the law has paid insufficient attention to the difficulties inherent in this translation process, we disagree with the notion that it is not possible. Cooke and Michie's statistical argument that confidence intervals about recidivism probabilities are nonsensical has been roundly debunked by noted statisticians Peter Imrey and Philip Dawid, who find their position "seriously mistaken in many particulars" and conclude that their analysis should "play no role in reasoned discussions about violence recidivism risk assessment."[22] As Karl Hanson and Philip Howard have noted, the declarations made by Cooke, Michie and Hart, "if true … would be a serious challenge to the applicability of any empirically based risk procedure to any individual for anything."[23]

I would go further. If these assertions against nomothetic risk assessment are true, any type of expert testimony – whether or not empirically based – would be suspect. Even the expert who purports to bottom his or her conclusions solely on an interview with the individual in question relies – consciously or not – on stereotypes, past experiences with "similar" individuals, and literature about related groups. In the specific context of risk assessments, to the extent facts such as age, gender, criminal history, and personality traits influence the evaluator's conclusions, they do so because they are "known" or intuited to have particular correlations with, or effects, on behavior. Barbara Underwood put it well in 1979: "Although the clinician need not identify in advance the characteristics he will regard as salient, he must nevertheless evaluate the applicant on the basis of a finite number of

[20] See Porter v. Comm, 661 S.E.2d 415 (Va. 2008) (excluding defense testimony on this ground); see also, United States v. Taylor, 583 F.Supp.2d 923 (E.D. Tenn. 2008) (excluding defense testimony that "invites the jury to make decisions based upon group characteristics and assumptions"); Rhodes v. State, 896 N.Ed.2d 1193 (Ind.Ct.App. 2008) (holding that using an LSI-R score as an aggravating factor at sentencing was impermissible).

[21] See David Faigman, John Monahan & Christopher Slobogin, Group to Individual (G2i) Inference in Scientific Expert Testimony, 81 U. Chi. L. Rev. 417 (2014).

[22] Peter B. Imrey & A. Philip Dawid, A Commentary on Statistical Assessment of Violence Recidivism Risk, 2 Stat. & Pub. Pol'y 1, 1 (2015).

[23] R. Karl Hanson & Philip D. Howard, Individual Confidence Intervals Do Not Inform Decision-Makers About the Accuracy of Risk Assessment Evaluations, 34 Law & Hum. Behav. 275, 277 (2010).

salient characteristics, and thus, like the statistical decisionmaker, he treats the applicant as a member of a class defined by those characteristics."[24]

This does not mean that a risk assessment based on an RAI should be blasé about the G2i issue. A risk estimate from an RAI (indeed, any conclusion about risk) should not purport to say that a particular offender has X probability of reoffending. Nor should it state that the person will, or will not, reoffend, a fact that, in almost all cases, *is* unknowable. Rather, an evaluator using an RAI to estimate the risk an offender poses should report that the offender received a risk score that is consistent with the scores of a group studied in previous research, X percent of which offended. So phrased, a conclusion about risk offered in a legal proceeding is not "irrelevant" on G2i grounds.[25]

However, such a conclusion could still be irrelevant on a number of other grounds. It is a constitutional axiom that the elements of crime be clearly delineated, in part to provide sufficient notice to the public about prohibited conduct, but primarily to control the discretion of police, prosecutors and judges, who otherwise might abuse vague laws.[26] Because risk assessments can have the same impact on liberty as a conviction for crime, legislatures and courts should similarly be obligated to set forth, as a matter law, the elements of risk that must be proven. Again, those elements are (1) the probability, preferably quantified in terms of a group, (2) of a particular outcome, (3) within a particular time frame, (4) in the absence of a given intervention (usually incarceration).

2.3 THE PROBABILITY CRITERION

If a decision whether to detain an arrestee or imprison a convicted offender depended entirely on the risk the person poses, a conclusion that the individual is within a group associated with a 0 percent risk would presumably result in a non-prison disposition, whereas a conclusion that 100 percent of the offender's group recidivated in the past might result in a pretrial detention or a prison term of some length. Of course, most offenders will pose a degree of

[24] Barbara Underwood, Law and the Crystal Ball: Predicting Behavior with Statistical Inference and Individualized Judgment, 88 Yale L.J. 1408, 1427 (1979).

[25] See Erica Beecher-Monas, Lost in Translation: Statistical Inference in Court, 46 Ariz. St. L.J. 1057, 1092 (2014) (calling this type of formulation a "solution to the G2i problem in the courts" because "the instrument does not say . . . that the tested individual is 26% likely to recidivate; rather it says [h]e is merely part of a group with an average recidivism rate of 26%. Some will recidivate more, some less. The inference about the tested individual's likelihood of recidivism is left to the factfinder.").

[26] See generally John C. Jeffries, Legality, Vagueness, and the Construction of Penal Statutes, 71 Va. L. Rev. 189 (1985).

risk somewhere between those two poles. What degree of risk justifies an enhanced deprivation of liberty?

To the extent there is law on this issue, it is almost useless. The Bail Reform Act of 1984, which governs in federal cases, allows pretrial detention if the judge finds that the arrestee poses "a danger to any person or the community."[27] While the judge is to consider the "nature and seriousness" of the danger, the statute provides no further help on how probable it must be.[28] The same vacuous statutory language appears in sentencing schemes. Even in capital sentencing proceedings, where life literally hangs in the balance, the legal standard is extremely vague—although not, according to the Supreme Court, unconstitutionally so. Under the Texas statute upheld by the Court in *Jurek v. Texas*,[29] a person convicted of capital murder may be sentenced to death if the jury finds beyond a reasonable doubt that there is "a probability that the individual will commit criminal acts of violence that constitute a continuing threat to society."[30] Although occasionally Texas courts have permitted the parties to stipulate that "probability" means more likely than not,[31] the Texas Court of Criminal Appeals has explicitly and repeatedly refused to quantify or define that word.[32]

That is an abdication of its responsibility. The beyond-a-reasonable doubt standard that applies at criminal trials is also a vague term, but all agree that it requires at least a 90 percent level of certainty that the defendant committed the crime charged.[33] Something similar is necessary at sentencing, not just when the death penalty is at stake but whenever a deprivation of liberty might result. More specific definitions of terms like "probability" are crucial if legal

27 18 U.S.C. § 3142 (d)(2).

28 Id., at (g)(4).

29 428 U.S. 262 (1976).

30 Tex. Code Crim. Proc., Art. 37.071(b)(2).

31 See Varga v. State, 2003 WL 21466926, at *4 (Tex. Crim. App., 2003) ("The appellant alleges that both parties agreed to instructing the jury that the term 'probability' meant "something that's more likely than not to occur.").

32 See Long v. State, 2009 WL 960598, at *3 (Tex. Crim. App. 2009); Chamberlain v. State, 998 S.W.2d 230, 237–38 (Tex. Crim. App. 1999); King v. State, 553 S.W.2d 105, 107 (Tex. Crim. App. 1977).

33 See, e.g., Hal R. Arkes & Barbara A. Mellers, Do Juries Meet Our Expectations?, 26 Law & Hum. Behav. 625, 631 (2002) (discussing several surveys in which the mean and median responses of federal judges questioned about the beyond-a-reasonable-doubt standard were around 90 percent certainty); C. M. A. McCauliff, Burdens of Proof: Degrees of Belief, Quanta of Evidence, or Constitutional Guarantees?, 35 Vand. L. Rev. 1293, 1322, 1332, tbl. 8 (1982) (showing results of a survey in which federal judges' mean estimate of the probability of certainty required for beyond-a-reasonable-doubt proof was 90.28 percent); Brown v. Bowen, 847 F.2d 342, 345–46 (7th Cir. 1988) (90 percent or better).

decision-makers are to make the difficult normative determination of whether the risk a person poses should affect his or her liberty.

Furthermore, with the advent of RAIs, a more-likely-than-not standard—if that is how probability is defined—need not be just another abstract judicial pronouncement that, in practice, places no limitations on judges or juries. Nor, despite judicial expressions of concern to the contrary,[34] would such a standard be unreachable, even in capital proceedings where the probability must be proven beyond a reasonable doubt. RAIs like the VRAG can provide specific group probability estimates of violent crime ranging from 0 percent to 100 percent within a ten-year period. If "probability" were defined as more-likely-than-not (which might be quantified at 51 percent), and that probability had to be proven beyond a reasonable doubt (which might be quantified at 90 percent), the state would need to show that roughly 45 percent (51 percent x 90 percent) of people in the offender's risk category will commit "a violent act constituting a threat to society."[35] Of the nine probability bins produced by the VRAG, the upper five meet that threshold (although, as the following discussion of the outcome criterion indicates, that number could be reduced considerably depending on how "violent act" is defined). In noncapital proceedings or pretrial settings, where a lower standard of proof—clear and convincing evidence or a preponderance of the evidence—might be countenanced, the proof requirement would be relaxed even further.

An additional advantage of specifying the risk threshold is that it would create pressure on the developers of RAIs to be more transparent about the information they provide. While the VRAG provides estimates that directly answer the probability question, many RAIs do not. Recall that "third decile" on the COMPAS does not refer to a group, 30 percent of whom will recidivate, but rather a group that, in the validation sample, posed a lower risk than roughly 70 percent of the sample; because even the highest decile group on the COMPAS is associated with a probability of reoffending considerably lower than 100 percent, the third decile group is very likely associated with a reoffending risk much lower than 30 percent. Yet the decision-maker does not know how much lower.

The risk designations produced by the HCR-20 (and many other RAIs) are even more problematic in this regard. While a designation of "high risk"

34 See Addington v. Texas, 441 U.S. 418, 432 (1979) ("We have concluded that the reasonable-doubt standard is inappropriate in civil commitment proceedings because, given the uncertainties of psychiatric diagnosis, it may impose a burden the state cannot meet and thereby erect an unreasonable barrier to needed medical treatment.").

35 See John Monahan & David Wexler, Proof of a Definite Maybe: Proof and Probability in Civil Commitment, 2 Law & Hum. Behav. 37 (1978) (making this type of calculation).

virtually always results in enhanced intervention,[36] surveys that ask clinicians and judges how they define that term show tremendous variation. The average percentage associated with the "high risk" label falls somewhere between 60 and 70 percent, but the range of answers varies from 5 percent to 100 percent and the variability between raters is very high.[37] More troubling, one study of evaluators found that the probability of recidivating associated with a "moderate or high" rating was more than twice the actual recidivism rate of those groups.[38] Lay decision-makers are even more generous in their definition of "likelihood," with one study finding that a 1 percent chance of a sexual offense meets that definition and should be sufficient to authorize indefinite confinement.[39] If the required probability is specified by the law, neither evaluators nor judges would be able to rest their conclusions on such unspecified categorical pronouncements.

Decision-makers must also pay careful attention to how probabilities are phrased to make sure they provide the relevant information. For instance, the manual for the federal pretrial risk assessment instrument states: "Defendants who had one or more misdemeanor or felony charges at the time of arrest were 20 percent more likely to fail pending trial when compared to defendants who did not have a pending charge."[40] That statement does not mean that arrestees with one or more charges have a 20 percent chance of "failing" (i.e., reoffending or not appearing for trial); in fact, if only 5 percent of those without charges fail then this statement means that only 6 percent of those *with* charges fail! Far better to know is the probability of offending associated with the group in question.

36 Nicolas Scurich, The Case Against Categorical Risk Assessments, 37 Beh. Sci. & L. 554, 559 (2018) ("Virtually never does an individual who is deemed 'high risk' avoid loss of liberty in sexually violent predator commitment proceedings, in parole hearings for indeterminately-sentenced inmates, or in psychiatric civil commitment hearings") (citations omitted).

37 Id. at 556–57 (reporting a study in which the "high risk" designation among clinicians ranged from 38 percent to 100 percent; a study where the mean percentage for high risk among evaluators was 63 percent with a very large standard deviation of 23.2 percent; and a study finding a range of 5 to 100 percent among a sample of judges and forensic clinicians asked to define high risk).

38 Daniel Krauss, Gabriel I. Cook &. Lucas Klapatch, Risk Assessment Communication Difficulties: An Empirical Examination of the Effects of Categorical versus Probabilistic Risk Communication in Sexually Violent Predator Decisions, 36 Behav. Sci. & L. 532, 544 (2018).

39 Jefferson Knighton et al., How Likely Is "Likely to Reoffend" in Sex Offender Civil Commitment Trials?, 38 L. & Hum. Behav. 293 (2014).

40 Marie VanNostrand & Gena Keebler, Pretrial Risk Assessment in the Federal Courts, 73 Fed. Probation 3, 13 (2009).

2.4 THE OUTCOME CRITERION

Recall that the Texas death penalty statute defines risk in terms of the probability that the offender will commit "a violent act constituting a threat to society." As with the term "probability," this phrase begs for a definition. Indeed, despite *Jurek*, it may be unconstitutionally opaque. Forty years after *Jurek*, in *Johnson v. United States*,[41] the Supreme Court held that the residual clause of the Armed Career Criminal Act that defines "violent felony" is void for vagueness. The Act allows enhancement of a sentence by fifteen years to life if the court finds that the offender committed three or more "violent felonies," which at the time of *Johnson* the Act described as any crime that includes as an element the use of "physical force" against another, as well as any crime "that is burglary, arson, or extortion, or *otherwise involves conduct that presents a serious potential risk of physical injury to another*" (emphasis supplied by the Court).[42] In finding the italicized phrase constitutionally deficient, the Supreme Court reasoned that there are literally hundreds of crimes—ranging from witness tampering, to failing to stop after seeing a police officer's signal, to attempted burglary—that could present a risk of physical injury, but no legitimate way for a court to determine the "seriousness" of the risk.[43] The Texas death penalty statute is even more suspect, because it tells the factfinder that the aggravating factor exists if there is a probability of a violent act that "constitutes a threat" to others.

Even if violence is defined more precisely to mean, for instance, the use of physical force against another, the law's normative job should not be done. For instance, physical force against another can include a simple assault, risk of which presumably should not be enough, by itself, to authorize the death penalty.[44] In fact, one might argue on proportionality grounds that a risk of this type of minor criminal behavior—even if the risk of it occurring is very high—does not justify *any* type of confinement, much less a decision about the death penalty.[45] If that argument is accepted, then the Bail Reform Act's language permitting preventive detention for

[41] 576 U.S. 591 (2015).

[42] 18 U.S.C. §924(e)(2)(B).

[43] 576 U.S. at 594.

[44] See Cecelia Klingele, Labeling Violence, 103 Marquette L. Rev. 847, 849 (2020) (noting that, in many jurisdictions, "crimes of violence" include not only those behaviors, but also many other, lesser forms of aggression, such as simple assaults, extortion, concealed weapons charges, and operating motor vehicles while intoxicated.).

[45] See, e.g., Andrew Ashworth & Lucia Zedner, Preventive Justice 260 (2014) (arguing that sentence enhancements based on risk should not occur unless the person "is adjudged to

arrestees who pose "a danger to any person or the community" is equally problematic.

At the same time, crime seriousness need not be measured entirely in terms of violence. Some nonviolent crimes (embezzlement of large sums of money; widespread violation of antipollution regulations) can be very serious, and a significant probability of reoccurrence in the absence of significant constraints might warrant detention. Further, a risk of less serious crime might be a permissible outcome in some nonsentencing settings in which risk is an issue. For instance, if the context is parole release for drug offenders, the outcome measure might focus on drug possession violations in the absence of participation in treatment programs.

And once again, RAIs can help make delineation of the outcome criterion more than an abstract exercise. If, for instance, the law adopts the position that risk-based sentence enhancements or parole board release denials may only occur upon a significant probability of serious physical violence, then developers of RAIs will know to use serious violence, not just any offense, as their outcome measure. Unfortunately, many of today's RAIs fall short in this regard. For instance, violence was defined in the original validation research for the VRAG to include arrest for simple assault (which could, in theory, be a punch in the nose or might not involve physical contact at all).[46] The COMPAS's violence recidivism scales were normed on "any arrest" for a "person offense," otherwise undefined, and its general recidivism scores were normed on arrest for any felony, prison disciplinary infraction, *or* misdemeanor,[47] despite the fact that, as Alexandra Natapoff points out, many misdemeanors "are crimes of poverty ..., such as driving on a suspended license for failure to pay fines or sleeping or urinating in public due to homelessness."[48] The HCR-20 includes in its definition of violent offense any willful action that caused or could cause "serious psychological

present a very serious danger to others" and the person "has a previous conviction for a very serious offence").

46 Harris et al., supra note 7, at 383. See also Grant T. Harris et al., Violent Offenders: Appraising and Managing Fear 122–23, 152 (3d ed. 2015) (also indicating that the developers counted institutional conduct that did not result in charges if the developers thought they would have resulted in charges had they been committed outside the institution).

47 Northpointe, COMPAS Risk and Needs Assessment System 15 (2012), available at http://www.northpointeinc.com/files/downloads/FAQ_ Document.pdf (speaking of "person offense arrests" in defining violence); Douglas & Webster, supra note 12, at 8 (speaking of "violence and antisocial behavior").

48 Alexandra Natapoff, The High Stakes of Low-Level Justice, 128 Yale L.J. 1648, 1663 (2018).

harm,"[49] and some pretrial assessment instruments include traffic violations in their definition of recidivism.[50]

Note also that many of these RAIs use arrest, not conviction, in determining recidivism. Yet, according to the Bureau of Justice Statistics's sampling of cases from the 75 largest counties in the U.S., approximately one-third of felony arrests do not result in convictions,[51] and more than 10 percent of arrests for felonies are subsequently converted to misdemeanors.[52] As Chapter 4 discusses in more detail, arrests for minor crimes can also be heavily racially skewed and do not always correlate with actual criminal activity. As a result, an RAI that relies on drug possession or misdemeanor arrests as an outcome variable may rate black defendants as higher risk than white defendants who will engage in similar criminal behavior.

Assume that, in light of these considerations, the relevant law adopts the position that recidivism should be measured only in terms of *conviction* for the *most serious* violent offenses (e.g., homicide, sexual assault, robbery, and aggravated assault). If this tack were taken, the number of people in the highest risk bins of RAIs like the VRAG would decline significantly, or those bins might even disappear entirely, given the relative rarity of convictions for these types of crimes. Rhys Hester has demonstrated this point by constructing an RAI consisting of just four variables (criminal history, juvenile adjudication, age and gender).[53] Using conviction of *any* offense as the outcome, Hester's RAI can produce nine bins that identify, in its three highest risk bins, groups of individuals with a 67 percent, 69 percent and 79 percent probability of reoffending. But those percentages are reduced to 13 percent, 14 percent and 18 percent, respectively, if the outcome measure is changed to violent reoffending. While the latter percentages might increase (and in fact, with tools like the VRAG and COMPAS, do increase) if more factors were added to the tool—and they certainly would increase if arrests rather than convictions were the measure of recidivism—this example dramatically demonstrates the

49 Kevin S. Douglas et al., Historical-Clinical-Risk Management-20, Version 3 (HCR-20v3): Development and Overview, 13 Int'l J. Forensic Mental Health 93, 100 (2014).

50 Chelsea Barabas et al., Technical Flaws of Pretrial Risk Assessments Raise Grave Concerns 1 n. 2 (July 17, 2019), https://dam-prod.media.mit.edu/x/2019/07/16/TechnicalFlawsOfPretrial_ML%20site.pdf (describing the California Pretrial Assessment Tool).

51 Brian A. Reaves, U.S. Dep't of Justice, NCJ 228944, Felony Defendants in Large Urban Counties, 2009, at 24 tbl. 21 (2013), available at https://www.bjs.gov/content/pub/pdf/fdluc09.pdf.

52 Id. See also Anna Roberts, Arrests as Guilt, 70 Ala. L. Rev. 987 (2019) (detailing the many reasons arrests should not be equated with findings of guilt).

53 Rhys Hester, Risk Assessment Savvy: The Imperative of Appreciating Accuracy and Outcome, 38 Beh. Sci. & L. 246, 250–52 (2020).

importance of determining, *as a legal-normative matter*, what the outcome measure should be.

2.5 THE DURATION CRITERION

A third risk criterion that requires more elaboration by policymakers is the time frame for the prediction. At capital sentencing, that time frame may be indefinite. But in noncapital cases, predictions that are meant to influence the sentence imposed at conviction should fit the relevant sentencing range. And if the issue is instead pretrial detention, the prediction frame should be three to six months, the period within which trial must take place under the typical speedy trial statute.[54]

Many RAIs do not have good fit on this criterion. Several instruments that purport to predict pretrial offending rely on unspecified follow-up periods.[55] The RAIs used at sentencing may also be deficient on this score. Recall that the VRAG predicts violence within a seven-year or ten-year period, the HCR-20 within two years. If a statutory sentence range ends before seven years (which is true of all misdemeanors and many felonies, including violent ones), the VRAG's outcome projection might be said to be irrelevant. Even the HCR-20's two-year period may be too long in cases involving minor offenses or where the issue is whether a person should be released on parole, a decision sometimes made on an annual basis.

2.6 THE INTERVENTION CRITERION

An individual's risk of reoffending can vary enormously depending on the law's response to the risk. While imprisonment might substantially reduce risk, it may not be any more effective at doing so than an effective substance abuse treatment program in the community, a vocational training program in a halfway house, or a job-release program coupled with an ankle monitor. Thus, even a finding that a person belongs to a group with a high probability of committing serious crime in the near future should not necessarily counsel *incarceration* on the basis of risk when good treatment services are available. Further, as developed in Chapter 5, a solid constitutional argument can be made that, when the state's goal is prevention of antisocial behavior, it *must* pursue the least drastic means of achieving it.

54 Under the Federal Speedy Trial Act, the presumptive period permitted between arrest and trial is 100 days. 18 U.S.C. § 3161(b)(c).

55 See Sandra Mayson, Dangerous Defendants, 127 Yale L. J. 490, 514 tbl. 2 (2017).

Consider in this regard research associated with the Legal Service/Case Management Inventory (LSCMI).[56] The LSCMI is a well-known RAI which its progenitors, James Andrews and Donald Bonta, refer to as a risk-needs-responsivity (RNR) instrument, because it not only endeavors to differentiate high and low risk offenders, but also to identify the behavior or traits that need to be addressed to reduce risk and the types of interventions that can respond to those needs. Like the HCR-20, the LSCMI contains a number of variable risk factors that research suggests are related to criminal behavior and that can be the focus of treatment, including "procriminal attitudes" (such as rationalizations for crime and negative attitudes toward the law), "social supports for crime" (such as criminal friends and isolation from prosocial people); substance abuse; poor family relationships; poor educational performance; and lack of involvement in prosocial activities (such as work). Research on programs with fidelity to the RNR approach indicates that the recidivism of high risk offender groups can be reduced by up to 35 percent, often through cognitive-behavioral techniques.[57] At the same time, even well-vetted RNR programs have only minimal effect on the recidivism of low risk offenders, with some research indicating these programs might even increase recidivism among that group, especially if it involves incarceration.[58]

The latter finding dovetails with the considerable amount of research alluded to in Chapter 1 that finds that incarceration can be criminogenic for a wide range of offenders, for a number of reasons, including the loss of connections with family, jobs, and community, and the development of relationships with other criminals that results from imprisonment.[59] It also

56 For a description of this instrument, see James Bonta & D. A. Andrews, Risk-Needs-Responsibility Model for Offender Assessment and Rehabilitation (2007), available at https://www.publicsafety.gc.ca/cnt/rsrcs/pblctns/rsk-nd-rspnsvty/rsk-nd-rspnsvty-eng.pdf.

57 D. A. Andrews & James Bonta, The Psychology of Criminal Conduct 242–43 (6th ed. 2017) (also noting, however, that most of these studies were carried out by the developer of the treatment; replications produce recidivism reduction rates closer to 15 percent).

58 See, e.g., James Bonta, Suzanne Wallace-Capretta & Jennifer, A Quasi-experimental Evaluation of an Intensive Rehabilitation Supervision Program, 27 Crim. Just. & Beh. 312 (2000) (finding, in an evaluation of a Canadian program, that low risk offenders who received minimal levels of treatment had a recidivism rate of 15 percent and low risk offenders who received intensive levels of services had more than double the recidivism rate (32 percent), while high risk offenders who did not receive any intensive treatment services had a recidivism rate of 51 percent but those who received treatment had almost half the recidivism rate (32 percent)); Phyllis Solomon, Jeffrey Draine & Stephen C. Marcus, Predicting Incarceration of Clients of a Psychiatric Probation and Parole Services, 53 Psychiatric Services 50 (2002) (finding that intensive surveillance can lead to rearrests for minor crimes that normally would not occasion incarceration).

59 See, e.g., Greg Pogarsky & Alex R. Piquero, Can Punishment Encourage Offending? Investigating the "Resetting" Effect, 40 J. Research in Crime and Delinquency 95 (2003); Travis C. Pratt & Francis T. Cullen, Assessing Macro-level Predictors and Theories of Crime:

coincides with Andrews and Bonta's assertion that "effectiveness is maximized when the treatment is in a community setting."[60] That conclusion, well-replicated by other researchers,[61] also makes sense because of the many factors associated with risk (including poor family relationships and low involvement in prosocial activities) that are difficult to address while the offender is incarcerated. Even potentially violent individuals might be better handled in the community rather than in custody. For instance, Multi-Systemic Therapy, which involves intense intervention with the offenders' family, peers, and schools and other facets of the community over a several-month period, is much more successful than prison programs at reducing violence among juveniles, at lower cost.[62]

A jurisprudence of risk ought to take this type of research into account. Of course, risk is not always the only consideration, especially at sentencing. Most obviously, retributive goals may demand that offenders spend a certain amount of time in prison. But to the extent risk is considered relevant either at the initial sentencing or after a minimum period of retributively-defined incarceration, courts, parole boards, and other decision-makers should demand not only information about the probability, type and duration of reoffending, but also whether prison will be the optimal means of preventing or reducing it. RAIs like the HCR-20 and the LSCMI can be of significant assistance in this regard.

At the same time, it is important to recognize that not all variable or dynamic risk factors that are found in the typical risk assessment instrument are *causal* factors that, when changed, demonstrably reduce risk.[63] An example of a causal factor is substance abuse; research shows not only

A Meta-analysis, in Crime and Justice: A Review of Research (Vol. 32), 373 (Michael Tonry, ed., 2005); Paula P. Smith, Claire Goggin & Paul Gendreau, The Effects of Prison Sentences and Intermediate Sanctions on Recidivism: General Effects and Individual Differences (2002); Patrice Villettaz, Martin Killias & Isabel Zoder, The Effects of Custodial vs. Non-custodial Sentences on Re-offending: A Systematic Review of the State of the Knowledge (2006).

60 Andrews & Bonta, supra note 57, at 12.

61 See Mark Lipsey & Francis Cullen, The Effectiveness of Correctional Rehabilitation: A Review of Systematic Reviews, 3 Ann. Rev. L. & Soc. Sci. 297, 302 (2008).

62 For a description of the program, similar programs, and relevant data, see Ctr. for the Study and Prevention of Violence, Blueprints for Violence Prevention (2004), at https://www.ncjrs.gov/pdffiles1/ojjdp/204274.pdf .

63 See generally, John Monahan & Jennifer Skeem, Risk Assessment in Criminal Sentencing, 12 Ann. Rev. Clinical Psych. 489, 506 (2016) ("although a wealth of empirical guidance is available for assessing adult offenders' risk of recidivism, far less is available for reducing that risk," although noting that substance abuse and "criminal thinking patterns" probably qualify as causal risk factors).

a clear link between use of alcohol and violence, but also that treating alcohol abuse reduces recidivism.[64] Not as clear is the extent to which many other dynamic factors that help predict risk, such as psychopathy, poor employment history, and low-level education, are causal as well.[65] As Jennifer Skeem and John Monahan point out, risk assessment is usually divorced from "needs" assessment; "in practice, . . . the former is often subject to empirical scrutiny while 'anything goes' for the latter,"[66] because validation is easier with respect to risk assessment than risk management. Thus, some variables that are called needs "do not even qualify as risk factors for recidivism, much less as 'causal' risk factors."[67]

Skeem and Monahan recommend that, if the goal is to inform risk reduction efforts, "needs assessments must prominently feature empirically supported, causal risk factors for recidivism."[68] Jodi Viljoen and her colleagues concur: "[R]esearchers need to pay greater attention to how tools are applied to guide real-world decisions, such as by testing the pathways between risk assessment and risk management, identifying areas of slippage, and developing strategies to facilitate the ability of risk assessments to translate into better risk management efforts."[69] The lesson is that, for the time being, some decisions about the appropriate intervention will be concededly experimental in nature; more is said about how legal decision-makers should confront this issue in Chapter 4's discussion of procedural justice.

Even in the absence of a full understanding of the mechanisms for reducing risk, the requirement that risk assessment engage in the intervention inquiry can have major consequences. Consider, for instance, capital sentencing proceedings at which risk is an aggravating factor, such as those that occur in Texas. In most death penalty states, including Texas, the only dispositional

64 See, e.g., Denise C. Gottfredson et al., Long-Term Effects of Participation in the Baltimore City Drug Treatment Court: Results from an Experimental Study, 2 J. Experimental Criminology 67 (2006).

65 Tony Ward, Detection of Dynamic Risk Factors and Correctional Practice, 14 Criminol. & Pub. Pol'y 105, 105 (2015); Faye S. Taxman & Michael S. Caudy, Risk Tells Us Who, But Not What or How: Empirical Assessment of the Complexity of Criminogenic Needs to Inform Correctional Programming, 14 Criminol. & Pub. Pol'y 71 (2015).

66 Skeem & Monahan, supra note 3, at 288.

67 Id.

68 Id.

69 Jodi L. Viljoen et al., Do Risk Assessment Tools Help Manage and Reduce Risk of Violence and Reoffending? A Systematic Review, 42 Law & Hum. Behav. 181, 210–11 (2018). See also Faye Taxman et al., Justice Reinvestment in the United States: An Empirical Assessment of the Potential Impact of Increased Correctional Programming on Recidivism, 9 Vict. Offenders 50 (2014) (arguing that effectiveness of RAIs should be measured by how well offender needs are met systemically).

alternative to the death penalty is life without parole.[70] Thus, in evaluating dangerousness, the factfinder's decision should focus on the probability of violent reoffending in prison, not in civilian society.[71] Even if, in the abstract, the risk posed by a person who has committed capital murder is high, a death sentence will often be unwarranted if it must be justified on the ground that it is necessary to prevent reoffending.[72]

The intervention question is of even more practical import at the other end of the punishment spectrum. Offenders who are low risk probably do not require prison to prevent recidivism. In fact, as suggested above, imprisonment of such offenders may exacerbate the risk they pose once released. In part for this reason, several commentators have proposed that, for individuals considered low risk, there be a presumption in favor of alternatives to prison or outright release.[73] As these examples illustrate, in a risk-oriented regime, the intervention question may well be the most important of the four fit issues discussed here.

2.7 CONCLUSION:IMPLEMENTING THE FIT CRITERIA

Jessica Eaglin has criticized the law's use of RAIs because their developers make policy decisions, often hidden, about how to define recidivism, where to get the relevant data, and what the risk categories should be.[74] She concludes that, while the judgments ingrained in "previous efforts to estimate risk at sentencing—like guidelines and mandatory penalties . . . were apparent on the

70 Life Without Parole, Death Penalty Information Center, https://deathpenaltyinfo.org/policy-issues/sentencing-alternatives/life-without-parole (last visited Mar. 24, 2020).

71 Recognizing this point is a white paper by a group of psychologists concluding that the Psychopathy Checklist-Revised, a popular risk assessment tool that is also incorporated in the VRAG, is not appropriate for use in capital sentencing proceedings, because it is not normed on that population. Jaymes Fairfax-Columbo & David De Matteo, Reducing the Dangers of Future Dangerousness Testimony: Applying the Federal Rules of Evidence to Capital Sentencing, 25 Wm. & Mary Bill Rts. J. 1047 (2017).

72 See Mark D. Cunningham, Thomas J. Reidy & Jon R. Sorenson, Is Death Row Obsolete? A Decade of Mainstreaming Death-sentenced Inmates in Missouri, 25 Beh. Sci. & L. 307 (2005) (finding that rates of institutional violence among death row inmates who were "mainstreamed" were similar to those of life-without-parole inmates, and well below those of fellow inmates who were sentenced to parole eligible terms).

73 Kevin R. Reitz, The Compelling Case for Low-Violence-Risk Preclusion in American Prison Policy, 38 Beh. Sci. & L. 207 (2020); Stephen D. Gottfredson & Michael Gottfredson, Selective Incapacitation?, 478 Annals of the American Acad. of Pol. & Soc. Sci. 135 (1985); Hennessey D. Hayes & Michael R. Geeken, The Idea of Selective Release, 14 Just. Quart. 353, 368–69 (1997).

74 Eaglin, supra note 13, at 59.

face of the mechanized tool, ...[w]ith actuarial risk tools, normative judgments are more difficult or even impossible to discern."[75]

If Eaglin is right, this normative opacity is the law's fault, not the developers'. For each setting in which risk is at issue, legislatures, agencies, or courts should define the legal threshold as precisely as possible, just as they try to define in a clear manner possible crimes, defenses, and desert-based sentencing criteria in their efforts to cabin government discretion. In particular, it is crucial, and perhaps even constitutionally required, that the relevant legal entity address four criteria: the probability of reoffending, the type of reoffending, when any reoffending is predicted to occur, and the type of intervention likely to reduce or prevent such reoffending.

Good precedent for this type of effort is found in the closely related domain of civil commitment, involving involuntary hospitalization of people with mental illness on dangerousness grounds. Most states prohibit commitment unless the state can show that the person poses a "significant" risk of "serious bodily injury to self or others" in the near or "imminent" future, and that hospitalization is the "least restrictive" intervention for dealing with the risk.[76] A sizeable jurisprudence has developed on these issues.[77] Further, the Supreme Court has held that these criteria must be proven by clear and convincing evidence.[78]

In the pretrial and post-conviction settings, in contrast, policymakers have dragged their feet in coming to grips when these issues. At one time, that abdication might have been understandable, if not excusable, on the ground that unstructured evidence purporting to address the probability, outcome, duration, and intervention issues was largely speculative and thus could not easily address questions raised by more concrete standards. But, with the advent of RAIs, that is no longer the case.

A second, more likely, reason for the policymaking failure—still not excusable, however—is that establishing these criteria requires, as one court put it, "a delicate balancing of society's interest in protection from harmful conduct against the individual's interest in personal liberty and autonomy."[79] The

75 Id. at 88.

76 See Gary Melton et al., Psychological Evaluations for the Courts: A Handbook for Mental Health Professionals and Lawyers ch. 8 (4th ed. 2018).

77 See Christopher Slobogin, Thomas Hafemeister & Douglas Mossman, Law and the Mental Health System: Civil and Criminal Aspects 839–57 (7th ed. 2020); In re M.B.K., 639 N.W.2d 473 (N.D. 2002) (holding that statistical evidence of a 37 to 45 percent chance of "reoffending" within ten years is "clear and convincing" proof sufficient to justify commitment).

78 Addington v. Texas, Addington v. Texas, 441 U.S. 418 (1979)

79 State v. Krol, 344 A.2d 289, 302 (N.J. 1975) (also recognizing that this decision is "is ultimately a legal one").

recent controversy over a Cook County, Chicago bail reform project that uses an RAI is illustrative of this last point. The initial claim about the program was that only 0.6 percent of the 24,504 defendants released during the first 15 months of its operation were rearrested for a violent crime prior to trial.[80] But "violent crime," as defined by the researchers, did not include domestic violence, battery, and simple assault. A subsequent study that included those crimes as outcome measures found that 2.4 percent of those released prior to trial were rearrested for violent crimes (for a difference of 1.8 percent from the initial study).[81] However, as proponents of the program pointed out, by either definition, the risk of violent crimes committed by released arrestees was low, and that "in order to eliminate the risk altogether, the justice system would have to needlessly jail about 24,000 additional people a year who we know will not be re-arrested for any type of a violent crime."[82] Knowing the potential effect on both crime rates and the number of people who are detained prior to trial on risk grounds, should policymakers now mandate that the probability, outcome and duration metrics of the Cook County RAI be adjusted? Or should they leave the RAI alone?

That may be a tough decision. But it should be made explicitly. And it should be made by policymakers and the affected communities,[83] not by the

80 Office of Chief Judge, State of Illinois Circuit Court of Cook Country, Bail Reform in Cook County: An Examination of General Order 18.8A and Bail in Felony Cases 35 (May, 2019), available at http://www.cookcountycourt.org/Portals/0/Statistics/Bail%20Reform/Bail%20Reform%20Report%20FINAL%20-%20%20Published%2005.9.19.pdf.

81 David Jackson, Todd Lightly & Gary Marx, Bail Reform Analysis by Cook County Chief Judge Based on Flawed Data, Undercounts New Murder Charges, Chicago Tribune, Feb. 13, 2020, available at https://www.chicagotribune.com/investigations/ct-cook-county-bail-bond-reform-tim-evans-20200213tkodxevlyvcp7k66q2v2ahboi4-story.html.

82 Another study criticizing the initial research on the program noted that its comparison of arrest rates prior to and after initiation of the program was flawed because the post-program period was eighty-nine days shorter than the pre-program period. Paul G. Cassell & Richard Fowles, Does Bail Reform Increase Crime? An Empirical Assessment of the Public Safety Implications of Bail Reform in Cook County (2020). But that finding itself was flawed in several ways. See James Austin & Wendy Naro-Ware, Why Bail Reform is Safe and Effective: The Case of Cook County 4 (2020), available at http://www.jfa-associates.com/publications/reduce/Cook_County_Bail_Report.pdf ("The Cassell and Fowles critique tries to standardize the follow-up period, but along the way makes several incorrect assumptions about re-arrest rates for defendants who are benefiting from the new Order and how to measure them, among other errors and omissions.").

83 Ngozi Okidegbe, The Democratizing Potential of Algorithms, 53 Conn. L. Rev. 42 (2021) (arguing that policymakers and developers of RAIs have seldom consulted the communities in which the tools will be used and that "resolving this ensuing democratic exclusion and its racially stratifying effects might be possible but requires shifting power over pretrial algorithms downward toward these communities"). See Section 4.3.3's discussion of procedural injustice for more on this particular point.

developers of RAIs. There follows a brief template of what that policymaking might look like, in a number of different settings.

2.7.1 *Prison Release/Diversion*

Assume first that the goal is to determine whether a convicted offender should be diverted or released from prison to a community-program. What probability (P) of what outcome (O) during what time period (T) must be shown if the government wants to continue to subject the individual to a confinement intervention (I) on risk grounds? Take the last three issues, O, T, and I, first. If hospitalization under civil commitment law requires a risk of serious bodily injury, presumably prolonging imprisonment based on risk should as well. If so, the value for O should probably be conviction—not arrest—for crimes like homicide, sexual assault, other serious assault, robbery, and attempts to commit these types of crimes. T might be the time associated with the offender's maximum sentence, and I would require factoring in the risk-reducing impact of available rehabilitative programs in the community if the offender were released.

That still leaves the value of P to be decided: of people released from prison, what percentage of those in the offender's group, subject to the designated rehabilitation programs, commit violent crime within a several-year period? Since the magnitude of the predicted harm is so serious, the probability threshold might be set lower than if the outcome measure were general recidivism. One candidate for that threshold is 30 percent, which, according to the Department of Justice's Bureau of Justice Statistics, is the approximate rate at which released prisoners commit homicide, rape, robbery, and assault within three years of their release (with assault, at 23 percent, making up the bulk of the reoffending).[84] From a risk perspective, it is difficult to justify incarcerating an individual who poses a lower risk than the average released prisoner.[85]

[84] U.S. Dep't of Justice, Office of Justice Programs, NCJ 244205 Recidivism of Prisoners Released in 30 States in 2005: Patterns from 2005 to 2010, tbl. 2 (2016), available at https://www.bjs.gov/content/pub/pdf/rprts05p0510_st.pdf.

[85] The DOJ reports only arrest rates, not conviction rates; thus, the 30% figure overestimates official recidivism. However, it must also be recognized that a significant amount of crime never results in arrest, much less conviction, see Melton et al., supra note 76, at 295–297, which means this figure could easily underestimate actual reoffending. Consistent with this analysis, the Post Conviction Risk Assessment (PCRA), an instrument used by the federal Bureau of Prisons to determine which probationers should be subject to intensive supervision, defines high risk as a 23 percent probability of an arrest for a violent crime (while equating that label with a 63 percent probability when the outcome is *any* arrest). See Jennifer Skeem &

Note that if this were the probability threshold, that does not mean that 30 percent of the people released are predicted to recidivate. Because everyone who poses *less* than a 30 percent likelihood of reoffending would also be released, including those who pose virtually no risk, the recidivism rate of the entire released group is likely to be much lower. (That is why the recidivism rate in Cook Country study was well below 3 percent despite an instrument with a release cutoff set at a much higher probability threshold.)

Of course, one could also make the argument that the probability criterion for diverting or releasing offenders from prison ought to be much higher than 30 percent, given that a deprivation of liberty—possibly quite prolonged—is involved in the sentencing context.[86] Or perhaps the probability threshold should be lower, on the theory that society cannot countenance release of those who have even a small chance of committing violent crime. Fiscal concerns, such as the expense of confinement or treatment programs, might also be taken into account. The important point is that policymakers, not RAI developers, need to make these choices and state them explicitly.

2.7.2 *Pretrial Detention Based on Risk of Offending*

Assume instead that the decision is whether to detain an arrestee prior to trial on the basis of risk. Here a jurisdiction might decide that the O value should be measured by arrest, not conviction, on the ground that conviction for a crime during the pretrial period is highly unlikely. In contrast to the assumptions built into the Cook County RAI, it might also relax the type of offense that can trigger detention, on the ground that detention prior to trial is not as significant a liberty deprivation as a sentence enhancement. At the same time, for reasons indicated earlier, defining the outcome measure to include minor misdemeanor arrests should be avoided. Further, given the pretrial setting, the duration criterion (T) should be no more than six months, and, as with the post-conviction scenario, risk-reducing interventions in the community should be considered.

Christopher Lowenkamp, Using Algorithms to Address Trade-Offs in Predicting Recidivism, 38 Beh. Sci. & L. 259, 266 (2020); Christopher Lowenkamp et al., The Federal Post Conviction Risk Assessment (PCRA): A Construction and Validation Study, 10 Psychological Services 87, 87–89 (2013).

86 In other work, I have argued that the threshold should initially be 50%, on the ground that the degree of risk required to continue imprisoning someone should be at least as high as that required for involuntary commitment, a much less significant liberty deprivation. Christopher Slobogin, Prevention as the Primary Goal of Sentencing: The Modern Case for Indeterminate Sentencing, 48 San Diego L. Rev. 1127, 1137 (2011).

With respect to the probability issue, if general rather than violent recidivism is the focus of the prediction, a higher threshold might be required. Surveys of citizens have found that, when asked to indicate the risk level at which a person should be confined prior to trial, the median answer was a 60 percent chance of arrest for any crime.[87] It is worth noting that even using arrest for any felony, rather than arrest for a violent felony, as the outcome measure, only a small percentage of arrestees (probably under 10 percent) would meet this 60 percent threshold.[88]

2.7.3 *Pretrial Detention Based on Flight Risk*

Pretrial detention can also occur if the arraignment court believes that the arrestee is a flight risk. Indeed, at least in theory, failure-to-appear (FTA) was the only outcome measure courts were permitted to consider at the pretrial stage until the 1970s and 1980s.[89] However, since then, most jurisdictions—heavily influenced by the federal Bail Reform Act of 1984,[90] and given the green light by the Supreme Court[91]—have enacted statutes that explicitly allow pretrial detention based on risk of reoffending.

As Lauryn Gouldin has argued, the risk factors that help predict the two types of risk can be quite different,[92] and the PSA now explicitly recognizes

87 Nicolas Scurich & Daniel Krauss, Public's Views of Risk Assessment Algorithms and Pretrial Decision Making, 26 Psychol., Pub. Pol'y & L. 1, 5 (2020); Pew Charitable Trusts, Americans Favor Expanded Pretrial Release, Limited Use of Jail, Fig. 8 at 9, Nov. 2018 (66 percent would be willing to release an individual with a 70 percent chance of no arrest during the pretrial period).

88 For instance, one study looking at data from the federal pretrial risk assessment instrument indicates that only the groups that received a score of four or five on the instrument (the two highest scores) pose a risk of 30 percent or more of *any* "adverse event" (which includes failure to appear and pretrial revocation as well as commission of violent and nonviolent offenses); combined, these two groups comprised under 15 percent of the sample. See Thomas H. Cohen & Christopher T. Lowenkamp, Revalidation of the Federal PTRA, 46 Crim. J. & Behav. 234, 245 (2019). The percentages of those arrested for violent offenses for the groups that score 4 and 5 were 2.1 and 2.9, and for any offense 13.0 and 16.5, respectively. Id. However, these percentages are deflated by the fact that many of these individuals were often detained and thus much less likely to reoffend.

89 According to Stack v. Boyle, 352 U.S. 1, 4 (1951). However, bail was often used sub rosa to detain "dangerous" individuals. See John Mitchell, Bail Reform and the Constitutionality of Preventive Detention, 55 Va. L. Rev. 1223, 1235 (1969).

90 18 U.S.C. § 3142(e).

91 United States v. Salerno, 481 U.S. 739 (1987).

92 Lauryn P. Gouldin, Disentangling Flight Risk from Dangerousness, BYU L. Rev. 838, 842 (2017) ("One key problem with most of the risk assessment tools employed in the federal system and around the country, however, is that they combine flight risk and dangerousness into a single 'risk of pretrial failure' score").

that fact. Perhaps most important to the FTA inquiry is the intervention (I) question. Research suggests that the probability of failing to appear falls below 5 percent if arrestees are provided reminders of their next court date,[93] afforded pretrial services, and provided with transportation and flexible scheduling.[94] If so, incarceration on the ground that the arrestee poses a risk of failure to appear should be rare.

2.7.4 *Prison Population Reduction*

For still another scenario, assume that the focus is not on individual cases but on system-wide adjustments to the number of individuals who end up in prison. In 1994, the Virginia legislature abolished parole and adopted a determinate sentencing regime.[95] However, anticipating that the increase in prison terms mandated by the statute would lead to fiscal "collapse" of the state's prison system, the legislature also directed the newly formed Virginia Criminal Sentencing Commission to develop an empirically-based risk-assessment instrument that would enable judges to divert 25 percent of the "lowest-risk, incarceration-bound, drug and property offenders" from prison to alternative sanctions such as jail, release, probation, community service, outpatient substance-abuse treatment, or electronic monitoring.[96] To meet the goal declared by the state legislature, the Commission in effect worked backward from practical considerations to normative ones. Instead of establishing a cut-point based on a balancing of the risk to the public posed by release against the cost to the individual and the prison system of detention, the Commission had to figure out the number of offenders who needed to be diverted from prison to accomplish the legislature's goal of a 25 percent reduction in prisoners, and then set the low risk cut point at a level that would meet that goal.

The result was the NVRA. Using Virginia's approach, a state that wanted to reduce prison populations more aggressively could expand the percentage to be released. Or it could extend risk assessment to all crimes, not just

93 See, e.g., Marie VanNostrand, Kenneth J. Rose & Kimberly Weibrecht, State of the Science of Pretrial Release Recommendations and Supervision *20 (Pretrial Justice Institute, June 2011), archived at http://perma.cc/QFK5-8UGG (finding that FTAs were reduced to 5 percent if arrestees are directly reminded of their court date).

94 See Lauryn P. Gouldin, Defining Flight Risk, 85 U. Chi. L. Rev. 678, 737–41 (2018) (discussing the impact of pretrial services and flexible scheduling).

95 Va. Code § 53.1–165.1.

96 Kern & Farrar-Owens, supra note 8, at 165.

nonviolent ones, and dictate more demanding probability, outcome, duration and intervention thresholds. The latter approach is discussed further in Chapter 5.

* * *

Specification of risk thresholds in the way outlined in this chapter may strike some as overly mechanistic. The alternative, however, is a regime governed by vague legal formulas referring to "danger to the community" or the "probability of criminal acts of violence" and by RAI results using undefined terms such as "high risk" or "eighth decile." When added to the uncertainty already inherent in evaluating risk, these types of phrases allow significant deprivations of liberty to be based on intuition and whim. Such language runs directly counter to the Supreme Court's repeated admonition, in its cases striking down vague statutes, that laws that "authorize or … encourage arbitrary and discriminatory enforcement" are invalid.[97]

RAIs can provide a concrete means of limiting arbitrariness and discrimination. The law should take advantage of that fact. It should provide judges and evaluators guidance that addresses, in each legal setting in which risk is an issue, the probability, outcome, timing and intervention criteria. Doing so is a crucial aspect of any serious jurisprudence of risk. It will also make the inner workings of the criminal justice system much more transparent.

97 Chicago v. Morales, 527 U.S. 41, 56 (1999) (citing Kolender v. Lawson, 461 U.S. 352, 357 (1983).

3

Validity

Figuring Out When Risk Algorithms Are Sufficiently Accurate

Assume a risk assessment instrument produces data that meets all of the fit requirements. It provides group probability estimates regarding outcomes, time frames, and interventions that fit the inquiries the law asks. Decision-makers still should not rely on these results unless they are reasonably accurate. What lawyers call accuracy or reliability, social scientists call validity. There are numerous measures of validity. As applied to RAIs, they are all aimed at determining the extent to which an instrument does what it purports to do.

As a matter of legal precedent, the validity inquiry is most sensibly framed under Federal Rule of Evidence 702 and analogous rules in virtually every state, which require experts to use "reliable principles and methods" that are "reliably applied."[1] This language was meant to operationalize the U.S. Supreme Court's decision in *Daubert v. Dow Chemical Co.*,[2] which tells courts to ensure that the basis of expert testimony has been subjected to some type of verification process, such as empirical testing, the generation of error rates, and peer review through publication in accepted journals. Many jurisdictions hold that Rule 702 and the *Daubert* criteria are inapposite in the pretrial and post-conviction settings at issue here, because they were devised as rules of evidence meant to apply at trials.[3] But that stance is hard to fathom; if the *Daubert* test must be met before evidence can be presented in a tort suit (the context of the *Daubert* case), it should certainly apply where weeks, months or years of jail or prison time are at stake.

[1] Fed. R. Evid. 702(c)–(d).

[2] 509 U.S. 579 (1993).

[3] United States v. Slager, 912 F.3d 224, 235 n.4 (4th Cir. 2019) ("Applying *Daubert* would run contrary to the sentencing court's 'wide discretion' to determine the 'sources and types of evidence,' which are relevant for defendants' individualized sentencing."); United States v. Fields, 483 F.3d 313, 342 (2007) ("No Circuit that we are aware of has applied *Daubert* to sentencing").

If *Daubert* and the rest of the rules of evidence did apply to RAIs, they would require: (1) that the probabilities the instrument generates be stated with an acceptable level of confidence (calibration validity); (2) that the RAI do a passable job at distinguishing high risk from low risk individuals (discriminant validity); (3) that the RAI be validated on a population similar to the population in question (external or local validity); (4) that it have satisfactory inter-rater agreement (implementation validity, or, in social science terms, reliability); and (5) that information about all of these factors be periodically updated (current validity). Notice that, as expressed here, all of these criteria leave considerable wiggle room ("acceptable level of confidence," "passable job at distinguishing risk," "similar populations," "satisfactory reliability," and "periodically update"). No instrument can achieve perfect predictive validity (an umbrella term for all five types of validity), and the extent to which an instrument should approximate that goal may, again, vary with the legal setting.

Before elaborating on these points, an important preliminary issue that is directly relevant to the use of RAIs is whether such instruments are *needed* to reach accurate results—whether, as a social scientist would put it, they provide "incremental validity." Rule 702 holds that expert testimony is admissible only if it based on "specialized knowledge" that is "helpful" to the trier of fact.[4] If laypeople unaided by experts are just as good at prediction as RAIs, then Rule 702 counsels against permitting the results of RAIs to be considered. And the same outcome might be appropriate if experts using clinical skills unaided by RAIs could do as well or better.

3.1 INCREMENTAL VALIDITY AND HELPFULNESS

One might think that the statistical expertise needed to put together an actuarial RAI or the familiarity with research literature that goes into the creation of SPJ instruments would be sufficient evidence of specialized knowledge. But if judges or lay-parole boards are just as able to figure out who will reoffend as evaluators using RAIs, then arguably that specialized knowledge is not helpful to the factfinder. One study purported to find just that. In 2018, Julia Dressel and Hany Farid conducted a study that led them to conclude that the COMPAS "is no more accurate or fair than predictions made by people with little or no criminal justice expertise."[5] Specifically they found, based on

[4] Fed. R. Evid. 702(a).

[5] Julia Dressel & Hany Farid, The Accuracy, Fairness, and Limits of Predciting Recidivism, 4 Sci. Adv. EAAO5580 (Jan. 18, 2018), available at https://advances.sciencemag.org/content/4/1/eaao5580.

a comparison of human predictions and COMPAS predictions for 1,000 defendants, that humans were correct in about 62 percent of the cases and the COMPAS was correct in 65 percent of the cases.[6]

Dressel and Farid's study had one significant problem, however. Given the way it was conducted, the humans essentially functioned like algorithms—they were each shown fifty mini-vignettes that listed only a few features of the defendant, all of which have a robust statistical relationship with reoffending; in effect the subjects were provided a "checklist" RAI. Further, after the subjects registered their opinion about whether the person in the vignette would recidivate, they were immediately told whether they were right or wrong, feedback that a judge or parole board virtually never receive but which, in the study, "trained" the participants about the most pertinent traits and how they are related to recidivism. As Sharad Goel and his colleagues concluded, "these boosted 'human predictions' are far removed from unaided human judgement."[7] A follow-up study by Zhiyan Lin and others found that when lay participants are *not* provided feedback, they do much more poorly than an RAI, even when they are given base rate information about the average rate of offending of the population in question.[8] The authors also found that when the information given the humans was "noisier" (that is, when a much richer set of facts was provided than the barebones list of traits Dressel and Farid used), the humans did barely better than chance, whereas the statistical model the authors created was much better at distinguishing recidivists and non-recidivists.[9]

These types of results replicate a large number of other studies finding that algorithms typically outperform human predictions, whether made by laypeople or trained clinicians.[10] For instance, a 2006 meta-analysis of forty-one studies

[6] Id. at 3.

[7] Sharad Goel et al., The Accuracy, Equity, and Jurisprudence of Criminal Risk Assessment, in Research Handbook on Big Data Law 9, 13 (Roland Vogl, ed., 2021).

[8] Zhiyuan "Jerry" Lin et al., The Limits of Human Predictions of Recidivism, 6 Science Advances EAAZ-0652, at 2–4 (Feb. 20, 2020), available at https://advances.sciencemag.org/content/6/7/eaaz0652.

[9] Id. at 5 ("we also found that algorithms tended to outperform humans in settings where decision-makers have access to extensive information and do not receive immediate feedback and base rates are far from balanced, features of many real-world scenarios").

[10] See Sarah J. Desmarais, Kiersten L. Johnson & Jay P. Singh, Performance of Recidivism Risk Assessment Instruments in U.S. Correctional Settings, 13 Psychological Services 206, 206 (2016)("There is overwhelming evidence that risk assessments completed using structured approaches produce estimates that are more reliable and more accurate than unstructured risk assessments."); R. Karl Hanson & Kelly E. Morton-Bourgon, The Accuracy of Recidivism Risk Assessments for Sexual Offenders: A Meta-analysis of 118 Prediction Studies, 21 Psychological Assessment 1, 6 (2009) ("For the prediction of sexual or violent recidivism, the actuarial measures designed for violent recidivism were superior to any of the other methods."); William M. Grove et al., Clinical Versus Mechanical Prediction: A Meta-analysis, 12

found that actuarial techniques routinely did better than clinical methods in every area investigated, and that with respect to predicting violent or criminal behavior in particular, the actuarial approach was "clearly superior to the clinical approach."[11] The meta-analysis also found that even subsets of "best professionals" designated as experts did not outperform statistical formulae.[12] Several studies that compare algorithms to judges, clinicians, and correctional officers obtain similar results, probably because, despite their official position,[13] the decisions of these people are like other peoples'—largely intuitive, heuristic-based, subject to bias, and inattentive to base rates.[14]

Psychological Assessment 19 (2000) (finding that actuarial predictions are about 10 percent more accurate than clinical predictions). See also Ben Green & Yiling Chen, Disparate Interactions: An Algorithm-in-the-Loop Analysis of Fairness in Risk Assessments (unpublished manuscript, 2019) available at https://scholar.harvard.edu/files/19-fat.pdf [https://perma.cc/Q8QA-AHHL] (presenting the results of an experimental study in which human subjects "underperformed the risk assessment even when presented with its predictions").

11 Stefania Ægisdóttir et al., The Meta-analysis of Clinical Judgment Project: Fifty-six Years of Accumulated Research on Clinical Versus Statistical Prediction, 34 The Counseling Psychologist 341, 368 (2006) (out of 1,000 predictions, statistical predictions of violence accurately identify 90 more violent clients than do clinical predictions).

12 Id.

13 Jongbin Jung et al., Simple Rules for Complex Decisions (2017), available at https://arxiv.org/pdf/1702.04690 (finding that when compared to judges in a pretrial setting a simple algorithm that only looked at two factors of arrestees—age and previous failures to appear—"consistently outperform[ed] the human decision-makers"); Jon Kleinberg et al., Human Decisions and Machine Predictions, 133 The Quarterly Journal of Economics 237, 241 (2017) (similar finding); Hanson & Morton-Bourgon, supra note 10; J. Stephen Wormith, Sara M. Hogg & Lina Guzzo, J. S. Wormith, S. Hogg & L. Guzzo, The Predictive Validity of a General Risk/Needs Assessment Inventory on Sexual Offender Recidivism and an Exploration of the Professional Override, 39 Criminal Justice & Behavior 1511–38 (2012) (finding that a professional override by probation officers, psychologists, or social workers on the result suggested by a risk assessment instrument designed to test sexual offense recidivism "led to a slight, but systematic, deterioration in the predictive validity"); Kathleen Spencer Gore, Adjusted Actuarial Assessment of Sex Offenders: The Impact of Clinical Overrides on Predictive Accuracy Gain (2007), available at https://lib.dr.iastate.edu/cgi/viewcontent.cgi?referer=&httpsredir=1&article=16536&context=rtd (finding that psychologist overrides on the results produced by an instrument designed to predict recidivism for sex offenders "failed to even nominally exceed the [instrument] in terms of overall predictive accuracy"). See generally, Stephen D. Gottfredson & Laura J. Moriarty, Clinical Versus Actuarial Judgments in Criminal Justice Decisions: Should One Replace the Other?, 70 Federal Probation 15, 15 (2006) (stating that over-reliance on human judgment may undermine the accuracy of risk assessment, because probation and parole officers may "concentrate on information that is demonstrably not predictive of offender behavioral outcomes.").

14 See Laurel Eckhouse et al., Layers of Bias: A Unified Approach for Understanding Problems with Risk Assessment, 46 Crim. Just. & Behav. 185, 186 (2019) (citing studies); R. Barry Ruback et al., Communicating Risk Information at Criminal Sentencing in Pennsylvania: An Experimental Analysis, 80 Fed. Prob. 47, 47 (2016) (noting that human judgments can be affected by extraneous factors such as hunger, fatigue and personal distractions).

This type of research is one of the principal reasons risk algorithms could help reduce mass incarceration. They can more accurately provide information about risk, and thus can pinpoint lower risk individuals who, with relative safety, can be released pretrial, diverted, given shorter sentences, or released on parole. For instance, Kleinberg et al. found that replacing judicial decisions with algorithmic decisions in the pretrial setting could reduce jailing rates by 40 percent without increasing pretrial crime rates (or reduce pretrial crime rates by 25 percent with no change in incarceration rates).[15]

In short, RAIs can be very helpful to the legal system, which otherwise must depend on inferior lay or clinical judgment. However, it is also important to recognize that RAIs vary immensely with respect to how well they are validated. Furthermore, accuracy needs to be considered from a number of angles to ensure the legal system gets the information it needs. Specifically, legal policymakers should demand data about what this book calls calibration validity, discriminant validity, external validity, implementation validity, and current validity.

3.2 CALIBRATION VALIDITY

There are two primary means of evaluating the accuracy of an algorithm: "calibration" and "discrimination."[16] Calibration, discussed here, measures the extent to which a positive finding (that a person will recidivate) is correct, and the extent to which a negative finding (that a person will not recidivate) is correct. Discriminant validity, discussed next, measures the extent to which an RAI has differentiated between recidivists and non-recidivists, and thus provides a measure of how much better than chance an RAI performs.

Among tool developers, the positive predictive value (PPV) and negative predictive value (NPV) are often thought to be the most relevant measures of calibration.[17] The question the PPV answers is how often a prediction that someone will recidivate is correct, and the NPV tells us how often a prediction that a person will not recidivate is correct. Usually the PPV is calculated with

[15] Kleinberg et al., supra note 13, at 240–41.

[16] For an in-depth treatment of differing calibration and discrimination measures of predictive validity, why some work better than others, and why no measure is perfect, see L. Maaike Helmus & Kelly M. Babchishin, Primer on Risk Assessment and the Statistics Use to Evaluate Accuracy, 44 Crim. Just. & Behav. 8 (2016). This chapter provides a discourse on the most legally relevant predictive validity measures.

[17] For further description of the PPV and NPV, see Jay P. Singh, Predictive Validity Performance Indicators in Violent Risk Assessment, 31 Behav. Sci. & L. 8, 18 (2013).

a confidence interval of 95 percent (meaning that the range provided by the interval has a 95 percent chance of identifying the correct risk level).

For instance, using a sample dataset from the COMPAS which divided offenders into high, medium, and low risk groups, Melissa Hamilton calculated that the PPV for those designated as a high risk of violent reoffending is 49 percent, with a confidence interval range of 43 percent to 55 percent; in other words, there is a 95 percent chance that a high risk score on the COMPAS is associated with a 43 to 55 percent probability of recidivating.[18] Hamilton also found that the NPV of the medium and low risk groups examined together was 86 percent, with a confidence interval range of 85 percent to 87 percent, meaning that there is a 95 percent chance that a medium or low risk score is associated with an 85 to 87 percent chance of not recidivating.[19] When, instead, Hamilton lumped together the medium and high risk groups, separate from the low risk group, the PPV with respect to whether the first group recidivated dropped to 31 percent (29 percent to 34 percent) and the NPV with respect to whether the second group did not recidivate went up slightly to 89 percent (88 percent to 91 percent).[20]

This example illustrates two important points. First, the PPV and NPV of an RAI can be manipulated by changing the cut point (for instance, as Hamilton did, from the bottom of the high category to the bottom of the high-medium category combined). Second, to arrive at PPV and NPV as traditionally calculated, one has to assume that there is a *single* cut point and that a score above that cut point is equivalent to a prediction that the individuals in that group *will* recidivate, while a score below it is equivalent to a prediction that the individuals in that group *will not* recidivate. In fact, that is not what most RAIs claim to be doing, or at least not what they should claim to be doing. Rather, for reasons discussed in the last chapter, they are associating a particular score or category with a *probability* of reoffending.

Thus, instead of the PPV, based on one cut point, a more legally relevant measure of calibration is what could be called the *category* positive predictive value or the category base rate (CBR),[21] which answers the following three-part question: (1) does the RAI associate a person with a category (a score or risk group); (2) if so, what percentage of people in the category does it predict will recidivate (as

[18] Melissa Hamilton, Judicial Gatekeeping on Scientific Validity with Risk Assessment Tools, 38 Behav. Sci. & L. 226 (2020).

[19] Id. at 234.

[20] Id.

[21] Interestingly, empiricists do not have a commonly accepted term for this concept, but category base rate is an accurate descriptor, and probably preferable to category positive predictive value, because PPV has an accepted meaning within the empirical world.

defined consistently with the fit criteria in Chapter 2) and (3) to what extent is that percentage correct, as measured by validation studies and confidence intervals? As an example of this type of RAI, recall the VRAG. That tool assigns people with certain scores to one of nine bins associated with specific probabilities of recidivating that have been validated on several different populations, so that, for instance, one can feel relatively confident that people who receive a score that puts them in the third bin belong to a group approximately 17 percent of whom recidivated in the relevant validation studies, while people whose score puts them in the seventh bin belong to a group 55 percent of whom recidivated in those studies.

Given the normative importance of determining a person's risk category, discussed in Chapter 2, the CBR is the key measure of validity. The CBR is also important from an evidentiary perspective, because it provides information about error rates, one of *Daubert's* desiderata. Yet, as Chapter 2 also noted, some RAIs do not use scores or other categories, or they do so without associating them with probabilities, but rather only with recommendations for or against detention, or only with deciles or high, medium, and low risk labels that are left undefined. These RAIs lack fit with the questions the law should be asking. And even if the RAI meets the first two criteria (that is, even if it produces risk categories associated with specific probabilities), it may not meet the third criterion: if the tool's probabilities have not been replicated outside the validation sample, or they have not been calculated with respect to important subgroupings, they cannot be accepted with confidence, a point explained further in the discussion of external validity. But first, discriminant validity.

3.3 DISCRIMINANT VALIDITY

An RAI can have very good positive and negative predictive values, in the sense that validation studies indicate that its probability forecasts about groups have been largely borne out, but still be problematic. For instance, as Lin et al. point out, when a given sample has a low base rate of offending (say 5 percent), even "a naïve classifier that predicts that no one recidivates" would be right 95 percent of the time, an overall accuracy rate that compares favorably to any RAI.[22] Yet the classifications so produced would be useless to legal decision-makers, who want to separate those who are high risk from those who are not. Thus, another measure of accuracy, one that examines the extent to which an RAI can differentiate between high and low risk individuals independently of how accurately it identifies absolute risk levels, can be useful.

[22] Lin et al., supra note 8, at 4.

The most popular such measure is called the AUC, for Area Under the Curve. The "curve" is created by plotting, for each point total or cut point (e.g., decile) of the instrument, the true positive rate or "sensitivity" (the rate at which those who recidivated received that score) against the true negative rate or "specificity" (the rate at which those who did not recidivate received that score).[23] If the curve created by this plot is a diagonal, bisecting the chart, the AUC is .5, and represents a finding that the tool does no better than chance at designating those who recidivated from those who did not, whereas a curve that looks like an "r" would indicate a perfect ability to do so. Social scientists have designated a .56 AUC as a small effect size, .64 as a moderate effect size, and .71 as a large effect size,[24] although legal policymakers are of course free to require higher discriminant validity.

Virtually all professionally developed RAIs have AUCs above .5, between .6 to .85.[25] The latter figure means that, 85 percent of the time, a randomly selected recidivist receives a higher score on the tool than a randomly selected non-recidivist. The naïve classifier described above, in contrast, would actually have an AUC *below* .5, since no recidivist would receive a higher score than a non-recidivist.

As an evidentiary matter, the AUC value can be thought of as a measure of relevance, which under the rules of every state requires that proffered evidence have a "tendency to make the existence of any fact that is of consequence to the determination of the action [here reoffending] more probable or less probable than it would be without the evidence."[26] Under this definition, the results of an RAI—even one that is well-calibrated—that has an AUC of .5 or close to it might be considered irrelevant. Such an instrument's risk designations are no more accurate than randomly labeling individuals as either high or low risk (the proverbial coin flip). A respectable AUC value is particularly important in settings known to involve populations with low base rates of offending (such as arrestees during the pretrial period, or offenders who will be incarcerated for the foreseeable future), where correctly identifying high risk individuals will be especially difficult.

23 Singh, supra note 17, at 15.

24 Helmus & Babchishin, supra note 16, at 12. These same authors state that other researchers are more likely to say that AUCs between .60 and .69 are poor, .70 to .79 are fair, .80 to .89 are good, and over .90 are excellent. Id. at 11.

25 See Taanvi Ramesh et al., Use of Risk Assessment Instruments to Predict Violence in Forensic Psychiatric Hospitals: A Systematic Review and Meta-analysis, 52 Eur. Psychiat. 47, 50 tbl. 3 (2018) (reporting AUCs for 9 instruments ranging from .71 to .85 for predictions of imminent offending risk and between .62 and .75 for longer-range predictions).

26 See, e.g., Fed. R. Evid. 401.

3.4 EXTERNAL VALIDITY (LOCAL AND GROUP VALIDATION)

External validity, in social science terms, refers to the extent to which a test or tool applies outside the context of the study, or generalizes to other situations or people. As used here, it encompasses two separate ideas—local validation and group validation—both of which have to do with how well the calibration and discriminant validity of an RAI translates beyond its validation sample. In evidentiary terms, external validity has to do with "empirical fit,"[27] in contrast to the legal fit issues discussed in Chapter 2.

RAIs are often developed on half a sample (the development sample) and then tested on the other half of the sample (the validation sample) to see how well it performs. But to be optimally useful in jurisdictions outside of the one in which the RAI was developed, the RAI should perform well in those jurisdictions as well.[28] The VRAG was validated on a sample of incarcerated white men with mental disability in Canada. Until it was tested on diverse populations here in the United States, its external validity with respect to those populations was suspect.[29] Likewise, RAI validation should be attentive to the type of population that will be evaluated. An RAI validated on a population of released sex offenders, using sexual assault as the outcome variable, will be of limited use assessing the risk of other types of offenders, and of no use in the pretrial detention context. An instrument validated on a sample in an urban area might not work well in rural areas with lower crime rates and fewer arrest and convictions.[30] If the validation sample is significantly different from the local population, the RAI should be revalidated locally.

27 David Faigman, John Monahan & Christopher Slobogin, Group to Individual (G2i) Inference in Scientific Expert Testimony, 81 U. Chi. L. Rev. 417, 442 (2014) ("Legal fit calls upon courts to determine whether the expert testimony proffered in the case is material to a factual question that the substantive law requires to be answered. . . . Empirical fit calls upon courts to determine whether the expert testimony proffered in the case is based on research methods that relate to the factual question in issue.").

28 Gina M. Vincent et al., The Use of Actuarial Risk Assessment Instruments in Sex Offenders, in Sex Offenders: Identification, Risk Assessment, Treatment, and Legal Issues 70, 81 (Fabian Saleh et al. eds., 2009)("[T]here is no way to tell in the development sample how much of the observed relation between the variables and recidivism is due to underlying associations that will be shared in new samples and how much is due to unique characteristics of the development sample.").

29 See Astrid Rossegger, Replicating the Violence Risk Appraisal Guide: A Total Forensic Cohort Study, 9 Plos One e91845 at 2 (2014) (stating that "[s]tudies that *have* investigated the goodness-of-fit between the rates of violent recidivism published in the VRAG manual and rates observed during the research have produced inconsistent findings," but finding acceptable predictive validity on European samples) (emphasis in original).

30 See John Logan Koepke & David G. Robinson, Danger Ahead: Risk Assessment and the Future of Bail Reform, 93 Wash. L. Rev. 1725, 1756 (2017) ("Using one jurisdiction's data to

Assessing predictive validity with respect to racial groups and gender may be of particular importance, because, as Chapter 4 discusses in detail, race and gender disparities in risk scores raise fairness issues of possibly constitutional magnitude. Although research for many of the most widely used instruments shows that predictive validity does not vary significantly among racial groups,[31] such outcomes cannot simply be assumed.[32] Using the COMPAS sample described above, Hamilton calculated that the AUC for blacks (at the 95 percent confidence level) is .71 (.68 to .74), for whites .68 (64 to .73) and for Hispanics .64 (.55 to .73). For Hispanics, the AUC on the COMPAS comes perilously close to dipping below an acceptable level of relevance.[33] In recognition of this type of problem, in 2018, the Canadian Supreme Court prohibited use of a risk assessment instrument validated on the majority population in that country to assess the risk of a person from an indigenous group.[34]

Gender differences might be even more of an issue. Hamilton demonstrates that, for the males in the COMPAS sample, the CBR goes up for each of the ten deciles, meaning that the predicted probability of recidivism and the actual rate of recidivism for each decile are fairly closely aligned. However, for the female part of the sample, the CBR does not align well with actual recidivism from the fourth decile on, and drops precipitously at the seventh through tenth deciles (with females in the higher risk categories recidivating at a much lower rate than males).[35]

In short, ideally an RAI should not only be validated locally, but also have similar predictive validity measures among major demographic groups.[36] This may require separate instruments (with different risk factors) for some groups,

predict outcomes in another is an inherently hazardous exercise, a challenge that is highlighted in the existing literature").

31 Jennifer L. Skeem & Christopher Lowenkamp, Risk, Race, and Recidivism: Predictive Bias and Disparate Impact, 54 Criminol. 680, 700 (2016) ("these results indicate that risk assessment is not 'race assessment'"); Desmarais, Johnson & Singh, supra note 10, at 216 (in metareview of 19 RAIs, of the three that permitted comparison of black and white AUCs, the measures were "identical" or "highly similar"); Jay Singh & Seena Fazel, Forensic Risk Assesment: A Metareview, 37 Crim. Just. & Beh. 965, 978 (2010) (finding that, of six meta-reviews, five found "no evidence that predictive validity varied by the ethnicity of participants").

32 See, e.g., Melissa Hamilton, Judicial Gatekeeping on Scientific Validity with Risk Assessment Tools, 38 Behav. Sci. & L. 226, 232–236 (2020) (providing several examples of how PPVs and AUCs can vary by race, sex and other variables).

33 Id. at 236.

34 Ewert v. Canada [2018] 2 S.C.R. 165 (Can.).

35 Hamilton, supra note 18, at 231–32.

36 See Pamela M. Casey et al., Nat'l Ctr. for State Courts, Using Offender Risk and Needs Assessment Information at Sentencing: Guidance for Courts from a National Working Group 29–30 (2011) ("After identifying the most promising tool for use in a jurisdiction, the

particularly people of color and women. Min Yang and his colleagues go further:

> [The] predictive efficacies of all tools must be eventually subjected to repeated empirical validation with client groups that differ in demographic characteristics (e.g., age, gender, socioeconomic status, ethnicity), level and type of past violence (e.g., criminal histories, sexual vs. nonsexual offenders), psychiatric diagnosis (e.g., presence of personality disorder, psychosis), intervention received (e.g., treated vs. untreated), the specific criterion being predicted (e.g., violent vs. nonviolent behavior or different types of violent behavior), environmental setting (e.g., clients residing in institutions vs. the community), countries of origin of the research, and so forth.[37]

Accomplishing what Yang and colleagues propose can be difficult, because it requires large enough samples to arrive at statistically useful findings in each of these types of categories. Nonetheless, from a legal perspective, the more effort made in this regard, the better. Otherwise, even a tool which, on its face, has satisfactory calibration and discriminant accuracy could verge on being irrelevant, a possibility that some American courts have noted.[38]

3.5 IMPLEMENTATION VALIDITY: INTER-RATER RELIABILITY AND "ADJUSTMENTS" OF SCORES

To a social scientist, reliability means repeatability, the ability to produce similar results under similar circumstances. An RAI that has good calibration, discriminant, and external validity may still not produce valid results if it cannot be administered reliably. Some RAIs, like the HCR-20, rely on numerous "soft variables," such as "lack of insight," "negative attitudes," and "impulsivity." These types of variables are subject to many interpretations. If evaluators have not been trained how to measure them, in a way that is consistent with how they were conceptualized by the tool's developers, the

supervising agency should validate the instrument on a sample that is representative of the local population before undertaking full-scale implementation. Importantly, this should include empirical efforts to norm the tool on different groups of offenders in the target population to ensure that the tool produces accurate risk classifications across subgroups.").

37 Min Yang et al., The Efficacy of Violence Prediction: A Meta-Analytic Comparison of Nine Risk Assessment Tools, 136 Psychol. Bull. 740, 741 (2010).

38 State v. Gordon, 919 N.W.2d 635, *9 (Iowa Ct. App.), vacated on other grounds, 921 N.W.2d 19 (Iowa S. Ct. 2018) ("Nothing in our record indicates the existence of validation studies for these tests or any cross validation for an Iowa population of offenders"); State v. Loomis, 881 N.W.2d 749, 764 (Wisc. 2016) (judges should be aware that a given instrument may not have been normed on local populations and "must be constantly monitored and re-normed for accuracy due to changing populations and subpopulations").

odds increase that the same individual will receive different scores from different evaluators or that similar individuals will receive different scores.[39] Even more objective instruments, such as the VRAG, include items that can suffer from poor inter-rater reliability, such as the individual's score on the Psychopathy Checklist-Revised and his or her psychiatric diagnosis. Only the NVRA and the PSA, which rely on factors such as prior convictions and failure to appear, are unlikely to have significant variation in application, and even here scoring errors can occur.[40]

Rule 702 states that expert testimony must be based on reliable methods and principles, "reliably applied." Applied to use of RAIs, this language makes it incumbent on the decision-maker to ensure that the evaluator has been trained and has relied on trustworthy information sources in gathering relevant data. It also requires some assessment of whether the scoring and assignment of the individual to a particular risk group was carried out in a competent manner. This inquiry may not be easy. A survey of fifty-three studies in 2013 found that only two provided reports on inter-rater reliability that could be consulted by decision-makers.[41]

Even testimony based on an RAI that has good inter-rater agreement and has been reliably scored can produce unreliable (and therefore likely invalid) results if the expert evaluator decides to adjust the score or the risk level based on his or her own judgment. Unfortunately, this is a common occurrence among evaluators.[42] And judges are even more likely to consider an RAI merely one factor among many. As one survey of judges who use the PSA

39 See Grant Duwe, Public Safety Clearinghouse, Why Inter-Rater Reliability Matters for Recidivism Risk Assessment 2 (2017), available at https://psrac.bja.ojp.gov/ojpasset/Documents/PB-Interrater-Reliability.pdf (explaining that few studies have adequately studied inter-rater reliability but of the few studies that exist several found "relatively low IRR for recidivism risk assessment tools"); Anthony W. Flores et al., Predicting Outcome with the Level of Services Inventory-Revised: The Importance of Implementation Integrity, 34 J. Crim. Justice 523, 528 (2006) (predictive validity of results under the LSI-R suffered when the instrument was administered by untrained personnel).

40 See Patrick J. Kennealy, Are Pretrial Services Officers Reliable in Rating Pretrial Assessment Tools? 82 Fed. Probation 37 (2018) (finding an "excellent" Kappa of .82 for the total risk score and a "good" Kappa of .72 for the summary risk classification).

41 Sarah L. Desmarais & Jay P. Singh, Risk Assessments Instruments Validated and Implemented in Correctional Settings in the United States (2013), available at https://doi.org/10.1002/9781119184256.ch1.

42 Thomas H. Cohen et al., Examining Overrides of Risk Classifications for Offenders on Federal Supervision, 80 Fed. Prob. 12, 15 tbl. 2 (2016) (estimating overrides in 10 to 15 percent of cases); Fred Schmidt et al., Predictive Validity of the Youth Level of Service/Case Management Inventory with Youth who have Committed Sexual and Non-Sexual Offenses: The Utility of Professional Override, 43 Crim. Just. & Behav. 413, 421 (2016) (estimating an even higher percentage of overrides).

found, even those who were highly favorable toward the instrument "were still inclined to consider recommendations in the context of their own judicial intuition and experience, and would request information that was not included in the risk assessment instrument when they deemed this to be necessary."[43] One judge remarked, "It's important to understand that it's just a tool and that judges are the definitive answer."[44] The judicial decisions that have analyzed the use of RAIs at sentencing have likewise emphasized that the results of an RAI are but one factor to consider and should not be dispositive.[45]

If these statements are meant merely to stress that sentencing judges should always consider other objectives besides reducing or preventing risk, they are unremarkable. Judges are clearly the ultimate decision-maker in the pretrial and sentencing contexts and may take multiple variables into account in making that decision. But they should be aware that, consistent with the findings about RAIs' incremental validity compared to decisions made by lay factfinders, evaluator and judicial adjustments concerning *risk* usually do not improve on the actuarial assessment. In fact, several studies find that professional "overrides" of an RAI's risk estimate, whether by judges, probation officers or other correctional professionals, *decrease* accuracy in predicting offending.[46] For example, based on a sample of 3,646 offenders, Guay and Parent found that adjustments to an RAI result made by probation officers were significantly less accurate than the unadjusted RAI.[47] A study by Schmidt et al. found that professional overrides decreased predictive validity and usually increased risk level.[48] The most recent study likewise found that

43 Matthew DeMichele, et al., The Intuitive Override Model: Nudging Judges Toward Pretrial Risk Assessment Instruments 18 (2018), available at https://craftmediabucket.s3.amazonaws.com/uploads/PDFs/5-Intuitive-Override-Model.pdf.

44 Id.

45 See, e.g., State v. Loomis, 881 N.W.2d 749, 769 (Wis. 2016); Malenchik v. State, 928 N.E.2d 564, 573 (Ind. 2010).

46 See sources cited supra notes 10–14; Cohen, supra note 42, at 20–21 (finding that overrides by probation officers were "almost all … an upward adjustment" and that these overrides "demonstrated a weaker correlation between the adjusted risk levels and recidivism compared to the original risk levels"); Grant Duwe & Michael Roque, The Home-field Advantage and the Perils of Professional Judgment: Evaluating the Performance of the Static-99R and the MnSOST-3 in Predicting Sexual Recidivism, 42 Law & Hum. Beh. 269 (2018) (concluding that "use of professional judgment led to a significant degradation in predictive performance.").

47 Jean-Pierre Guay & Genevieve Parent, Broken Legs, Clinical Overrides, and Recidivism Risk: An Analysis of Decisions to Adjust Risk Levels With the LS/CMI, 45 Crim.l Just. & Behavior 82, 97 (2018).

48 Fred Schmidt, Sarah M. Sinclair & Solveig M. Thomasdót, Predictive Validity of the Youth Level of Service/Case Management Inventory with Youth Who have Committed Sexual and

overrides typically result in an "upward reshuffling" of risk, and a loss of predictive accuracy.[49] The pretrial setting is no different. One study found that judges agreed with 84 percent of the relevant RAI's "detain" recommendations, but only 47 percent of its "release" recommendations.[50]

There are likely several explanations for these types of findings. Adjustments to RAI results may be based on unverified speculation about the traits that might affect risk, a belief that "special circumstances" (e.g., contriteness or surliness) warrant ignoring the risk score, or simple mistrust of quantified decision-making.[51] Or they may stem from extraneous considerations. Erroneous adjustments upward, to a higher risk label, may be influenced by knowledge that a false negative decision (that is, a decision to release a person who ends up offending), is much more likely to be discovered than a false positive decision that results in incarceration; moreover, of course, these types of errors are much more likely to have professional and societal consequences.[52] In contrast, erroneous decisions downward may reflect concern about whether sufficient treatment resources are available in prison; if not, judges have been known to opt for a prison alternative that appears to better serve the individual (although here the override might be proper, if the RAI has not taken the community treatment into account).[53] Evaluators, judges, and parole board members might also dislike the idea of surrendering a significant amount of their discretion to a table; as one Virginia judge put it,

Sexual Offenses: The Utility of Professional Override, 43 Criminal Justice & Behav. 413, 413 (2016).

49 Thomas H. Cohen et al., Risk Assessment Overrides: Shuffling the Risk Deck Without Any Improvements in Prediction, 20 Crim. Just. & Behavior 1 (2020).

50 "Not in it for Justice:" How California's Pretrial Detention and Bail System Unfairly Punishes Poor People, Human Rights Watch (2017), available at https://www.hrw.org/report/2017/04/11/not-it-justice/how-californias-pretrial-detention-and-bail-system-unfairly.

51 R. Karl Hanson, What Do We Know about Sex Offender Risk Assessment, 4 Psychol., Pub. Pol'y & L. 50, 65 (1998)(recommending that clinicians be "exceedingly cautious" in making adjustments, but noting that "[t]hose skeptical of actuarial predictions will always find reasons to adjust actuarial estimates").

52 Katherine E. McCallum et al., The Influence of Risk Assessment Instrument Scores on Evaluators' Risk Opinions and Sexual Offender Containment Recommendations, 44 Crim. Just. & Behav. 1213, 1214 (2017).

53 See Cohen et al., supra note 49 (finding this to be the case in a study of probation officers). But a concern about lack of resources *in the community* could also have the opposite effect. See Brandon Garrett & John Monahan, Assessing Risk: The Use of Risk Assessment in Sentencing, 103 Judicature (2019), available at https://judicature.duke.edu/articles/assessing-risk-the-use-of-risk-assessment-in-sentencing/#_ednref21 ("Our findings confirm the 'treatment resource hypothesis' to be one factor accounting for the wide variation among courts and individual judges in the extent to which drug and property offenders assessed as low risk of recidivism actually receive a sentence of community treatment that does not include incarceration in a local jail.").

"I don't do voodoo."[54] Unfortunately, because these adjustments to the RAI result are subjective, or at most are based on untested assumptions based on experience or found in the literature, they may not only be wrong but also infected by racial and other biases, a possibility some courts have noted.[55]

At the same time, adjustments to the RAI result should not be prohibited in all circumstances. For instance, if two different RAIs are administered in the same case and arrive at different results, and both RAIs are well-validated, appropriate adjustments might be made (although research indicates that RAIs with good psychometric properties tend to arrive at similar results).[56] Additionally, occasionally the basis of the adjustment is a variable that was not considered by the developers of the instrument but that other research has shown can improve its accuracy. The developers of the STATIC-99—an RAI used to evaluate the risk of sexual reoffending that, as the name implies, relies entirely on static factors—provide an example of this latter situation. Several years after the instrument had been introduced, the developers candidly admitted that new research showed that a high score on the STATIC-99 should not be considered a sufficient basis for commitment of a person as a dangerous sex offender; rather, only if a high score was accompanied by the presence of "unusually high levels of psychological risk factors," as measured through structured interviews, should commitment be considered.[57]

However, this modification was itself an across-the-board change to the STATIC-99 instrument. If the Rule 702/*Daubert* reliability standard is taken seriously, case-by-case modifications should be rare, based on unique circumstances or obvious anomalies (such as when a person designated as high risk for violence has since become disabled, or when a person considered low risk

[54] Anne Metz et al., Valid or Voodoo: A Qualitative Study of Attorney Attitudes Towards Risk Assessment in Sentencing and Plea Bargaining (2020), available at https://ssrn.com/abstract=3552018.

[55] State v. Loomis, 881 N.W.2d 749, 758 (Wisc. 2016) (favorably contrasting "evidence-based sentencing" with "ad hoc decision making"); Malenchik v. State, 928 N.E.2d 564, 573 (Ind. 2010) ("Having been determined to be statistically valid, reliable, and effective in forecasting recidivism, the assessment tool scores may, and if possible should, be considered to supplement and enhance a judge's evaluation, weighing, and application of the other sentencing evidence in the formulation of an individualized sentencing program appropriate for each defendant").

[56] See Daryl G. Kroner, Jeremy F. Mills & John R. Reddon, A Coffee Can, Factor Analysis, and Prediction of Antisocial Behavior: The Structure of Criminal Risk, 28 Int'l J. L. & Psychiatry 360 (2005).

[57] David Thornton, R. Karl Hanson & Leslie Hemus, The Standard Model for Adjusted Actuarial Assessment, CiteSeer, (2010), available at http://citeseerx.ist.psu.edu/viewdoc/summary?doi=10.1.1.357.3622.

voices a genuine threat to another).[58] It is important to remember that carefully constructed RAIs are the product of considering and discarding scores of variables during development. The authors of the VRAG, for instance, analyzed approximately fifty possible risk and protective factors before paring them down to twelve;[59] the developers of the PSA tested hundreds of factors.[60] Some of these variables were rejected for practical reasons (e.g., the difficulty of finding the relevant data) rather than empirical ones (i.e., no correlation with risk). Adjustments based on the former variables should be fair game for litigants. But relying on a variable that was found to have no predictive value to change a person's risk score does not make empirical sense.

The dangers of adjusting a risk level in the absence of supporting research is particularly high with upward adjustments, which are the most common.[61] Most RAIs consist primarily of risk factors, not protective factors, so the reason for rating a person as a higher risk than the RAI indicates can easily be something that has already been taken into account. One of the common mistakes in this regard is to "double-count" criminal history. For instance, a judge might decide that even though an RAI indicates an offender is a low risk, the sentence should be enhanced because the offender has committed two prior offenses; research in Virginia indicates that is precisely what happens there.[62] Since every RAI already incorporates criminal history into its

58 Paul Meehl, Clinical Versus Statistical Prediction: A Theoretical Analysis and a Review of the Evidence 24–28 (1954) (making this point). Some courts appear to agree. See, e.g., State v. Loomis, 881 N.W.2d 749, 758 (Wis. 2016) (contrasting "evidence-based sentencing" with "ad hoc decision making" and noting the state's "commitment" to evidence-based practices). See also, Malenchik v. State, 928 N.E.2d 564, 573 (Ind. 2010).

59 Marnie E. Rice & Grant T. Harris, Violence Risk Appraisal Guide (VRAG), in Encyclopedia of Psychology and Law 847, 847 (Brian L. Cutler ed., 2008).

60 Laura & John Arnold Found., About the Public Safety Assessment: What is the PSA?, APPR, available at https://advancingpretrial.org/psa/about/ (stating that the PSA consists of nine factors, "narrowed down from hundreds").

61 Angèle Christin et al., Courts and Predictive Algorithms 7, Data Society (Oct. 27, 2015), available at http://www.datacivilrights.org/pubs/2015-1027/Courts_and_Predictive_Algorithms.pdf; Steven J. Wormith et al., The Predictive Validity of a General Risk/Needs Assessment Inventory on Sexual Offender Recidivism and an Exploration of the Professional Override, 39 Crim. Just. & Behav. 1511, 1516 (2012).

62 Anne Metz et al., Risk and Resources: A Qualitative Perspective on Low-Level Sentencing in Virginia 15 (2019), available at https://papers.ssrn.com/sol3/papers.cfm?abstract_id=3437750 (finding that 83 percent of judges considered the results of the NVRA as a "validating data point" but not "dispositive," because they also consider "the facts of the case and the defendant's criminal history"); see also Green & Chen, supra note 10 (finding that "participants responded to particularly salient features that are unevenly distributed by race (such as number of prior convictions)—essentially double-counting features for which the risk assessment had already accounted").

algorithm, this type of assessment will almost certainly be less accurate, and thus decrease the reliability/validity of the risk assessment enterprise.

In contrast, protective factors—that is, again, traits that are correlated with lower risk—are less likely to have been considered during the development of an RAI. Further, if an individual is able to produce evidence showing the presence of protective factors not considered in the RAI's development, or that a particular intervention that fits his or her "needs" is available, a downward adjustment or some alternative to prison may be indicated. In practice, justifiable RAI-overrides are likely to be in the downward direction.

3.6 CURRENT VALIDITY/RE-VALIDATION

All of the measures of accuracy discussed to this point can change for a particular instrument if, for instance, the population in the relevant jurisdiction changes significantly, the jurisdiction's crime, arrest or conviction rates go up or down substantially, the jurisdiction's policing practices change (as is occurring right now in some jurisdictions in response to the Movement for Black Lives), or the jurisdiction begins implementing innovative alternatives to prison that can reduce risk.[63] Because the potential for offending is affected by these types of factors, a person rated high risk on an outdated instrument may actually belong to a group that is low risk, or vice versa. For that reason, RAIs should be revalidated periodically. All of the instruments discussed to this point have been revised based on new data. For instance, Virginia's sentencing RAIs have been revalidated twice since 2001, and its pretrial tool twice since 2005.[64]

Other measures of current validity include auditing and peer review.[65] Tools tested in the field rarely do as well as they did during validation. They

63 See, e.g., Leslie Helmus et al., Reporting Static-99 in Light of New Research on Recidivism Norms, 21 The Forum 38 (2009) (describing how sex offender RAIs had to be renormed given dropping crime rates); Koepke & Robinson, supra note 30, at 1764–65 (pointing out that reforms designed to remind arrestees of their trial dates decreased failures-to-appear but that the effects of this innovation are not taken into account in pretrial RAIs).

64 See Virginia Criminal Sentencing Commission, 2012 Annual Report 31, 48 (2012), available at http://www.vcsc.virginia.gov/2012VCSCAnnualReport.pdf (detailing the history of the first revalidation study and implementing the results of a revalidation study started in 2010); Kenneth Rose, Virginia Department of Criminal Justice Services, Risk Assessment Factsheet: Virginia Pretrial Risk Assessment Instrument 1 (2019), available at https://www-cdn.law.stanford.edu/wp-content/uploads/2019/06/VPRAI-Factsheet-FINAL-6-20.pdf ("Though the VPRAI was first developed in 2003, the tool was revised in 2007 to remove the 'Outstanding Warrants' factor and was further revised in 2016").

65 See Brandon Garrett & John Monahan, Judging Risk, 108 Calif. L. Rev. 439, 487 (2020) (calling for "(1) publicly specifying the criteria for risk assessment instruments; (2) defining the relevant risks and needs to be measured; (3) making the risk instrument public and accessible

should be audited periodically to ensure they are performing adequately. Virginia, for instance, provides annual reports on its RAIs.[66] RAIs should also be subject to peer review, by researchers who did not develop the instrument. University-based researchers are often ideally situated to carry out such a review.[67] CBRs, AUCs, rater reliability, and override data that have been replicated by such experts, ideally in the same setting in which the RAI is being used, instill confidence that the RAI is reliable in both the legal and scientific sense. Several guides for conducting such audits exist.[68]

3.7 THE MEANING OF PREDICTIVE VALIDITY

In much of the empirical literature, the term "predictive validity" refers to calibration and discriminant validity. But, from a legal perspective, predictive validity should also encompass what this chapter has called external, implementation, and current validity. Validity in each of these respects is required to ensure that an RAI does what it purports to do.

In recent years, social scientists have focused on AUC values as the principal means of evaluating predictive validity.[69] While discriminant validity can be important for determining whether a tool has any predictive validity above chance levels, from a legal perspective accurate CBRs are much more important, because they signal the proportion of people in a given risk category who will recidivate.[70] Further, if an instrument's categories have ascending CBRs (e.g., a score of one has a CBR of 10 percent, a score of two a CBR of 20 percent

to researchers; (4) presenting risk information in a comprehensible way to decision-makers; (5) structuring decision-making to make better use of that information; and (6) accompanying these reforms with ongoing monitoring, through judicial review and by making data accessible to researchers").

66 See, e.g., Brandon Garrett, Alexander Jakubow & John Monahan, A Report of the Virginia Criminal Justice Policy Reform Project (2018), available at vcsc.virginia.gov/2018meetings/UVA%20Law%20School%20-%20NVRA%20Sentencing%20Analysis%20and%20Judicial%20Survey%20(Mar%201%202018).pdf.

67 Examples of university-based studies carried out by scholars such as Sarah Desmarais, Melissa Hamilton, and Jennifer Skeem appear throughout this book.

68 See e.g., Melissa Hamilton, Risk Assessment Tools in the Criminal Justice System: Theory and Practice—a Resource Guide 95–113 (2020), www.nacdl.org/RiskAssessmentReport (report commissioned by the National Association of Criminal Defense Lawyers).

69 Singh, supra note 17, at 16–18.

70 Indeed, some scholars have suggested that even a significant AUC value, by itself, is "not practically meaningful" for the purpose of determining a tool's legal usefulness. KiDuek Kim & Grant Duwe, Improving the Performance of Risk Assessments, in Handbook of Risk and Need Assessment: Theory and Practice 189, 217–18 (Faye S. Taxman ed., 2017). Others have characterized a good AUC as a "trivial and unexceptional accomplishment." Zachary Hamilton et al., Customizing Criminal Justice Assessments, in Handbook, supra, at 536, 536.

and so on), the AUC value is likely to be quite good, because randomly selected recidivists are likely to have higher scores than randomly selected non-recidivists.

Much of the older legal literature about prediction focused on false positive and false negative rates (the rates at which positive predictions and negative predictions are accurate).[71] This type of information can be very useful in gauging the extent to which predictions lead to unnecessary confinement (in the case of false positives) and avoidable harm to others (in the case of false negatives). But those rates, like the single PPV and NPV values that social scientists use, are based on one cut-point; that is, they assume that people who fall above a given score will recidivate and those who fall below it will not. As should be clear by now, that is not what scores on RAIs actually mean, and they should not be used in that manner. Rather, each score or category should be associated with a specific PPV (a CBR) that can tell decisionmakers, within specified confidence intervals, the proportion of people with that score who will recidivate (and thus the proportion who will not). Those are the data about risk that, as the previous chapter explained, are most relevant to the normative fit analysis.

3.8 CONCLUSION: ASSURING ACCURACY

While much of the content of this chapter is familiar to social scientists, it may be new to many legally-trained individuals. A natural question is whether judges and correctional officials have to master the nuances of CBRs, confidence intervals, AUC values, reference group concerns, and reliability and revalidation requirements. The answer to that question is nuanced.

Daubert clearly demands that legal decision-makers have a certain amount of familiarity with scientific concepts, regardless of the type of expertise involved. Even if *Daubert* does not apply, some understanding of these measures is important if RAIs are going to be used to determine whether or not people are released or confined. Indeed, the Constitution may require close assessments of accuracy even if the rules of evidence do not.

Admittedly, in *Barefoot v. Estelle*,[72] the Supreme Court held that suspect testimony about dangerousness does not violate the due process clause even when proffered by the state in an effort to obtain a death sentence. But *Barefoot*

[71] Much of my earlier work provides an example. See Christopher Slobogin, Dangerousness and Expertise, 133 U. Pa. L. Rev. 97, 110–11 (1994) (stating that "high 'false positive' rates have been characterized as the central problem in dangerousness prediction").

[72] 463 U.S. 880 (1983).

was decided in 1981, well before the modern era of RAIs. In that case, the expert, a psychiatrist named Dr. James Grigson, offered the type of clinical, non-actuarial testimony common at the time. Grigson, who had testified in scores of other capital cases—always for the prosecution—opined that there was a "one hundred and absolute chance" Barefoot would commit future acts of violence, based solely on a hypothetical question about the defendant's four previous non-violent offenses, a prison escape, and the circumstances of the murder.[73] On cross-examination, Grigson admitted that he was not familiar with the literature on risk assessment, and stated, contrary to fact, that the American Psychiatric Association did not agree with the proposition that dangerousness predictions are often wrong.[74] The Supreme Court may have been willing to permit such obviously speculative, ill-informed testimony because it saw no alternative; as the majority put it, "the suggestion that no psychiatrist's testimony may be presented with respect to a defendant's future dangerousness is somewhat like asking us to disinvent the wheel."[75] In any event, it concluded that, "at least as of now," the adversary process can be trusted "to sort out the reliable from the unreliable evidence and opinion about future dangerousness."[76]

Now is the time to reconsider *Barefoot*, because the wheel has been reinvented. RAIs expose the speciousness of testimony like Grigson's in a concrete way that cross-examination based on vague assertions about the uncertainty of risk assessment cannot. And, of course, in most of the settings in which risk is considered today, there is no real adversary process, a point taken up further in the next chapter. Thus, if risk is the question, well-validated RAIs should usually be the answer.

In *O'Donnell v. Harris County*,[77] the Fifth Circuit edged toward recognizing these points, at least in the pretrial detention setting. *O'Donnell* held that the cash bail system in operation in Harris County, Texas, violated due process because judges departed from release recommendations made by pretrial services as much as 66 percent of the time.[78] Further, the court found, judges insisted on bail even when they knew this decision would lead to incarceration because of the arrestee's indigency. The Fifth Circuit concluded that this "unwritten custom and practice" was "marred by gross inefficiencies, did not achieve any individualized assessment in setting bail, and was incompetent to

73 Id. at 919 (Blackmun, J., dissenting).
74 Id.
75 Id. at 896 (majority opinion).
76 Id. at 901.
77 892 F.3d 147 (5th Cir. 2018).
78 Id. at 154, 158.

do so."[79] While the court did not require that an RAI be used in such circumstances, the litigation in the case led to a consent decree in which Harris Countrry agreed to adopt an RAI and to carry out ongoing data collection and monitoring of pretrial outcomes.[80]

If arbitrary decision-making is unconstitutional in the pretrial setting it ought to be impermissible in the post-conviction process as well. Even the Texas Court of Criminal Appeals, which historically has been astonishingly lenient toward dangerousness testimony in capital cases, seems to be moving toward that conclusion. In the 1998 decision of *Nenno v. State*,[81] it permitted capital sentencing testimony from an expert who offered no studies to back up his opinion and admitted that he did not follow any "particular methodology for determining future dangerousness" but rather relied on his experience evaluating "thousands of cases."[82] But twelve years later, the court excluded testimony on essentially the same facts (facts, note, that are remarkably similar to *Barefoot*'s).[83]

In theory, at least, the validity of clinical testimony like Dr. Grigson's in *Barefoot* should be analyzed every time it is presented. Another advantage of RAIs, besides the delivery of more precise information about risk, is that now the decision-maker—whether it is a court or a correctional official—need not evaluate every aspect of accuracy every time an RAI is used. Rather issues of general validity should be resolved by upper level policymakers and treated as precedent, just as the fit issues discussed in the previous chapter should be.

More specifically, in answer to the question that began this concluding section of the chapter, calibration, discriminant, external, and current validity are all aspects of accuracy that can be evaluated by an extrajudicial body such as a sentencing commission or multidisciplinary panel, or by an upper level court through the appellate process, aided, ideally, by university-based or similarly independent researchers. If such a state- or region-wide entity finds the RAI to be satisfactory in these respects, the instrument itself should be considered an "admissible" source of information under *Daubert* or as a matter of due process, in all judicial or quasi-judicial proceedings in that jurisdiction. Thus, typically, the only issue that the factfinder will have to decide on a case-by-case basis is whether the RAI was reliably applied by a trained individual who used the tool appropriately and without making

79 Id. at 153.

80 Mary Moreno, Harris County Should be Proud of Bail Reform Package, Houston Chronicle (Aug. 3, 2019).

81 970 S.W.2d 549 (Tex. Crim. App 1998).

82 Id. at 562.

83 Coble v. State, 330 S.W.3d 253 (Tex. Crim. App. 2010).

unjustified adjustments; if so, the RAI's results should be given presumptive effect.[84]

Much more can be said about the precise nature of the body that might provide general validation, and the manner in which reliability can be gauged in individual cases. But those topics are best discussed in connection with fairness concerns, to which we now turn.

84 The procedure outlined here is based on a conceptual scheme that should apply to all expert testimony and is laid out in more detail in David L. Faigman, Christopher Slobogin & John Monahan, Gatekeeping Science: Using the Structure of Scientific Research to Distinguish between Admissibility and Weight in Expert Testimony, 110 Nw. U. L. Rev. 859 (2016) (distinguishing between "framework testimony" of general significance that is the province of appellate judges and "diagnostic" testimony that is the province of juries or bench judges).

4

Fairness

Avoiding Unjust Algorithms

While critics of risk algorithms in the criminal justice system have often complained about "off-label" uses of RAIs (the fit problem) or the difficulty of getting risk right (the validity problem), they have aimed their heaviest artillery at what they perceive to be the unfairness of using actuarial tools to determine risk. Even if RAIs were to satisfy the most stringent fit and validity requirements, critics argue, their use should be avoided or minimized because they exacerbate racial and other biases, justify liberty deprivations using factors that are irrelevant to blameworthiness, and allow incarceration to be based on dehumanizing, nonindividualized determinations. In the following discussion, these claims are labeled the egalitarian injustice, retributive injustice, and procedural injustice critiques.

There is more than a grain of truth to all of these critiques. They have important implications for the jurisprudence of risk. But none of them should sound the death knell for RAIs. Each can be countered through careful construction and use of risk assessment tools and transparency about their inner workings.

4.1 EGALITARIAN INJUSTICE

As a matter of formal legal doctrine, the Equal Protection Clause of the Fourteenth Amendment is the focal point of discussion about the extent to which the government must treat its citizens equitably. Generally, the Clause has been construed to permit government statutes and practices that discriminate between similarly situated individuals as long as they are based on some rational reason, which need not be empirically supported but rather can rest simply on "common sense."[1] However, certain legal classifications—most prominently,

[1] FCC v. Beach Communications, Inc., 508 U.S. 307, 313 (1993) (under rational basis review, a law "must be upheld against Equal Protection challenge if there is any reasonably conceivable state of facts that could provide a rational basis for the classification" made by the law).

race and sex, but also including alienage and religion—are "suspect" because of their historical association with political and social oppression. Thus, a statute or practice that discriminates on those grounds is subject to "strict scrutiny" (in the case of race) or "intermediate scrutiny" (in the case of sex).[2] The state may discriminate on the basis of race only if it can demonstrate that it has a compelling reason for doing so, using a means narrowly tailored to meet its objective, and discrimination on the basis of gender is permitted only upon a similar showing, albeit not quite as demanding.[3]

This interpretation of the Equal Protection Clause is usually called "anti-classification," because it limits the government's ability to engage in classification on the basis of a person's race and sex, regardless of which race or gender is at issue. It is often distinguished from the "anti-subordination" approach to equal protection, which focuses on whether the government is discriminating against a group that has historically been oppressed or subordinated to more privileged groups; under this approach, and in contrast to the anti-classification principle, race and sex may be taken into account to the extent doing so will rectify wrongs against people of color and women.[4] *Brown v. Board of Education*,[5] which famously found "separate but equal" white and black schools to be a violation of equal protection, could be seen as an illustration of either principle; under the educational system declared unconstitutional in the case, schools were classified on the basis of race, and that classification significantly disadvantaged a race that had been enslaved and then subject to Jim Crow laws.[6]

When the Court has been confronted with cases that required a choice between these two equal protection theories, however, it has usually chosen the anti-classification approach.[7] For instance, affirmative action programs for blacks could be seen as an implementation of the anti-subordination version of

2 See Clark v. Jeter, 486 U.S. 456, 461 (1988).

3 Id.

4 On the distinctions between anticlassification and antisubordination approaches, see Jack M. Balkin & Reva B. Siegel, The American Civil Rights Tradition: Anticlassification or Antisubordination? 58 U. Miami L. Rev. 9, 9–10 (2003).

5 347 U.S. 483 (1954).

6 See Reva B. Siegel, Equality Talk: Antisubordination and Anticlassification Values in Constitutional Struggles over Brown, 117 Harv. L. Rev. 1470, 1484–99 (2004) (noting that, immediately after *Brown*, some scholars interpreted the decision consistently with the anticlassification theory and others with antisubordination theory).

7 Kimberly Jenkins Robinson, The Constitutional Future of Race-Neutral Efforts to Achieve Diversity and Avoid Racial Isolation in Elementary and Secondary Schools, 50 B.C. L. Rev. 277, 315 (2009). ("The Court's current approach to equal protection, which has been labeled an antidiscrimination, anticlassification, or color-blind approach, emphasizes the impropriety of government use of racial classifications.")

equal protection, but the Court over time has held that, under most circumstances, they are unconstitutional because they classify on the basis of race. The Court's current position is summed up in Chief Justice Roberts statement that "[t]he way to stop discrimination on the basis of race is to stop discriminating on the basis of race."[8]

When a statute or practice does not explicitly differentiate on the basis of race or sex, but rather simply has a disparate racial or sex-based impact, it is usually not considered violative of equal protection, unless animus toward the racial or sex-based group is shown.[9] As the Supreme Court put it, "our cases have not embraced the proposition that a law or other official act, without regard to whether it reflects a racially discriminatory purpose, is unconstitutional solely because it has a racially disproportionate impact."[10] This test recognizes that the absence of an explicit race or sex classification usually passes constitutional muster.

Application of these concepts to RAIs is not an easy task, but the overall conclusion should be that, with a few caveats, such instruments do not violate equal protection if they are valid in the senses discussed in the previous chapter. A number of courts, including the Supreme Court, have held that protecting the public from dangerous individuals is a compelling state interest.[11] On that assumption, traditional anti-classification theory might permit even explicit use of race in a risk algorithm if it has significant

8 Parents Involved in Cmty. Schools v. Seattle Sch. Dist. No. 1, 551 U.S. 701, 748 (2007) (plurality opinion). See also Grutter v. Bollinger, 539 U.S. 306, 329–330 (2003) (stating that enrolling a specified percentage of a particular group merely because of its race or ethnic origin "would be patently unconstitutional").

9 Michael Selmi, Was the Disparate Impact Theory a Mistake?, 53 UCLA L. Rev. 701, 727 (2006) (discussing the history of disparate impact litigation and noting that a contrary approach "could have prompted a significant amount of litigation and social restructuring").

10 Washington v. Davis, 426 U.S. 229, 239 (1976).

11 See United States v. Salerno, 481 U.S. 739, 745 (1987) (stating, in the pretrial detention context, that the federal government has "compelling interests in public safety"); Schall v. Martin, 467 U.S. 253, 264 (1984) (same, and collecting cases standing for the proposition that "[t]he 'legitimate and compelling state interest' in protecting the community from crime cannot be doubted" and is "a weighty social objective"). Lower courts have even found a compelling interest in preventing relatively minor crimes or speculative risks. United States v. Chappell, 691 F.3d 388, 399 (4th Cir. 2012) ("The Virginia statute serves the important—indeed compelling—interest of promoting public safety by prohibiting an individual from intentionally impersonating a peace officer for a broad range of improper aims"); Kachalsky v. Cacace, 817 F.Supp.2d 235, 269 (S.D.N.Y. 2011) ("[T]he state has an important government interest in promoting public safety and preventing crime"); May v. Hunter, 451 F.Supp.2d 1084, 1088 (D. D. Cal. 2006) (stating that "the state has a compelling interest to protect the public from those prisoners who are not in remission, and that in order to protect the public, it is necessary to provide those prisoners continuing mental health treatment until the underlying condition can be kept in remission").

predictive validity and if alternatives to using it could not as effectively achieve the state's aims. However, race, by itself, is not a particularly strong predictor.[12] In any event, in the 2017 decision of *Buck v. Davis*,[13] a capital sentencing case, the Supreme Court declared, without even mentioning any possible state interest that might thereby be undermined, that "it would be patently unconstitutional for a state to argue that a defendant is liable to be a future danger because of his race."[14] Perhaps anticipating that conclusion, no mainstream RAI incorporates race into its algorithm. Nor, with one notable exception, do these RAIs use ethnicity, alienage, or religion, which are also suspect classes and closely aligned with race in many circumstances.[15]

Several RAIs do, however, use gender to help differentiate risk levels. Not clear, post-*Davis*, is how the Court would react to that fact. Pending a Supreme Court case that directly addresses the issue, under current doctrine sex can only be used as a risk factor if there is a strong justification for doing so (as one lower court decision, discussed in Section 4.2.1, has found).

If instead an RAI uses neither race nor sex as a risk factor, but only produces results that have a disparate racial or gender impact, then formal classification is not occurring, and use of the RAI is permissible if there is any rational basis for doing so, unless a discriminatory purpose can be shown. While the Supreme Court has not always required serious animus in its disparate impact jurisprudence, it has tended to mandate strong proof of discriminatory purpose in the criminal justice setting.[16] In any event, developers of RAIs are not likely to have harbored or intended to implement animus toward any given racial group, and in fact probably want to avoid disproportionate outcomes.[17] Thus, a disparate impact argument against RAIs is unlikely to prevail.

12 Michael T. Kirkpatrick & Margaret B. Kwoka, Title VI Disparate Impact Claims Would Not Hurt National Security, 46 Harv. J. Leg. Harv. 503, 524 (2009) ("Although there are data showing correlations between arrest rates and race, and incarceration rates and race," no data demonstrate "either a general or a circumstantial correlation between race and crime").

13 137 S.Ct. 759 (2017).

14 Id. at 775.

15 Timothy Cadigan & James L. Johnson, The Re-Validation of the Federal Pretrial Risk Assessment (PTRA): A Research Summary, 82 Fed. Prob. 23, 24 (2018), available at https://www.uscourts.gov/federal-probation-journal/2012/09/re-validation-federal-pretrial-services-risk-assessment-ptra (noting that the PTRA instrument includes "citizenship" as a variable).

16 Michael Coenen, Spillover Across Remedies, 98 Minn. L. Rev. 1211, 1229–1230 (2014) (stating that "the discriminatory purpose rule applies with equal force in criminal cases," noting, for instance, that notwithstanding powerful evidence of discrimination against blacks in cocaine prosecutions, "Washington v. Davis and its progeny stood as an impenetrable barrier to equal protection relief, as black crack-cocaine defendants never managed to gather enough evidence to satisfy the discriminatory purpose requirement").

17 Cary Coglianese & David Lehr, Regulating by Robot: Administrative Decision Making in the Machine-Learning Era, 105 Geo. L. J. 1147, 1193 (2017) (so stating).

A number of writers have nonetheless insisted that RAIs violate related subconstitutional norms when they have a disparate racial impact,[18] and some have argued that these norms are also violated when there is disparate impact on other grounds, such as poverty.[19] Some state statutes could also be interpreted to take this position by stipulating that, to use Ohio's language, a court "shall not base the sentence upon the race, ethnic background, gender, or religion of the offender."[20] Surfacing these concerns and responding to them is an important aspect of exploring the justness of algorithmic risk assessment. The overall conclusion reached here is that, given the importance of valid RAIs to achieving the state's goals of protecting the public and reducing incarceration, neither formal equal protection doctrine nor other inequality concerns should derail development of RAIs.

However, the balancing of state and individual interests of the type that is inherent in equal protection analysis does trigger fairness concerns. Specifically, it raises questions about whether certain outcome variables—most predominately, certain types of criminal history—are out-of-bounds on race discrimination grounds; whether constitutionally protected characteristics—particularly sex—can nonetheless be explicitly considered in developing RAIs; and whether other characteristics—for instance, being unemployed—are so weakly predictive that they cannot survive even the minimal rational basis test.

4.1.1 *Race*

Probably the best-known critique of risk assessment instruments came in 2016, in an article published in ProPublica about the COMPAS.[21] The article reported that the instrument was "biased against blacks" because it produced a false positive rate for that group that was twice the false positive rate for whites when the cut-off was "medium" risk (45 percent to 23 percent) and three times

18 Anupam Chander, The Racist Algorithm? 115 Mich. L. Rev. 1023 (2017) (arguing for "algorithmic affirmative action"); Bernard Harcourt, Risk as a Proxy for Race: The Dangers of Risk Assessment, 27 Fed. Sent Rpt. 237 (2015).

19 See Sonia B. Starr, Evidence-Based Sentencing and the Scientific Rationalization of Discrimination, 66 Stan. L. Rev. 803, 805 (2014).

20 Ohio Rev. Code Ann. 2929.11(C) ("A court that imposes a sentence upon an offender for a felony shall not base the sentence upon the race, ethnic background, gender, or religion of the offender"). See also, Tenn. Code Ann. 40–35-102(4) ("Sentencing should exclude all considerations respecting race, gender, creed, religion, national origin, and social status of the individual").

21 Julia Angwin et al., Machine Bias, ProPublica (May 23, 2016), available at https://www.propublica.org/article/machine-bias-risk-assessments-in-criminal-sentencing.

the white false positive rate for those rated "high" risk (16 percent to 5 percent). The developer of the COMPAS did not disagree with these conclusions, but pointed out that the CBRs of the COMPAS were almost equal for both groups: among blacks, 21 percent of the high risk group reoffended, whereas among whites, 17 percent of those designated high risk recidivated.[22] Further, as other commentators pointed out, the differential false positive rates produced by a reasonably well-calibrated instrument like the COMPAS are inevitable as a statistical matter when, as the data from the sample used by ProPublica seemed to indicate,[23] the black crime rate is higher than the white crime. When black defendants have a higher rate of reoffending, a well-calibrated algorithm will classify a greater proportion of black defendants as high risk, and thus a greater proportion of black defendants who ultimately do not reoffend will have been classified as high risk.[24] (The same phenomenon would occur, for instance, with age and sex: because young people and males commit more crimes, a well-calibrated RAI will produce more false positives at each score among youth and men than among older people and women.)

The COMPAS abides by the anti-classification principle; race is not considered. Nonetheless, it has been lambasted by a number of commentators. For instance, the RAND Corporation stated:

> By accurately reflecting base rate criminality and thereby treating black people as higher risk than white people, COMPAS perpetuates a disproportionate impact along racial lines. . . . If existing base rates are unjust (because of historical factors and structural racism), it can be argued that accurate algorithms, such as COMPAS, are complicit in and contribute to this society-wide injustice.[25]

22 Sam Corbett-Davies et al., What Makes an Algorithm Fair? Medium (Oct. 28, 2016), available at https://medium.com/soal-food/what-makes-an-algorithm-fair-6ad64d75ddoc (pointing out that "[d]efendants assigned the highest risk score [on the COMPAS] reoffended at almost four times the rate as those assigned the lowest score (81 percent versus 22 percent)," and that "among defendants who scored a seven on the COMPAS scale, 60 percent of white defendants reoffended, which is nearly identical to the 61 percent of black defendants who reoffended").

23 Jeff Larson et al., How We Analyzed the COMPAS Recidivism Algorithm, ProPublica (May 23, 2016), available at https://www.propublica.org/article/how-we-analyzed-the-compas-recidivism-algorithm. ("Across every risk category, black defendants recidivated at higher rates.")

24 Corbett-Davies et al., supra note 22 ("If the recidivism rate for white and black defendants is the same within each risk category, and if black defendants have a higher overall recidivism rate, then a greater share of black defendants will be classified as high risk. And if a greater share of black defendants are classified as high risk, then . . . a greater share of black defendants *who do not reoffend* will also be classified as high risk.") (Emphasis in original).

25 Osonde A. Osba et al., Algorithmic Equity—A Framework for Social Applications (2019); Michael Tonry, Doing Justice, Preventing Crime 180–82 (2020).

This language mischaracterizes the interaction of race and risk on the COMPAS in several ways. First, the algorithm does not "treat[] black people as higher risk than white people." It treats people with risk factors X, Y, and Z as higher risk than those who do not have those risk factors, a greater proportion of whom happen to be black. Second, its impact is not "disproportionate" to the amount of crime blacks commit; as RAND admits, COMPAS accurately reflects base rate criminality. Third, if that base rate criminality is unjust because of structural racism, risk assessment is not the central problem; rather the entire criminal justice system, which assumes people can be punished for their crimes, is "complicit in and contributes to this society wide injustice." While there is a strong basis for calling the black crime rate "unjust" from a sociological point of view, that critique carried to its logical limit would end far more than risk assessment; indeed, it is the predicate for the Abolish Prison movement.[26]

ProPublica's less radical solution to the problem—equalizing false positive rates for both races—has its own difficulties. This approach, sometimes called *classification parity*, would mean that more whites would be classified as high risk when in fact they are not, or that more people of color who are high risk would be classified as low risk, or both. Additionally, as Richard Berk has suggested, that route would probably result in more victims of color, as individuals who should have been detained are released back into their communities;[27] if so, classification parity will have a disproportionately harmful effect on those who live in disadvantaged areas.[28] In any event, simultaneous equalization of both false positive and false negative rates will usually be impossible.[29]

The approach taken by the COMPAS, which tries to ensure that people who pose the same degree of risk are in the same risk category, regardless of

26 See Paul Butler, Chokehold: Policing Black Men 229–230 (2018) (arguing that prisons are agencies of white supremacy and their abolition would be "the third gift people who fight for African American freedom will have provided the country, after they defeated slavery and Jim Crow.").

27 Richard Berk, Accuracy and Fairness for Juvenile Justice Risk Assessments, 16 J. Empirical Legal Studies 175, 191 (2019). ("When one adjusts algorithms to make them more fair for black perpetrators, one risks increasing unfairness for black crime victims.")

28 Cf. see Mark A. R. Kleiman, When Brute Force Fails: How to Have Less Crime and Less Punishment 23 (2009) (noting that if law enforcement is evenly distributed, people who commit crime in high crime areas will be less subject to arrest and prosecution, which arguably violates equal protection "if 'equal protection' means that a crime against a poor or black person will be investigated as diligently, prosecuted as forcefully, and punished as severely as the same crime against a rich or white person").

29 Sandra G. Mayson, Bias In, Bias Out, 128 Yale L. J. 2218, 2271 (2019) ("it may not even be possible to equalize both error rates at once. An effort to equalize false-positive rates may widen the disparity in false-negative rates, or vice versa").

race, is a preferable method of ensuring fairness.[30] First, it sidesteps possible concerns about violating the Equal Protection Clause by avoiding intentional misclassification of whites or blacks. Second, it avoids the political blowback that is likely to accompany migrating affirmative action principles to the criminal context. Third, and most importantly, it treats people of equal risk equally. Each risk classification represents the same risk, regardless of race. Pro-publica's anti-subordinationist approach clearly violates not just anti-classification principles but also calibration principles.

At the same time, caution is necessary in evaluating the racial impact of RAIs. For instance, it is well-documented that people of color are more likely to be arrested for drug-possession crime than whites who engage in the same behavior, in part because of biased policing practices and in part because such crimes, when committed by poorer individuals, are more likely to be publicly observable;[31] the same is probably also true of many misdemeanors.[32] If an RAI uses *arrests* for these types of crimes as an outcome variable, as the COMPAS appears to do, it will be predicting that people of color commit more of these crimes than whites, when in fact they do not.[33] Sandra Mayson makes the point with an antidote: in New Orleans, where she practiced law, a black with

30 See id., at 2272 ("[A]lgorithmic affirmative action, in essence, constitutes a rejection of actuarial risk assessment itself"); Gina Vincent & Jodi Viljoen, Racist Algorithms or Systemic Problems? Risk Assessments and Racial Disparities, 20 Crim. J. & Behav. 1, 5 (2020) (describing the views of several empiricists on the issue of racial bias and concluding "by our ethical standards, there is currently no valid evidence that instruments in general are biased against individuals of color. Where bias has been found, it appears to have more to do with the specific risk instrument").

31 See Ojmarrh Mitchell & Michael S. Caudy, Examining Racial Disparities in Drug Arrests, Just. Q., Jan. 2013, at 22. ("[R]acial disparity in drug arrests between black and whites cannot be explained by race differences in the extent of drug offending, nor the nature of drug offending.") Some studies have suggested that white people use and sell drugs at even higher rates than black people. Jonathan Rothwell, How the War on Drugs Damages Black Social Mobility, Brookings Inst. (Sept. 30, 2014), available at http://www.brookings.edu/blogs/social-mobility-memos/posts/2014/09/30/how-the-war-on-drugs-damages-black-socialmobility [https://perma.cc/9KX3-UJ6B]. See also, Katherine Beckett, Kris Nyrop & Lori Pfingst, Race, Drug and Policing: Understanding Disparities in Drug Delivery Arrests, 44 Criminol. 105 (2006); Peter Reuter, Paul Hirschfield & Curt Davies, Assessing the Crack-Down on Marijuana in Maryland (Abell Foundation, 2001), available at http://citeseerx.ist.psu.edu/viewdoc/summary?doi=10.1.1.608.4702.

32 Megan Stevenson & Sandra G. Mayson, The Scale of Misdemeanor Justice, 98 B.U. L. Rev. 731, 769–70 (2018).

33 This appears to be the main concern of many who criticize RAIs on racial grounds. See Chelsea Barabas, Karthik Dinakar & Colin Doyle, the Problems with Risk Assessment Tools, N.Y. Times (July 17, 2019), available at https://dam-prod.media.mit.edu/x/2019/07/16/TechnicalFlawsOfPretrial_ML%20site.pdf.

three arrests was not much of a concern—but a white with three arrests was "really bad news."[34]

There are two solutions to this problem. The first is to change the outcome variable—to either convictions rather than arrests (on the assumption that convictions more accurately indicate criminal activity between races), or to arrests or convictions for violent crimes only. The latter choice is preferable, not only for empirical reasons (arrests and convictions for violent crimes are less likely to be racially contingent)[35] but also because, as Chapter 2 argued, confining people on the ground that they might commit a misdemeanor or low level felony is not justifiable as a normative matter, even if the risk of such reoffending is high. Several recent studies have found that the RAIs so constructed (by using arrests for serious crimes as the outcome measure) do not produce racial bias even in the sense highlighted by the ProPublica study.[36]

The second solution to the policing disparity problem—in addition to or instead of changing the outcome measure—is what could be called *race-conscious* calibration of the RAI, which involves creating different algorithms for different ethnicities or races, as described in Chapter 3. In Mayson's New Orleans, the race-conscious approach might put blacks with three arrests in a much lower risk category than whites with three arrests. The possible problem with this approach, of course, is that, like classification parity, it violates the anti-classification principle; it explicitly takes race into account.

However, unlike Propublica's classification parity approach—which to achieve its version of fairness must undermine accurate conclusions about propensity to commit crime—race-conscious calibration serves the important state interests of protecting the public and avoiding unnecessary incarceration, by rectifying the impact of discriminatory practices that unfairly raise one's risk score. The classification parity approach nullifies a person's real risk level. In contrast, race-conscious calibration that corrects for racially biased policing works to nullify a person's *erroneous* risk level, one that is a consequence of

34 Mayson, supra note 29, at 2264.

35 See generally Jason Schultz & Kate Crawford, Dirty Data, Bad Predictions: How Civil Rights Violations Impact Police Data, Predictive Policing Systems and Justice, 94 NYU L. Rev. 192 (2019) (noting that police data may include arrests of people known to be innocent, false claims of criminal activity, and doctored arrest statistics).

36 Sarah L. Desmarais et al., Predictive Validity of Pretrial Risk Assessments: A Systematic Review of the Literature, Crim. Just. & Beh. (2020), available at https://doi.org/10.1177/0093854820932959; Douglas B. Marlowe et al., Employing Standardized Risk Assessment in Pretrial Release Decisions: Association with Criminal Justice Outcomes and Racial Equity, 44 L. & Hum. Behav. 361 (2020); Evan M. Lowder et al., Differential Prediction and Disparate Impact of Pretrial Risk Assessments in Practice: A Multisite Evaluation (under review, 2021).

prior government malfeasance and that cannot be justified by any legitimate state interest; thus, it should not be considered a violation of the Equal Protection Clause.[37]

Note that this entire discussion about inequality and risk factors is only possible when risk assessment is a product of an RAI. If instead a risk assessment is the product of human judgment, taking any type of ameliorative action would be much more difficult. Even with implicit bias training, humans are often heavily influenced by race or race proxies.[38] And even with a requirement that reasons for acting be documented, human intuitive predictions of reoffending are opaque, which makes them difficult to challenge. In contrast, an RAI displays its stereotyping assumptions on its face. Thus, compared to human-driven risk assessment, RAIs allow bias to be more easily discovered. And because of that transparency, RAIs can take racial biases into account.

For example, using the Post-Conviction Risk Assessment tool (a federal probation instrument) and large samples, Jennifer Skeem and Christopher Lowenkamp have shown a number of ways race can be used in constructing a well-calibrated RAI that reduces significantly the "proxy effect" of race.[39] Crystal Yan and Will Dobbie were able to do the same thing in the pretrial setting with the PSA, with only minimal impact on predictive validity.[40] These types of efforts illustrate the fact that, as Sendhil Mullainathan has noted, "biased algorithms are easier to fix than biased people."[41]

37 See Aziz Z. Huq, Constitutional Rights in the Machine Learning State, 105 Cornell L. Rev. 1875, 1920 (2020) ("an official's mere awareness of race raises no constitutional problem. By analogy, it may also be that mere inclusion of race as a feature of training data should not be per se problematic"). This line of argument also finds some support in the "injustice-compounding" theories of Deborah Hellman. See, e.g., Deborah Hellman, Sex, Causation and Algorithms: Equal Protection in the Age of Machine Learning, 98 Wash. U. L. Rev. 481, 521 (2020) (arguing that it should be permissible to use sex in the "training data").

38 Adam Benforado summarizes this point as follows: "Studies on sentencing have shown that judges are influenced by the race of the defendant . . . . [T]he latest psychological research suggests that much of the skew is not susceptible to conscious control. There is no magic switch to erase a lifetime of exposure to damaging stereotypes that link the concepts of blackness and violence . . . ." Adam Benforado, Can Science Save Justice? 101 Judicature 25, 28 (2017).

39 Jennifer Skeem & Christopher Lowenkamp, Using Algorithms to Address Trade-Offs in Predicting Recidivism, 38 Beh. Sci. & L. 259 (2020).

40 Crystal Yang & Will Dobbie, Equal Protection Under Algorithms: A New Statistical and Legal Framework, 119 Mich. Lev. 291, 343–357 (2020).

41 Sendhil Mullainathan, Biased Algorithms Are Easier to Fix Than Biased People, N.Y. Times (Dec. 6, 2019), available at https://www.nytimes.com/2019/12/06/business/algorithm-bias-fix.html. See also, Jon Kleinberg et al., Discrimination in the Age of Algorithms, 10 J. Legal Analysis 113, 115 (2019) ("[g]etting the proper regulatory system in place . . . has the potential to turn algorithms into a powerful counterweight to human discrimination and a positive force for social good of multiple kinds").

4.1.2 *Sex*

While race is not explicitly incorporated into any commonly used RAI, sex—specifically, maleness—is a risk factor in several RAIs. In part, that is because developers have realized that an RAI that is well-calibrated for men may not be well-calibrated for women; as illustrated by Hamilton's example using the COMPAS, described in the previous chapter, women do not recidivate as much as men, apparently even when they are otherwise associated with identical risk factors. From an empirical point of view, that situation calls for an RAI validated on a female population. But, just as with race, while this sex-conscious classification approach assures better calibration, it may violate the anti-classification principle. For instance, in *Craig v. Boren*,[42] the Supreme Court struck down a law that allowed women to buy alcohol at age eighteen while prohibiting alcohol sales to males until they were twenty-one, despite evidence that men have higher rates of drunk driving. Apparently relying on similar reasoning, statutes in some states specifically ban use of gender in imposing a sentence.[43]

Nonetheless, in *Wisconsin v. Loomis*[44] the Wisconsin Supreme Court suggested that discriminating on the basis of sex is permissible if it validly helps distinguish between males and females in terms of risk. Loomis's sentence had been enhanced using the COMPAS, which specifically took gender into account; Loomis argued that this disposition violated due process. Although as a result of this framing, the Wisconsin court did not explicitly address the equal protection issue, it did state, in the course of rejecting Loomis's claim, that "it appears that any risk assessment tool which fails to differentiate between men and women will misclassify both genders."[45] In essence, the court was saying, because of its enhancement to accuracy, incorporating gender was a narrowly tailored means of meeting the state's interest in preventing harm to the public in a cost-efficient manner.

Had the court directly addressed the equal protection issue, would it have had to decide otherwise? *Boren* might be distinguished on the ground that the statistical evidence in that case about the difference between men and women

42 429 U.S. 190 (1976).

43 See supra note 20.

44 881 N.W.2d 749 (Wis. 2016).

45 Id. at 766. Other courts have recognized this point. See Karsjens v. Jesson, 6 F. Supp.3d 958, 967–68 (D. Minn. 2015) (in case challenging female sex offender civil commitment programming, calling attention to expert testimony that actuarial risk tools normed on male sex offenders are inapplicable to females); In re Risk Level Determination of S.S., 726 N.W.2d 121, 123 (Minn. Ct. App. 2007) (noting that expert declined to score a sexual recidivism risk tool for a female defendant because the tool had not been validated on women).

was weak; as Justice Brennan pointed out for the majority, the data showing that men are arrested for drunk driving more often than women might merely mean that "'reckless' young men who drink and drive are transformed into arrest statistics, while their female counterparts are chivalrously escorted home."[46] But in two cases applying Title VII, the federal anti-discrimination statute, the Court held that employers may not require women to pay more into, or receive less from, retirement accounts than men, despite strong data showing that women live longer and thus that, without those adjustments, they will cost the employer more money than men.[47] Although Title VII does not apply to the criminal justice system and recognizes a broader scope to discrimination claims, these cases signal the Court's concern with explicit use of sex as a discriminator.

At the same time, the state's interest in keeping the female drinking age at eighteen that was at issue in *Boren*, and even the employer's interest in saving money in the Title VII cases, pale in comparison to the state's twin interests that are inevitably at stake in cases like *Loomis*—protecting the public and avoiding unnecessary incarceration (in this case, of women). If Virginia's NVRA instrument is any guide (recall that, under that instrument, being male brings ten points, being female only one), sex is a powerful predictor that can help effectuate both interests. Like race-conscious calibration, sex-conscious calibration makes empirical sense, and should not be considered violative of equal protection.

4.1.3 *Other Traits*

Of the factors typically found in RAIs, only race and sex trigger Fourteenth Amendment protection and thus require more than a rational basis for their use under current law. Nonetheless, Sonya Starr has argued that the Fourteenth Amendment also bars RAIs from using poverty or proxies for it (e.g., unemployment, location, or house ownership),[48] based primarily on the Supreme Court's pronouncement in *Bearden v. Georgia*[49] that revoking parole for an offender who has failed to pay a fine "would be little more than punishing him for his poverty," and "is contrary to fundamental fairness."[50]

46 429 U.S. at 203 n.14.
47 City of Los Angeles, Dep't Water & Power v. Manhart, 425 U.S. 702 (1978); Arizona Governing Comm. for Tax Deferred Annuity and Deferred Compensation Plans v. Norris, 463 U.S. 1073 (1983).
48 Starr, supra note 19, at 830–36.
49 461 U.S. 660 (1983).
50 Id. at 671–72.

However, no court has interpreted *Bearden* to mean that factors *related* to poverty are anathema in assessing either risk or punishment generally.[51] Furthermore, *Bearden* itself stated that "a sentencing court can consider a defendant's employment history and financial resources in setting an initial punishment,"[52] and emphasized that the only sentencing practice it was barring was the use of poverty "as the sole justification for imprisonment,"[53] which no risk assessment instrument comes close to doing.

This does not mean that any wealth-related risk factor is fair game; the state still must demonstrate a rational basis for its use. The rationale developed above for permitting reliance on risk factors like sex or that correlate with race rested on the assumption that these factors are powerful predictors that help achieve the compelling state interest of protecting society. Following equal protection's tiered analysis, the relevance to risk assessment of other factors—such as age, employment status, home life as a child, diagnosis, or marital status—need not be as robust. At the same time, however, these types of factors should add some nontrivial predictive weight to the algorithm. Because of their minimal predictive value, for instance, employment and marital status were eventually dropped from Virginia's NVRA.[54] The developers of the PSA excluded drug and alcohol use, mental health, employment and residence as risk factors, despite the likelihood they were somewhat predictive, because they did not add appreciably to the usefulness of the RAI.[55]

In contrast, some RAIs explicitly treat these types of factors as strong predictors of reoffending. For instance, the VRAG includes as risk factors psychopathy, personality disorder, the presence of parents in the home when the subject was sixteen, and marital status, and the first three of these factors are given significant weight in the algorithm.[56] In contrast to some types of arrests, these traits cannot easily be attributed to discrimination, even on the part of society as a whole, much less the government. If one's intuition remains

51 See, e.g., United States v. Flowers, 946 F. Supp. 2d 1295, 1300 (M.D. Ala. 2013) ("[R]elative wealth and poverty will inevitably have some effect on the administration of justice"); State v. Johnson, 315 P.3d 1090, 1099 (Wash. 2014) (interpreting *Bearden* to mean solely that a person cannot be imprisoned for failure to pay a fine).

52 461 U.S. at 670.

53 Id. at 671.

54 Personal communication with Meredith Farrar-Owens, March 25, 2020 (memo indicating that these two factors were dropped on July 1, 2013, "based on a study of new felony cases").

55 Laura & John Arnold Found., About the Public Safety Assessment: How It Works, APPR, available at https://advancingpretrial.org/psa/factors/#psa-factors; https://craftmediabucket.s3.amazonaws.com/uploads/Public-Safety-Assessment-101_190319_140124.pdf (last visited May 31, 2020).

56 See Chapter 2, text accompanying note 7.

that it is an injustice to base confinement on such factors even when they clearly improve calibration, it probably stems not from concerns about egalitarian injustice, but rather from worries about what could be called retributive injustice.

4.2 RETRIBUTIVE INJUSTICE

While good calibration, adapted to ensure that algorithms are not tainted by state-enabled discrimination, can minimize egalitarian injustice, it may not assuage those who voice a closely related fairness objection, to the effect that many risk factors have nothing to do with individual blameworthiness. Hollywood's images of futuristic societies in which prisoners are selected according to genetic makeup or brain chemistry are far from current reality. But the difference between bio-prediction of this sort and an actuarial score, which often relies on static or congenital factors, is one of degree, not kind.

The retributive injustice claim addressed here is not the argument—to be addressed in Chapter 5—that risk is never a legitimate consideration in the criminal process. Rather, it is the claim that, even if risk can in whole or part justify criminal punishment, this type of deprivation of liberty must be based solely on culpable conduct.[57] At its broadest reach, that claim would mean that RAIs cannot rely on conduct that is not criminally blameworthy—such as substance abuse, remaining single, or choosing not to work—nor on circumstances that are not blameworthy in any sense—such as being abandoned by one's parents before majority or living in a particular area. Even more obviously for those who take this perspective, RAIs cannot incorporate traits, such as gender, age, or diagnosis, that have nothing to do with any type of conduct, blameworthy or not. Perhaps the RAI that most dramatically transgresses this point of view is provided by Virginia's NVRA, which, as mentioned in Chapter 2, recommends a prison sentence simply for those who are twenty-one, male, and have one prior conviction.

In *Buck v. Davis*,[58] the Supreme Court appeared to recognize the retributive injustice concern. As noted earlier, the thrust of *Davis* was a rebuke of egalitarian injustice; the Court stated that using the fact of being black as a risk factor "appealed to a powerful racial stereotype" and "coincided precisely with a particularly noxious strain of racial prejudice."[59] But the Court went on to

57 Michael Tonry, Legal and Ethical Issues in the Prediction of Recidivism, 26 Federal Sentencing Rep. 167, 171 (2014). ("Ascribed characteristics for which individuals bear no responsibility, such as race, ethnicity, gender, and age, should not be included.")

58 137 S.Ct. 759 (2017).

59 Id. at 776.

say that sentencing a person on the basis of race "is a disturbing departure from a basic premise of our criminal justice system: Our law punishes people for what they do, not who they are."[60] Taken literally, this latter sentiment would prohibit punishers from relying not only on race, but also on risk factors such as gender and age, and probably on factors involving current mental state, such as diagnosis or lack of insight as well, since none of these variables involves conduct.

At the same time, on several occasions the Supreme Court has explicitly permitted death sentences to be imposed on the ground that the offender is "dangerous,"[61] including in *Barefoot v. Estelle*, where Dr. Grigson's conclusion about Barefoot was predicated on a diagnosis.[62] Furthermore, the provenance for the Court's declaration in *Davis* that people cannot be punished for "who they are" is not at all clear. While *Davis*'s ban on race presumably comes from the Equal Protection Clause, the opinion did not identify any particular constitutional provision when it made its more general pronouncement about the proper basis of punishment. The most likely candidate is the Eighth Amendment's ban on cruel and unusual punishment, which has been construed to forbid criminalizing status, specifically the status of being addicted.[63] But the people who are subjected to risk assessment in the criminal justice system have already been convicted, or at least arrested, for criminal *conduct*, defined by statutes that are presumably constitutional. And the courts, including the Supreme Court, have long permitted both sentences and pretrial detention to be based on risk.[64] So in the end, the *Davis* decision is most accurately described as a prohibition on the use of race in sentencing, rather than as a wholesale rejection of incarceration based on the status of being high risk, or on having a certain age, sex, or condition.

60 Id. at 778.

61 Jurek v. Texas, 428 U.S. 262, 275-76 (1976) (stating that "prediction of future criminal conduct is an essential element in many of the decisions rendered throughout our criminal justice system [mentioning bail, sentencing and parole determinations as examples of such decisions]. . . . The task that a Texas jury must perform in answering the statutory question [about dangerousness of a capital defendant] is thus basically no different from the task performed countless times each day throughout the American system of criminal justice").

62 463 U.S. 880, 919 (1981) (Blackmun, J., dissenting) (noting that Dr. Grigson "placed Barefoot in the 'most severe category' of sociopaths (on a scale of one to ten, Barefoot was 'above ten'), and stat[ed] that there was no known cure for the condition").

63 Robinson v. California, 370 U.S. 660, 667 (1962) (holding that criminalizing the status of being a narcotics addict violates the Eighth Amendment).

64 Pennsylvania ex rel. Sullivan v. Ashe, 302 U.S. 51, 55 (1937) (the government "may inflict a deserved penalty merely to vindicate the law or to deter or to reform the offender or for all of these purposes. . . . [The offender's] past may be taken to indicate his present purposes and tendencies and significantly to suggest the period of restraint and the kind of discipline that ought to be imposed upon him"); United States v. Salerno, 481 U.S. 739, 749 (1987) (allowing pretrial detention to be based on risk); see also supra note 61.

While *Davis* may not squarely pose a retributive injustice challenge to RAIs, some scholars have done so, arguing that a criminal justice system unmoored from just desert is immoral, because of its insult to autonomy and dignity. The point was put succinctly by Andrew von Hirsch, a noted retributivist, who posited that "[u]nless the person actually made the wrongful choice he was predicted to make, he ought not to be condemned for that choice—and hence should not suffer punishment for it."[65] That view might permit risk-oriented punishment based on prior crimes as well as the crime of conviction. But, as applied to RAIs, it would prohibit not only risk factors that do not consist of conduct, but also risk factors based on conduct that is not criminally blameworthy, such as choices about psychoactive substance use, employment, or education. Accordingly, it would put an end to modern risk assessment.

From a risk assessment perspective, there are two significant practical problems with limiting risk factors to criminal conduct. First, removal of all noncrime factors from an RAI is likely to substantially reduce accuracy. Second, restricting RAIs to crime-only risk factors is also likely to create egalitarian injustice. A young male with psychopathic tendencies and one prior crime represents a much higher risk than an older female suffering from anxiety who has committed the same crime; yet, under a crime-only approach, both would be treated identically in terms of risk.

A true retributivist worried about risk's insult to blameworthiness would not be dissuaded by these types of concerns. Rather, more conceptual counterarguments are required. A first such response to the retributive injustice claim is that it is based on a category mistake. Interventions based on risk are not about culpability for past conduct, they are focused on preventing future conduct. Culpability assessments are the province of trial and, as discussed in more detail in the next chapter, they should also be crucial in setting the range of sentencing options. But if, as we are assuming here, risk is a legitimate consideration at the pretrial and post-trial stages, it is a separate inquiry from blameworthiness and should not be entangled with it.

The retributive inquiry and the risk inquiry are usually orthogonal to one another. While youth is often considered a mitigating factor from a retributive point of a few, it is clearly an aggravating factor from a risk perspective. The fact that one was abandoned by one's parents at age sixteen might be considered a mitigator when focused on culpability, but to the developers of the VRAG it is a risk factor. Or consider criminal history itself. It may be an aggravator from both a blameworthiness and a risk perspective, but rarely in precisely the same

65 Andrew von Hirsch, Past or Future Crimes: Deservedness and Dangerousness in the Sentencing of Criminals 11 (1985).

way. A third property crime might be considered highly blameworthy nose-thumbing to a retributivist, but not particularly indicative of high risk; alternatively, a retributivist might consider the two previous convictions irrelevant once the associated sentences are served, but if risk assessment is the goal these crimes presumably would be highly probative of future conduct.[66] Risk and culpability are clearly conceptually separate inquiries.

The first two examples also put the lie to the implicit claim by those who make the retributive injustice argument that culpability assessments are never based on status. Youth is a status. Yet it is routinely treated as a mitigator by retributivists;[67] indeed, in his latest work von Hirsch himself has proposed a "youth discount" for punishment, and argued that it should be "categorical," not individualized, which means that simply being youthful would require leniency.[68] Likewise, parental abandonment is a status. But a retributivist might treat it as a mitigator.

One cannot avoid this contradiction by claiming that, as long as noncriminal factors are used *only* as a mitigator, the damage to dignity and autonomy is minimized. If people are provided leniency based in part on their youth, older people are being treated more harshly because of their status. If people who were left by their parents are given a break, people with intact families are not. Status permeates both risk-based and retribution-based regimes.

At the same time, contrary to the literal interpretation of the Supreme Court's decision in *Buck v. Davis*, a person's risk categorization is not *simply* a status, but rather is closely associated with blameworthy choices, in two ways. First, risk assessment is, in large part, an evaluation of what a person has chosen to do. That is because it is, in essence, an evaluation of one's character, which on many accounts, including from scholars such as Peter Arenella, James Whitman, and Kyron Huigens, is directly relevant to desert.[69] The

66 The debate among retributivist as to how to treat punishment for multiple crimes has produced numerous positions which are not reconcilable with one another. See generally, Jesper Ryberg, Julian V. Roberts & Jan. W. de Keijser, Sentencing Multiple Crimes (2017) (edited volume).

67 See, e.g., Roper v. Simmons, 543 U.S. 551, 571–573 (2005) (stating "Once the diminished culpability of juveniles is recognized, it is evident that the penological justifications for the death penalty apply to them with lesser force than to adults," and rejecting the argument that it is "arbitrary and unnecessary to adopt a categorical rule barring imposition of the death penalty on any offender under 18 years of age").

68 Andrew von Hirsch, Deserved Criminal Sentences 134–35 (2017).

69 Peter Arenella, Character, Choice and Moral Agency: The Relevance of Character to Our Moral Culpability Judgments, 2 Soc. Phil. & Pol'y 59 (1990) (arguing that there is no means of judging persons except through assessing their character); James Q. Whitman, The Case for Penal Modernism: Beyond Utility and Desert, 1:2 Critical Analysis of the Law 178 (2014) (arguing for a European style trial mixing assessment of desert and character, because such

Supreme Court itself has made the connection, when it stated in *Deck v. Missouri* that "character and propensities of the defendant are part of a 'unique, individualized judgment regarding the punishment that a particular person *deserves*.'"[70] Character is an amalgam of choices, choices that are often constrained by circumstances (a point expanded upon in the next chapter), but choices nonetheless. People make decisions not only about whether to engage in antisocial conduct, but about their friends, family life, education and work; the places they frequent; the amount of drugs or alcohol they ingest; and whether to seek treatment for emotional problems such as anger and impulsivity—all of which are examples of precisely the types of activities captured in the most sophisticated RAIs. If these choices combine to make one's character high risk, they could be said to be blameworthy, even if individually they do not involve criminal activity.[71]

Of course, character analysis alone does not justify using risk factors that have nothing to do with choice, such as age, gender, and diagnosis. But the ultimate and best argument against the retributive injustice claim is that, viewed properly, risk factors—whether or not they are the product of choice—are not the *reason* for a high risk arrestee's detention or a high risk offender's sentence. Rather, they are merely *evidence* of what a person will decide to do in the future, in the same way that a finding of blameworthy choice in the past may rely on various facts that are not culpable in themselves, like being married to the victim, presence near the scene of the crime, or possession of a weapon. Risk assessments try to predict future culpable choices, just as circumstantial evidence about actus reus and mens rea tries to postdict culpable choices. Consider again the Virginia instrument that puts so much weight on age and gender. While it is extremely unlikely that those two variables alone provide sufficient

a trial "makes it possible to consider the full spectrum of information about individual blameworthiness, including both dangerousness and deservingness"); Kyron Huigens, The End of Deterrence and Beyond, 41 Wm. & Mary L. Rev. 943, 1022–34 (2000) (describing the aretaic theory of punishment, which aims at improving character).

70 544 U.S. 622, 633 (2005) (emphasis added). Making the link between risk and character even more explicit, just prior to this statement, the Court stated, "danger to the community . . . almost inevitably affects adversely the jury's perception of the character of the defendant." Id. at 622–23. The Court has even adhered to this sentiment in cases involving young offenders, whose character is typically in its formative stages; thus, for instance, while emphasizing such situations should be rare, in *Graham v. Florida* the Court stated: "Those who commit truly horrifying crimes as juveniles may turn out to be irredeemable, and thus *deserving* of incarceration for the duration of their lives." 560 U.S. 48, 75 (2010) (emphasis supplied).

71 Cf. Douglas Husak, Lifting the Cloak: Preventive Detention as Punishment, 48 San Diego L. Rev. 1173, 1195 (2011). ("As long as the possession of the characteristics x, y, and z are under the control of persons the state preventively detains—as I would insist—punishment would be compatible with the principle I propose to substitute for the act requirement.")

predictive power to meet the fit criteria proposed in Chapter 2, if they did and a person was imprisoned rather than diverted to the community as a result, it would not be because of youth and maleness. Rather, it would be because the RAI indicates he belongs to a group of people who pose a high probability of choosing to reoffend.

Risk is not pristine desert, but it is not some soulless mechanical assessment of humans-as-machines either. The debate on this score has been more hyperbolic than productive.

4.3 PROCEDURAL INJUSTICE

The fact that risk assessment does not consist simply of converting people into probability numbers or abstract categories such as high or low risk does not mean it is not perceived that way. Underlying much of the Bill of Rights is the notion that according dignity to people suspected or convicted of crime is intrinsically valuable. A suspect may not be subject to search or seizure without strong justification, those who are accused have the rights to counsel, public trial and confrontation, and punishment cannot be cruel and unusual, but rather must be consistent with "evolving standards of decency."[72] Additionally, the procedural justice literature suggests that for a legal process to be considered legitimate—especially by those enmeshed in it—it must treat people with respect, through giving them voice, ensuring a transparent process, and providing explanations of any decisions made.[73] Adhering to those goals can promote compliance with legal decisions and a more general sense of an obligation to obey the law, whereas a failure to do so may lead to less cooperation, not only with the particular decision, but with the government that permits it to happen.[74]

[72] See Judith Resnick & Julie Chi-hye Suk, Adding Insult to Injury: Questioning the Role of Dignity in Conceptions of Sovereignty, 55 Stanford L. Rev. 1921, 1935 (2003). ("[W]e find dignity mentioned in relation to the Eighth Amendment prohibition on cruel and unusual punishment; the Fourth Amendment protection against unlawful searches and seizures; the Fourteenth and Fifteenth Amendment rights to be free from discrimination, and the Ninth and Fourteenth Amendment rights to make one's own decisions on procreation.") The quoted language is from Trop v. Dulles, 356 U.S. 86, 101 (1958), which interpreted the scope of the Eighth Amendment's cruel and unusual punishment clause.

[73] The foundational research comes from Tom Tyler, Why People Obey the Law 115–57 (1990) (describing studies that suggest that perceptions of fairness hinge on whether disputants feel they have been given a voice in the process and are treated with dignity, as well as whether outcomes are fair over time).

[74] Id. at 56 (suggesting that people comply with the law for a complex set of reasons that include cost-benefit analysis, the norms of peers, one's own norms, and the perceived legitimacy of the

Procedural injustice could be a real danger in an RAI-oriented regime, unless certain precautions are taken. As Michael O'Hear notes about RAIs used at sentencing, in language that could also apply to pretrial detention:

> If a sentencing decision is driven entirely or overwhelmingly by a mechanically applied formula, then the decision would not seem to provide a meaningful voice opportunity. Likewise, a decision that imposes or prolongs incarceration based on factors beyond the offender's control or, more generally, on an expectation that the offender will fail again may seem inconsistent with the ideal of a caring decisionmaker following a respectful process. Perceived bias may also be a concern to the extent that an RAI relies on factors that are closely tied to historical discrimination and structural disadvantage.[75]

While, compared to RAIs, clinical predictions may be more susceptible to bias, less accurate, and equally influenced by stereotypes, they *appear* to be more individualized, especially when framed in psychological terms. That apparent difference may be exacerbated if, as this book recommends, RAI results are given presumptive effect on the issue of risk.

Two other realities give the procedural injustice claim particular force. First, the typical proceeding in which risk is considered is very informal, and in some settings cannot be called a proceeding at all. Second, for both proprietary and scientific reasons, the "mechanically applied formula" to which O'Hear refers may not even be accessible. Before discussing O'Hear's concerns, these other reasons that RAIs might deprive litigants of "a meaningful voice opportunity" need to be addressed.

4.3.1 *Process*

The adversarial process we associate with criminal trials is absent both prior to and after trial. Despite the significant consequences that can result from denial of pretrial release, many jurisdictions do not provide counsel at the bail hearing, taking a cue from the Supreme Court's reminder in *United States v. Salerno*[76] that, at the analogous probable cause hearing that takes place after warrantless arrests, counsel and cross-examination rights "far exceed what we

authorities, but concluding that the last reason is the most important for policymakers, because both titrating deterrence and changing individual and group norms are difficult). See also Tom R. Tyler, Procedural Justice, Legitimacy, and the Effective Rule of Law, 30 Crime & Just. 283, 286, 297 (2003).

75 Michael O'Hear, Actuarial Risk Assessment at Sentencing: Potential Consequences for Mass Incarceration and Legitimacy, 38 Beh. Sci. & L. 193, 195–96 (2020).

76 481 U.S. 739 (1987).

found necessary";[77] accordingly, pretrial detention decisions can be made in a matter of minutes.[78] Parole hearings, according to the Supreme Court, at most need to provide the prisoner with "an effective opportunity, first, to insure that the records before the Board are in fact the records relating to his case; and, second, to present any special considerations demonstrating why he is an appropriate candidate for parole."[79] Prisoners at these hearings are not entitled to counsel or an opportunity to cross-examine (indeed, there are often no witnesses); while the parole board has to provide some reason for its decision, there need be no "summary of the evidence."[80] The Court has been similarly tolerant of within-prison decision-making. Because "[c]onfinement in any of the State's institutions is within the normal limits or range of custody which the conviction has authorized the state to impose,"[81] transfer from a low security to a high security setting can be a purely administrative decision, unless the transfer is to a super-max facility or a mental hospital, and even in the latter settings the proceedings may be informal and in the absence of counsel.[82] In none of these situations is a judge involved or appeal to a court routinely available. As the Court has summarized these cases, "due process is not so rigid as to require that the significant interests in informality, flexibility, and economy must always be sacrificed."[83]

Only at sentencing is some semblance of a real adversarial process required, in that defendants are entitled to counsel, a judge presides, and a decision can often be appealed. However, even here there is no right to confront accusers or to compulsory process: "sentencing decisions may be based upon unsworn written assertions by probation officers, prosecutors, police, victims and others in pre-sentence reports, sentencing worksheets, or other documents that are never made public and that the defendant and his counsel never see."[84] Defendants are entitled to be present during sentencing, but do not have a right to testify in the normal sense, only a right to "allocution" (a statement by

77 Id. at 752.

78 See Douglas L. Colbert et al., Do Attorneys Really Matter? The Empirical and Legal Case for the Right to Counsel at Bail, 23 Cardozo L. Rev. 1719, 1755 (2002).

79 Greenholtz v. Inmates of Nebraska Penal and Correctional Complex, 442 U.S. 1, 15 (1979).

80 Id.

81 Meachum v. Fano, 427 U.S. 215, 225 (1976).

82 Vitek v. Jones, 445 U.S. 480, 495–96 (1980) (requiring, in the transfer from prison to hospital context, notice, a hearing, and an opportunity to present evidence in front of an independent decision-maker, but refusing to find a right to counsel); Wilkinson v. Austin, 545 U.S. 209, 228–30 (2005) (reaching essentially the same holding when a prisoner is placed in a "supermax" prison).

83 Gagnon v. Scarpelli, 411 U.S. 778,788 (1973).

84 Nancy King, Procedure at Sentencing, in Oxford Handbook of Sentencing and Corrections 317, 320 (Kevin Reitz & Joan Petersilia, eds., 2012).

the defendant that can be restricted to a plea for mercy);[85] funding for expert testimony is also minimal or nonexistent outside of capital cases.[86] As Chapter 3 noted, in many states neither *Daubert* nor any rule resembling it applies at sentencing,[87] which makes fit and validity challenges difficult.

Only at capital sentencing has the Supreme Court come close to requiring the type of process that is typical at trial. The rights to counsel, confrontation, and appeal are aggressively protected in death penalty cases.[88] The Court has also been attentive to matters relating to risk. For instance, in *Ake v. Oklahoma*,[89] the Supreme Court held that, when the state asserts that dangerousness is an aggravating factor, due process requires the state to provide indigent defendants an expert, because "the consequence of error is so great, the relevance of responsive [expert] testimony is so evident, and the burden on the state is so slim."[90] Likewise, in *Barefoot*, while the Court allowed speculative clinical prediction testimony in capital proceedings, it made clear that its holding was contingent on the existence of an adversarial process.[91]

Unfortunately, the sentiments expressed in *Ake* and other death penalty cases have yet to migrate to noncapital sentencing, much less to other proceedings in which RAIs might be used. This is not for want of good arguments. Scholars have pointed out that pretrial detention, sentence enhancements, and denials of parole are all deprivations of liberty which should be predicated on a hearing that, at a minimum, provides individuals with counsel and confrontation rights.[92] And the point made by Judge Appel

85 McGautha v. California, 402 U.S. 183, 218–220 (1971).

86 Brandon L. Garrett & Peter J. Neufeld, Invalid Forensic Science Testimony and Wrongful Convictions, 95 Va. L. Rev. 1, 33–34 (2009) (stating that most states do not provide any funding to indigent defendants for forensic testimony and that, "[a]s a result, indigent defendants are routinely denied funding to hire their own forensic expert").

87 Daniel A. Krauss & Nicholas Scurich, Risk Assessment in the Law: Legal Admissibility, Scientific Validity, and Some Disparities Between Research and Practice, 31 Behav. Sci. L. 215, 220 (2013) (nineteen states hold that admissibility rules governing expert evidence do not apply at sentencing or that the rules are relaxed sufficiently to allow testimony based on RAIs).

88 See generally John Douglass, Confronting Death: Six Amendment Rights at Capital Sentencing, 105 Colum. L. Rev. 1967, 1973–74 (2005) (making this point, but also noting that even in capital cases the extension of trial rights to sentencing is "fragmentary," in part because the Supreme Court is concerned about turning sentencing proceedings into trials).

89 470 U.S. 68 (1985).

90 Id. at 84.

91 463 U.S. at 901. ("We are unconvinced, however, at least as of now, that the adversary process cannot be trusted to sort out the reliable from the unreliable evidence and opinion about future dangerousness, particularly when the convicted felon has the opportunity to present his own side of the case.")

92 See Douglas Colbert, When the Cheering (for Gideon) Stops: The Defense Bar and Representation at Initial Bail Hearings, 36 Champion 10 (2012) (arguing for a right to counsel at initial bail hearings).

in *State v. Guise* applies in all of these contexts: "one thing is clear: if the state intends to offer risk assessments for the court to rely upon in sentencing, the defendant has a right to an adequate opportunity to attack it. If the court does not give the defendant an adequate opportunity to attack the statistical evidence, it should not be utilized in sentencing."[93] Chapter 5 of this book develops this theme further with respect to the post-conviction process. In the meantime, however, the informality of pretrial and post-trial processes must be taken into consideration in fashioning any process that relies on RAIs.

4.3.2 *Transparency*

A second obstacle to procedural justice is that RAIs themselves can undercut fair process when they are opaque, which is unfortunately a common occurrence. Recall that the company that produces the COMPAS refuses to reveal its algorithm or the weights assigned risk factors, claiming trade secret protection, a claim that the Wisconsin Supreme Court has upheld.[94] Thus, the inner workings of the instrument are hidden. For instance, sophisticated reverse engineering, well beyond the pay grade of defense attorneys, judges or correctional officials, is needed to figure out the fact that, while the COMPAS contains more than 100 factors, over half of the risk score is attributable to a single factor, the offender's age.[95]

Even purportedly publicly developed instruments can be less than transparent. Congress required that the PATTERN—the federal RAI developed under the First Step Act—be made public,[96] but did not require that the validation procedure that led to development of the instrument nor the data underlying it be disclosed. When asked for more information, the authors of the instrument stated that state law-driven privacy concerns prevented release even of anonymized versions of the data to outside researchers.[97] A number of states

93 State v. Guise, 921 N.W.2d 26 (Iowa 2018) (Appel, J., concurring).

94 State v. Loomis, 881 N.W.2d 759, 761 (Wis. 2016) (holding that, because Loomis had access to the questions the COMPAS asked and the risk assessment itself, he did not need access to "how the risk scores were determined or how the factors are weighed").

95 As shown in Megan T. Stevenson & Christopher Slobogin, Algorithmic Risk Assessments and the Double-Edged Sword of Youth, 96 Wash. U. L. Rev. 681, 688–98 (2018).

96 18 U.S.C. § 3631(b)(4) (requiring the Attorney General, inter alia, to "on an annual basis, review, validate, and release publicly on the Department of Justice website the risk and needs assessment system").

97 Department of Justice, The First Step Act Risk and Needs Assessment System—Update 14 (Jan., 2020) (hereafter First Step Act—Update), available at https://www.bop.gov/inmates/fsa/docs/the-first-step-act-of-2018-risk-and-needs-assessment-system-updated.pdf.

have responded in the same fashion to requests for data about the RAIs they use.[98]

Reliance on sophisticated machine learning in constructing RAIs could make matters worse, since under some versions of that technique the weights assigned risk factors and even the identity of those factors are inaccessible to humans.[99] Furthermore, even if the black box can be opened, serious interpretation problems can arise. More specifically, as Andrew Selbst and Simon Barocas note, some versions of machine learning can be either "inscrutable"—meaning that even when a model is available for direct inspection it may "defy understanding"—or "non-intuitive"—meaning that even where a model is understandable it may "rest on apparent statistical relationships that defy intuition."[100]

Proprietary interests and algorithmic opacity will often stymie meaningful challenges, even if competent counsel *is* present and empiricists stand ready to investigate. Egalitarian and retributive justice cannot be evaluated without knowing whether risk scores are based on race, gender, age, wealth classifications, or proxies for them, and the extent to which they purport to help the state achieve its aim in evaluating risk. The accuracy of the probabilities and other results reached by an RAI cannot be confirmed unless the underlying data and the empirical analysis using it can be evaluated by others. And if, as the previous chapter argued, decision-makers should only engage in "adjustments" to a risk assessment based on factors that were not considered in developing the instrument, they need to know what those factors are.

Once again, the Court's death penalty jurisprudence provides grounds for contesting this situation. In *Gardner v. Florida*,[101] the defendant argued that,

98 Nicholas Diakopoulos, We Need to Know the Algorithms the Government Uses to Make Important Decisions About Us, *Conversation* (May 23, 2016, 8:48 PM), available at https://theconversation.com/we-need-to-know-the-algorithms-the-government-uses-to-make-important-decisions-about-us-57869 (noting that only one state responded fully to Freedom of Information Act requests for algorithm documents and source codes). The developers of the PSA have given the same explanation. See Arnold Ventures, Public Safety Assessment FAQs, at 3, available at https://craftmediabucket.s3.amazonaws.com/uploads/Public-Safety-Assessment-101_190319_140124.pdf.

99 See generally, Doaa Abu Elyounes, Bail or Jail? Judicial versus Algorithmic Decision-Making in the Pretrial System, 21 Colum. Sci. & Tech. L. Rev. 376 (2020) (describing various types of machine learning algorithms and possible difficulties with discerning how they work). However, this article also notes that the seven most common pretrial RAIs today rely on traditional regression analysis, and are transparent with respect to the factors considered and the weight they are given. Id. at 426–27.

100 Andrew Selbst & Simon Barocas, The Intuitive Appeal of Explainable Machines, 87 Ford. L. Rev. 1085, 1091 (2018).

101 430 U.S. 360 (1977).

before his sentence was imposed, he had a due process right to discover and rebut the contents of his presentence report. The government objected to this claim on a number of grounds: discovery of the report, it claimed, would make sources reluctant to provide information, would delay the process, might disrupt rehabilitation given the psychological information contained in such reports, and was not necessary given the expertise of judges. But the Supreme Court rejected all of these arguments (many of which might be made in defending use of undisclosed RAIs as well), stating: "Our belief that debate between adversaries is often essential to the truth-seeking function of trials requires us also to recognize the importance of giving counsel an opportunity to comment on facts which may influence the sentencing decision."[102]

Gardner involved capital punishment, where the Supreme Court is admittedly particularly meticulous about accuracy. But in *Roviaro v. United States*,[103] involving a simple drug case, the Court similarly held that the identity of confidential informants must be revealed to the defendant when the informant possesses facts that are relevant to the defense. Although it involved a confidential informant rather than a confidential algorithm, *Roviaro* establishes that even strong claims of a need for secrecy (here protecting an informant) should not prevail when the information is crucial to the case. While *Roviaro* has been given short shrift in more recent lower court decisions,[104] its central rationale has not been abandoned.[105] Some lower courts have followed the logic of these opinions in requiring that defendants be given the facts and opinions underlying their proposed sentences and an opportunity to rebut them.[106]

Scholars have also made subconstitutional arguments in favor of open algorithms. Danielle Citron has contended that private companies that seek public money for products that affect public policy should not be able to hide behind trade secret laws,[107] and Rebecca Wexler has noted that companies' concern about giving competitors an advantage or discouraging innovation are overblown, especially if protective orders or *in camera* review requirements are

102 Id. at 361.

103 353 U.S. 53 (1961).

104 See Z. A. G. Perez, Piercing the Veil of Informant Confidentiality: The Role of In Camera Hearings in the *Roviaro* Determination, 46 Am. Crim. Law Rev. 179, 202–13 (2009) (describing Federal Circuit of Appeals approaches to *Roviaro*).

105 Id.

106 United States v. Millán-Isaac, 749 F.3d 57, 70 (1st Cir. 2014); Smith v. Woods, 505 F. App'x 560, 568 (6th Cir. 2012); United States v. Hayes, 171 F.3d 389, 394 (6th Cir. 1999).

107 Danielle Keats Citron, Technological Due Process, 85 Wash. U. L. Rev. 1249, 1290–91 (2008) ("the public [and] government actors are unable to influence policy when it is shrouded in closed code").

imposed.[108] Special attention has been paid to the opacity problems created by machine learning. Most prominently, scholars have argued for a "right to explanation,"[109] a right that the European Union has explicitly recognized in its General Data Privacy Regulation.[110]

That right is particularly important in the criminal context, for the reasons advanced in *Gardner*. Even if it turns out that advanced machine-learning RAIs are demonstrably more accurate than simpler versions (which is unlikely),[111] they should be banned from criminal proceedings, at least when they are "inscrutable"; litigants, policymakers and decision-makers must be provided information about how they work.[112] Specifically—summarizing the

108 See Rebecca Wexler, Life, Liberty and Trade Secrets: Intellectual Property in the Criminal Justice System, 17 Stan. L. Rev. 1343, 1403–13 (2018) (arguing that, given protective orders and other procedural devices, "trade secret protection is unnecessary in criminal cases"); see also, Danielle Keats Citron & Frank Pasquale, The Scored Society: Due Process for Automated Predictions, 89 Wash. L. Rev. 1, 26 (2014). ("There is little evidence that the inability to keep such systems secret would diminish innovation.") It is noteworthy that intellectual property claims have also been rejected in civil cases when the potential for error as a result of secrecy is "obvious" and "substantial." See K.W. v. Armstrong, 180 F.Supp3d. 703, 716–17 (D. Idaho 2016).

109 See generally, Margot E. Kaminski, The Right to Explanation, Explained, 34 Berkeley Tech. L. J. 189, 209–17 (2019) (reviewing the literature).

110 Regulation 2016/679 of the European Parliament and of the Council of 27 April 2016 on the Protection of Natural Persons with Regard to the Processing of Personal Data and on the Free Movement of Such Data, and Repealing Directive 95/46/EC, 2016 O. J. (L 119) 1 (EU), articles 13–15.

111 Alexandra Chouldechova, Estella Loomis McCandless & Kristian Lum, The Present and Future of AI in Pretrial Risk Assessment Instruments (June, 2020), available at http://www.safetyandjusticechallenge.org/2020/07/considering-the-present-and-future-of-ai-in-pretrial-risk-assessments/ ("AI technologies are not likely to achieve considerably greater predictive accuracy than currently available risk assessment instruments"); Cynthia Rudin and Berk Ustun, Optimized Scoring Systems: Toward Trust in Machine Learning for Healthcare and Criminal Justice, 48 Interfaces 449 (2018)(absent the inclusion of more complex unstructured input data, simple models that rely on a small set of factors such as age and prior system involvement can perform just as well); Elaine Angelino et al., Learning Certifiably Optimal Rule Lists for Categorical Data, 18 J. Machine Learning Research 8753 (2017); see generally, Sarah Desmarais & Samantha A . Zottola, Violent Risk Assessment: Current Status and Contemporary Issues, 103 Marquette L. Rev. 793, 813–16 (2020) (surveying research and concluding that "these findings suggest that there is no real advantage to using complex statistical models that are challenging for the layperson to understand").

112 Selbst & Barocas points out that, with respect to providing transparency, "researchers have developed at least three different ways to respond to the demand for explanations: (1) purposefully orchestrating the machine learning process such that the resulting model is interpretable; (2) applying special techniques after model creation to approximate the model in a more readily intelligible form or identify features that are most salient for specific decisions; and (3) providing tools that allow people to interact with the model and get a sense of its operation." Selbst & Barocas, supra note 100, at 1110.

types of information described in Chapters 2 and 3—developers ought to provide:

> a complete description of the design and testing process . . ., [a] list of factors that the tool uses and how it weighs them, [t]he thresholds and data used to determine labels for risk scores, . . . [t]he outcome data used to develop and validate the tool at an aggregate and privacy-protecting level—disclosing breakdown of rearrests by charge, severity of charge, failures to appear, age, race, and gender—[and] clear definitions of what an instrument forecasts and for what time period.[113]

Without the ability to investigate the basis of decisions about risk, not only procedural injustice, but egalitarian and retributive injustice, will have fertile ground in which to flourish.

4.3.3 *Voice*

If there were a right to counsel, a truly adversarial process, and transparent algorithms, O'Hear's concerns about procedural injustice would be substantially diminished. RAIs could be challenged in several ways. First, arrestees and offenders (hereafter, lumped together as "defendants") would be able to present results from their own RAI evaluations. Second, in the absence of precedent to the contrary, defendants would be able to challenge an RAI on the grounds summarized in Chapter 2, to the effect that it lacks legal fit because it does not meet the probability, outcome, durational, or intervention thresholds required in the legal proceeding at hand. Third, unless the validity and fairness issues canvassed in Chapter 3 and previous sections of this chapter are already settled by the relevant authority, defendants could argue that the RAI is not sufficiently accurate on calibration, discriminant, implementation, external, or current validity grounds, or that one or more of its risk factors offends egalitarian justice.

Most importantly from the perspective of providing voice, regardless of precedent, defendants could challenge whether the RAI was reliably administered, in two ways. First, the defense could attack the accuracy of a conclusion that a particular risk factor is present (e.g., the validity of an assumed arrest or conviction, the applicability of a diagnosis, or the failure to complete a program that in fact was not available to the offender). Second, defendants

113 David G. Robinson & Logan Koepke, Civil Rights and Pretrial Risk Assessment Instruments 11 (2019). See generally Kleinberg et al., supra note 41 (arguing that "all the components of an algorithm (including the training data) must be stored and made available for examination and experimentation").

could proffer protective factors that were not considered by the developers of the instrument (e.g., completion of a treatment or educational program, changes in employment status); researchers are beginning to identify a number of such factors.[114] The latter type of evidence should be particularly useful in humanizing and individualizing the process. It would also help combat adversarial bias, which research has shown afflicts even testimony based on relatively objective RAIs.[115]

Current reality, however, is that counsel and a true adversarial process are rare in most of the proceedings relevant to this book. Two other procedural components are thus crucial, so much so that they should be required even if the risk assessment process becomes more formalized: there must be robust independent review of the RAI by an independent body, and legal decision-makers must explain their RAI-based decisions.

First, as suggested at the end of Chapter 3, RAIs should be subject to legislative and administrative review. For instance, in authorizing creation of the PATTERN in the First Step Act, Congress directed that: (1) the Attorney General develop and release a "risk and needs assessment system" to determine the "recidivism risk of each prisoner" following "an objective and statistically validated method"; (2) a panel of researchers approve the instrument; (3) the instrument be annually validated; and (4) Bureau of Prison staff "demonstrate competence in administering the [PATTERN], including inter-rater reliability, on a biannual basis."[116] Given that such an instrument is, in effect, an "informal rule" governing "the rights and obligations" of citizens, such a system could be subject to notice and comment requirements under the Administrative Procedure Act;[117] in fact, the Bureau of Prisons did call for public comment and responded to criticisms,[118] criticisms not only about the validity of the PATTERN but about its fit and fairness as well. Ideally, any

[114] Richard B. A. Coupland & Mark E. Olver, Assessing Protective Factors in Treated Violent Offenders: Associations with Recidivism Reduction and Positive Community Outcomes, 32 Psychological Assessment 493 (2020).

[115] Stephane M. Shepherd & Danny Sullivan, Covert and Implicit Influences on the Interpretation of Violence Risk Instruments, 24 Psychiatry Psychol. & L. 292, 297 (2017) (citing studies).

[116] 18 U.S.C. § 3632(f)(4).

[117] Long Island Care at Home, Ltd. v. Coke, 551 U.S. 158, 172–73 (2007) (associating notice-and-comment rulemaking with a regulation that "directly governs the conduct of members of the public, 'affecting individual rights and obligations'") (quoting Chrysler Corp. v. Brown, 441 U.S. 281, 302 (1979)); cf. Richard A. Bierschbach & Stephanos Bibas, Notice-and-Comment Sentencing, 97 Minn. L. Rev. 1 (2012).

[118] I was one of those who testified, on behalf of the American Bar Association's Criminal Justice Section, consistently with the points made in this book. A summary of the responses to the notice and comment period can be found at The First Step Act Risk and Needs Assessment

instrument produced through such a process would also be subject to judicial hard look review to ensure that the government can demonstrate it is rationally related to the state's objectives.[119] Where those instruments are produced by private companies, Andrea Nishi has made the argument that the private non-delegation doctrine—the "lesser-known cousin" of the doctrine applicable to government agencies[120]—applies in this setting, and requires that "grants of government power to private entities are adequately structured to preserve constitutional accountability."[121]

This upper level review of fit, validity, and fairness issues is essential. A federal panel such as that created by the First Step Act is one possibility; the now defunct National Commission of Forensic Science would have been another.[122] European countries have forensic institutes that are established to investigate science used in the courts; for instance, in the United Kingdom, the Ministry of Justice houses the Correctional Services Accreditation and Advice Panel, which evaluates a tool in terms of whether it "does what it aims to do."[123] However, for empirical reasons having to do with local validation requirements, situating review responsibility at the state level, and ensuring that the state entity takes into account significant jurisdictional differences (particularly urban-rural divides), makes the most sense.[124] In fact, a number of state legislatures have mandated that sentencing judges or corrections officials use a "validated risk assessment tool,"[125] and in other states the state sentencing

System, supra note 97. The DOJ's Internal Review Committee did not accept all of the suggestions, but is committed to continually receiving feedback and re-validation efforts. Id.

119 Kevin M. Stack, Interpreting Regulations, 111 Mich. L. Rev. 355, 378–79 (2012). ("[H]ard-look review … has long been understood as requiring a higher standard of rationality than the minimum rational basis standard of constitutional review.")

120 Ass'n of Am. R.Rs. v. U.S. Dep't of Transp. (Amtrak I), 721 F.3d 666, 670 (D.C. Cir. 2013).

121 Andrea Nishi, Privatizing Sentencing: A Delegation Framework for Recidivism Risk Assessment, 119 Colum. L. Rev. 1671, 1695 (2019) (quoting Gillian E. Metzger, Privatization as Delegation, 103 Colum. L. Rev. 1367, 1456 (2003)).

122 See generally, Jules Epstein, The National Commission on Forensic Science: Impactful or Ineffectual? 48 Seton Hall L.Rev. 743 (2018) (describing the short-lived commission, disbanded in 2017 by Attorney General Jeff Sessions).

123 Her Majesty's Prison and Probation Service, Guidance: Risk Assessment of Offenders, available at https://www.gov.uk/guidance/risk-assessment-of-offenders#what-makes-a-good-risk-assessment-tool (last accessed April 15, 2020).

124 See Alica Solow-Niederman, Yoojung Choi and Guy Van den Broeck, The Institutional Life of Algorithmic Risk Assessment, 34 Berkeley Tech. L. J. 705 (2019) (noting that the effects of proxies, Simpson's paradox and thresholding decisions need to be considered in designing risk assessment instruments that will be used in diverse jurisdictions).

125 See, e.g., Ky. Rev. Stat. § 439.335(1). ("In considering the granting of parole and the terms of parole, the parole board shall use the results from an inmate's validated risk and needs assessment and any other scientific means for personality analysis that may hereafter be developed.")

commission,[126] the department of corrections,[127] the state courts generally,[128] or, as California has done with respect to pretrial risk assessments, the courts in each jurisdiction,[129] have taken on the task. As long as the entity employs or can pay for experts who can develop and validate RAIs, and ensure that the validation is peer-reviewed by independent experts, it could fulfill a vital procedural role in a risk assessment regime.

Serious consideration should also be given to including nonexperts on the RAI review panel. Especially since the racial justice movement caught fire in the wake of the death of George Floyd, there has been a major push toward "democratization" of the criminal justice system, aimed most prominently at regulation of the police, but also at the pretrial detention process and the prosecution function.[130] The goal is to shift power from the elites and "experts" to those affected by law enforcement. Some have even argued that decision-making processes should be *dominated* by the formerly incarcerated.[131] That would be going too far in the risk assessment setting; experts need to be heavily involved. But, as Chapter 2 indicated, the polity affected by algorithmic risk assessment programs ought to have a say in determining risk thresholds (the probability criterion). Community representatives, as well as other stakeholders in the system such as prosecutors, defense attorneys, and victims' groups, might also be allowed to weigh in on the types of risk factors and criterion variables used in RAIs,[132] although community views of "fairness" should be balanced against legal requisites and accuracy concerns.[133] In other

126 See, e.g., Kansas Sentencing Commission, Justice Reinvestment Initiative in Kansas (2015) at 3; Utah Sentencing Commission, 2017 Adult Sentencing and Release Guidelines (2017).

127 Wash. Rev Code § 9.94A.500 (2013).

128 Arizona Judicial Branch, Presentence Report, available at www.azcourts.gov/apsd/Evidence-Based-Practice/PresentenceReport.

129 Pretrial Detention Reform Workgroup, Pretrial Detention Reform: Recommendations to the Chief Justice 52–53 (2017), available at http://www.courts.ca.gov/documents/PDRReport-20171023.pdf.

130 See generally Jocelyn Simonson, Democratizing Criminal Justice Through Contestation and Resistance, 111 Nw. U. L. Rev. 1609, 1612–13 (2017); K. Sabeel Rahman, Policymaking as Power-building, 27 S. Cal. Interdisc. L. J. 315 (2018).

131 Jocelyn Simonson, Police Reform through a Power Lens, 130 Yale L. J. 778 (2021).

132 This is the suggestion of Ngozi Okidegbe in The Democratizing Potential of Algorithms? 53 Conn. L. Rev. 42, 45 (2021) (stating that "the exclusion of these communities within algorithmic governance operates to reinforce and legitimize the barriers that already impede these communities' ability to challenge or gain control over the very criminal justice institutions responsible for their oversurveillance, overcriminalization, and overincarceration"). See also, Jessica M. Eaglin, Constructing Recidivism Risk, 67 Emory L. J. 59, 88–99 (2017) (describing the lack of democratic input that goes into the construction and implementation of algorithmic tools used in the criminal justice system).

133 Cf. Trevor Gardner, By Any Means: A Philosophical Frame for Rulemaking Reform in Criminal Law, Yale L. J. Forum (forthcoming, 2021) (arguing that "crime policy reform

words, review panels ought to be multi-disciplinary in the broadest sense of that word.

The type of instrument vetting just described may be an adequate substitute for, and in some ways may be preferable to, *Daubert*-type challenges in individual proceedings in front of generalist judges. However, it does not directly address the "hard-variable" orientation of RAI-dominated proceedings that is the core of the procedural injustice claim. In the absence of counsel, the role of the decision-maker becomes even more important in dealing with this legitimate concern. Thus, a second crucial requirement is that evaluators, judges, and parole boards lay out for defendants how the RAI works and why it reached the conclusions about risk it did. Assuming trade secret claims are ignored and the algorithm is both scrutable and intuitive, RAIs can tell a story similar to one that a clinical expert would tell.

This is true even if risk factors are primarily static. While such factors usually only correlate with risk rather than explain it, theories do exist as to why they are relevant to predictive validity (e.g., youth are more impulsive and subject to peer pressure; people with poor childhoods have fewer adaptive skills; people with criminal histories tend to repeat them). Explanation along these lines can meaningfully diminish the perception of robot justice. For instance, one study of the procedural justice implications of risk algorithms found that, while lay subjects preferred clinical to actuarial judgment in the abstract, their preferences were reversed when they were informed that the algorithm was more accurate, and they were even more likely to prefer algorithms when the factors used to construct them were made transparent.[134]

At the same time, RAIs ideally should contain dynamic factors as well, because these signal that the individual has some control over his or her fate. Evaluators and decision-makers should make sure to describe these factors, particularly protective ones. Likewise, if the determination is made that intervention is necessary because of the person's risk, procedural justice would be enhanced if the decision-maker specifies the types of actions the individual can take to reduce that risk (e.g., substance abuse treatment, cognitive therapy, employment). Some RAIs, such as the HCR-20 and the LSCMI, are more attuned to this goal, because they include dynamic or variable factors that the defendant can do something about. Even though—as noted in Chapter 2—not all of these dynamic factors are demonstrably

should be centered on the principle of process efficacy rather than the principle of process equity").

134 A. J. Wang, Procedural Justice and Risk Assessment Algorithms (2018), available at https://papers.ssrn.com/abstract=3170136.

"causal,"[135] the fact that they are mutable can help humanize the process. Under the PATTERN, for instance, prisoners are told the number and type of programs they must complete to reduce their risk.[136] This information can communicate to the individual that, whatever the numbers may say, he or she has the ability to change them.

In practice, evidence proffered in a risk assessment hearing, whether or not truly adversarial, should follow the character evidence model that applies at criminal trials, which allows the defendant to control when evidence of character is admissible. Under that model as applied to risk assessment proceedings, the state would initially be limited to presenting algorithmic evidence, which the subject can directly rebut by challenging its factual basis. Additionally, however, defendants should have the option of presenting, in their own case-in-chief, "softer" clinical evidence of protective factors that suggests the algorithmic estimate is wrong. Only once that door is open may the state respond in kind.[137]

4.4 CONCLUSION: ONE COURT'S STRUGGLE WITH ASSURING FAIRNESS

In *Wisconsin v. Loomis*,[138] the Wisconsin Supreme Court upheld the trial court's consideration of Loomis' COMPAS score in setting his sentence. In doing so, it permitted consideration of sex as part of the assessment process, a conclusion that, under the analysis proposed here, is permissible if it robustly improves the algorithm. The court also appropriately cautioned trial court judges that the COMPAS was not yet validated on a Wisconsin population, and stated that "risk assessment tools must be constantly monitored and re-normed for accuracy due to changing populations and subpopulations."[139] So far, so good.

But the court then went on to impose several additional, more problematic conditions on use of the COMPAS. First, because, according to the court, the

135 For an elaboration of the problems with the assumption that dynamic or needs factors are causal, see Seth J. Prins & Adam Reich, Can We Avoid Reductionism in Risk Reduction?, 22 Theoretical Criminology 258, 264–67 (2017) (noting that there could be an underlying cause for both the risk factor and recidivism, in which case treating the risk factor is akin to treating a symptom, not the disease).

136 First Step Act—Update, supra note 97, at 6–7, 11–12; 27–34 (Appendix A).

137 I flesh out this "subject-first" approach to risk evidence in Christopher Slobogin, Proving the Unprovable: The Role of Law, Science and Speculation in Adjudicating Culpability and Dangerousness 125–29 (2007).

138 881 N.W.2d 749 (2016).

139 Id. at 764.

COMPAS risk score is a "poor fit" for determining the length and severity of sentence, it could be used only for such matters as "(1) diverting low-risk prison-bound offenders to a non-prison alternative; (2) assessing whether an offender can be supervised safely and effectively in the community; and (3) imposing terms and conditions of probation, supervision, and responses to violations."[140] Second, the court stated, sentencing courts should be alert to research indicating that the COMPAS may "disproportionately classify minority offenders as having a higher risk of recidivism."[141] Third, sentencing courts should be told that the "proprietary nature of COMPAS has been invoked to prevent disclosure of information relating to how factors are weighed or risk scores are determined,"[142] but could still use the instrument on that condition.

For reasons that should be clear from the foregoing pages, all three of these aspects of *Loomis* are questionable. Taking them in reverse order, the court's acceptance of equivant's trade secret claim makes meaningful evaluation of the validity and fairness of the COMPAS impossible, and thus significantly undermines any possibility of procedural justice; telling courts that the COMPAS's algorithm is secret does nothing to solve this problem. The court's vague warning about the COMPAS's disproportionate impact on minorities, and implicit message that high risk scores among blacks should be discounted, essentially endorses the classification parity approach; as this chapter demonstrated, while concerns about racialized policing may require finetuning RAIs, the court's undifferentiated admonition is antithetical to both calibration and anti-classification principles, and thus undermines egalitarian justice. And the final limitation, which appears to be bottomed on concern about retributive injustice, is incoherent from a risk perspective. If the COMPAS should not be used to determine the length and severity of sentence, as the court dictates, it should not be used to determine whether a person can be diverted from prison (despite the court's statement otherwise), since those who are *not* diverted because of their COMPAS score are having the severity, if not the length, of their sentence determined by it. Further, mandating, as *Loomis* does, that the COMPAS not be "determinative" of one's risk or one's sentence disingenuously avoids the issue of when and to what extent RAI results are relevant.

In fairness to the Wisconsin Supreme Court, its statement that the COMPAS is a "poor fit" with respect to determining sentence length and severity was also meant to refer to the fact that sentencing involves more than

140 Id. at 769.
141 Id.
142 Id.

consideration of risk; retributive and deterrence concerns are also relevant.[143] But that is simply the recognition that risk should not be determinative of sentence, not that the COMPAS score should not be determinative of risk. And in fact, as I have argued in this book, if the goal is accuracy, it is preferable to make the score of a well-validated instrument (not necessarily the COMPAS) *determinative* on the issue of risk, in the absence of countervailing protective factors that were not considered in the instrument. Telling judges they can substitute their own risk assessment for a risk score does not make sense from a scientific point of view, and could well reintroduce the bias and other causes of inaccuracy that instruments are designed to prevent.

This discussion of *Loomis* highlights another point. Because of RAIs' empirical basis, which allows more concrete argumentation about risk, and because of the egalitarian, retributive and procedural justice controversies RAIs spawn, their introduction into the criminal process will spur much-needed litigation, not only about RAIs specifically, but about sentencing practices generally, and in particular about the relationship between risk and retribution. RAIs are going to help bring sentencing and other risk-infused proceedings out of the shadows. In the course of doing so, they may force, or at least encourage, rethinking about how the entire criminal justice system should be organized.

143 Id. (after describing the various goals of sentencing, stating "because of these disparate goals, using a risk assessment tool to determine the length and severity of a sentence is a poor fit").

5

Structure

Limiting Retributivism and Individual Prevention

To this point, this book has assumed that risk is a legitimate consideration in the criminal justice system. That assumption is on solid constitutional footing. In *United States v. Salerno*, the Supreme Court stated "[t]he government's interest in preventing crime by arrestees is both legitimate and compelling."[1] In *Jurek v. Texas*, the Court declared that "prediction of future criminal conduct is an essential element in many of the decisions rendered throughout our criminal justice system," including in capital sentencing proceedings.[2] Taking that constitutional case law as a baseline, this book has advanced a jurisprudence of risk that should apply in the pretrial and post-conviction settings, and has further hypothesized that, if risk assessment is carried out properly, it can reap major practical benefits. The contention has been that, if the fit, validity, and fairness principles are followed, incarceration rates can be reduced in a relatively unbiased manner without appreciably increasing crime rates.

Even if that contention turns out to be true, a number of thinkers resist the thrust of the foregoing pages, because they dispute the underlying assumption that dangerousness is relevant to punishment. Rather, they insist that, despite possible improvements brought by RAIs, risk assessment must be abandoned by the criminal justice system, because it is still too inaccurate, too likely to result in disparate results, and too divorced from what is perceived to be the central value of the criminal justice system—the principle that punishment should be based on culpability, or just desert. The latter argument is perhaps not as powerful in the pretrial setting, given the Supreme Court's holding in *Salerno* that, given the absence of vindictive legislative intent and the limitations posed by speedy trial rules, pretrial detention is "regulatory" rather than

1 481 U.S. 739, 749 (1987).
2 428 U.S. 262, 275 (1976).

"punitive" in nature;[3] nor is it salient in the within-prison setting where security concerns clearly may govern.[4] In the sentencing context, however, the desert-only stance has become increasingly popular in spite of the Court's decisions that refuse to require it. To some this stance ensures that people will "get what they deserve," to others it guarantees they will receive *solely* what they deserve and thus limit the duration of government-imposed deprivations of liberty, and to many it enhances dignity and autonomy by ensuring those liberty deprivations are triggered only after a choice to do wrong, not before. Thus, this view would not accept the previous chapter's response to the retributive injustice critique (which is based on the conception of risk as a prediction of future choice), nor does it accept the Supreme Court's position that risk is a permissible consideration at sentencing.

This chapter will not engage fully in the debate about the legitimacy of risk assessment in criminal justice, which has been carried out elsewhere.[5] But, in the first section below, it does stress that, whatever the flaws of risk assessment, desert-based punishment is no less rife with inaccuracy, disparity and unfairness issues. A system based on desert is not a panacea for either the practical or normative conundra faced by the criminal justice system.

At the same time, the criminal justice system clearly should not abandon desert as the focal point of criminal justice. Along with the courts,[6] virtually every modern criminal law scholar believes that, if criminal punishment is to occur, it must be cabined by retributive considerations. In particular, there is general consensus that an offender should never be punished more than he or she deserves.[7] At least until science (including the science of risk assessment)

3 481 U.S. 747–48 (holding that pretrial detention is "regulatory," not punitive, in part on the ground that "the maximum length of pretrial detention is limited by the stringent time limitations of the Speedy Trial Act").

4 Turner v. Safley, 482 U.S. 78, 91–92 (1987) (permitting, over a First Amendment objection, limitations on correspondence for "security" reasons); Bell v. Wolfish, 441 U.S. 520, 546 (1979) (permitting body cavity searches, cell searches, and limitations on packages and hard back books because "maintaining institutional security and preserving internal order and discipline are essential goals that may require limitation or retraction of the retained constitutional rights of both convicted prisoners and pretrial detainees").

5 For some of my contributions to the debate, see Christopher Slobogin, Prevention as the Primary Goal of Sentencing: The Modern Case for Indeterminate Sentencing, 48 San Diego L. Rev. 1127 (2011), and Christopher Slobogin, Empirical Desert and Preventive Justice: A Comment, 17 New Criminal L. Rev. 376 (2014).

6 Roper v. Simmons, 543 U.S. 551, 560 (2005) (noting that the Eighth Amendment's ban on excessive punishment "flows from the basic 'precept of justice that punishment for crime should be graduated and proportioned' to both the offender and the offense") (quoting Weems v. United States, 217 U.S. 349 (1910).

7 See, e.g., Michael Tonry, Introduction: Thinking about Punishment, in Why Punish? How Much? A Reader on Punishment 3, 6 (Michael Tonry, ed., 2011) ("By 1980 .... [m]ost writing

convincingly challenges the predicate that we control our actions, assessments of culpability are essential not just at the adjudication stage but also post-conviction.

In the end, both desert and risk are crucial considerations in fashioning sentences in individual cases, and arguably are the principal considerations in that context. General deterrence is, course, another important goal, and it certainly mandates that some type of punishment be imposed for those who violate the criminal law. But its relevance to individual sentences is probably minimal; as Michael Tonry summarized the findings of three National Academy of Sciences panels, "[i]maginable increases in severity of punishments do not yield significant (if any) marginal deterrence effects."[8] Retribution and individual prevention goals are, and should be, the key considerations in determining the dispositions of particular individuals.

On that assumption, the bulk of this chapter proffers a structure for combining the best aspects of both desert and risk, in a version of limiting retributivism that uses RAIs to promote what I call "preventive justice."[9] As outlined in the second and third sections of the chapter, preventive justice is, in essence, a modern form of indeterminate sentencing which relies heavily on parole boards informed by RAIs. The final two sections of the chapter then consider how preventive justice would interact with the most important structural feature of American criminal justice, plea bargaining—the much-maligned subterranean process that resolves over 90 percent of all criminal cases. Although our system probably could not function without plea bargaining, a preventive justice regime might minimize many of its more repugnant aspects.

on punishment philosophy and theory had a pronounced retributive slant," which takes desert as the starting point); Youngjae Lee, Why Proportionality Matters, 160 U. Pa. L. Rev. 1835, 1838 (2012) (calling a "fundamental legal protection" the principle that "people be punished no more than they deserve"); Richard A. Bierschbach & Stephanos Bibas, Constitutionally Tailoring Punishment, 112 Mich. L. Rev. 397, 428 (2013) ("Scholars agree somewhat on negative retributivism–that defendants should be punished no more than they deserve—but much less on positive retributivism—that they should ordinarily be punished as much as they deserve").

8 Michael Tonry, Purposes and Functions of Sentencing, 34 Crime & Just. 1, 28 (2006).

9 I coined this phrase in 2011 to refer to the type of sentencing described in the text. See Christopher Slobogin & Mark R. Fondacaro, Juveniles at Risk: A Plea for Preventive Justice (Oxford University Press, 2011). Other authors have used it in a pejorative sense, primarily as a synonym for preventive detention. See Andrew Ashworth & Lucia Zedner, Preventive Justice (2014); chapters by Markus Dubber, David Dyzenhaus, Matt Matravers, Bernard Harcourt, and Pat O'Malley, in Prevention and the Limits of the Criminal Law (Andrew Ashworth, Lucia Zedner & Patrick Tomlin, eds., 2013).

The main goal of this chapter is to make the case for preventive justice on conceptual grounds. But, again, the practical reason for doing so is that a system of preventive justice has the potential to make a serious dent in our incarcerated populations. A sentencing system that is driven by well-informed, accountable back-end decision-makers can reduce prison populations in a way that sentences dictated by legislatures, judges and prosecutors cannot.

Countering that claim, Kevin Reitz has made the argument that much of our prison growth since the 1990s has been in states with indeterminate systems controlled by parole boards, which increasingly refused to release prisoners who were eligible for parole.[10] But he does not mention the fact that the same pressures that led to truth-in-sentencing, mandatory minima, and three-strikes laws also made "indeterminate" sentencing regimes much more determinate; legislative initiatives in these jurisdictions significantly increased the proportion of prisoners who are ineligible for parole, to anywhere from 55 percent to 95 percent.[11] And while parole boards are certainly easily vulnerable to political pressures from governors and legislatures, that malleability works both ways; Reitz's work acknowledges that, before the tough-on-crime movement in the 1980s and 1990s, parole boards were much more willing to release prisoners early,[12] and that today the states that are

[10] Kevin Reitz, Don't Blame Determinancy: Incarceration Growth Has Been Driven by Other Forces, 84 Texas L. Rev. 1787, 1794 (2006).

[11] For instance, Reitz says that the top four "carceral powerhouses" were "Texas, Louisana, Oklahoma and Georgia, all indeterminate jurisdictions." Id. at 1795. But all of these states significantly limit the proportion of the prison population that is eligible for parole—Texas (to 55 percent), Louisiana (7 percent), Oklahoma (17 percent) and Georgia (39 percent)—and none of them recognize presumptive parole (requiring automatic release if certain criteria are met). See Jorge Renaud, Grading the Parole Release Systems of All 50 States, Prison Pol'y Initiative (2019), available at https://www.prisonpolicy.org/reports/parole_grades_table.html.

[12] Kevin Reitz, Prison Release Reform and American Decarceration, 104 Minn. L. Rev. 2741, 2745 (2020). ("During the thirty-five year buildup period, ... parole boards ... became progressively more risk-averse in their decision-making and ever more fearful of external scrutiny and condemnation. Instead of using their release discretion as often as they had done in the earlier twentieth century, parole boards transformed themselves into agencies of "release-denial discretion.") This is also why attempts to compare the effects of "determinate" and "indeterminate" sentencing regimes are so conflicted. Don Stemen & Andres F. Rengifo, Policies and Imprisonment: The Impact of Structured Sentencing and Determinate Sentencing on State Incarceration Rates, 1978–2004, 28 Just. Q. 174, 174–77 (2011) (finding mixed results when measuring the two regimes in terms of percentage of released prisoners who commit violent crimes) with Yan Zhang, Lening Zhang & Michael S. Vaughn, Indeterminate and Determinate Sentencing Models: A State-Specific Analysis of Their Effects on Recidivism, 60 Crime & Delinquency 693, 711 (2009) (also obtaining mixed results, and concluding that "the effects of different sentencing models on reoffending may be largely contingent on ... supervision approaches ..., differing expertise of state parole boards, or differing crime categories that are legislatively mandated").

leading the charge in the decarceration movement are those with indeterminate sentencing.[13] If, as this chapter proposes, parole board decision-making is constrained by RAIs, the membership of parole boards consists of expert panels rather than partisan appointees with no training, and the parole process is formalized with rights to counsel and appeal, the parole process will be much less vulnerable to political pressure, and can take a leading role in rationalizing our punishment system.

5.1 THE PROBLEMS WITH DESERT

Resisting the contentions made in this book, many scholars of sentencing have argued that no amount of regulation will sufficiently reduce the inaccuracy of risk assessment or mitigate its unfairness. They contend that eradicating false positives is impossible, pointing to evidence that, even at its best, risk assessment science will produce inaccurate predictions in one-third of the cases.[14] And they argue that it is fundamentally unjust to "punish" someone for something they have not yet done.[15]

It cannot be denied that prediction of reoffending is far from an exact science and that sentences based on risk are a form of preventive detention. Before declaring that these facts doom risk-based sentencing as a normative matter, however, the worthiness of RAI-driven sentencing should be compared to sentences based on backward-looking culpability assessments. If the former is no worse than the latter with respect to either accuracy or fairness considerations, then the criticisms of risk-based sentencing ought, at the least, to be

[13] Reitz, supra note 12, at 2776 ("it is intriguing that indeterminate states have had more than twice as much prison-rate decline as determinate states in the post-growth period. This raises the possibility that the low-friction quality of indeterminate prison-release systems could make it easier to reverse course than in stickier determinate regimes"); Kevin Reitz et al., Prison-Release Discretion and Prison Population Size State Report: Texas (2020). ("Texas is (undisputably) an example of a jurisdiction with an extremely high degree of indeterminacy overall in its framework for prison-release decision making, even when compared with other paroling states. It is also (undisputably) an example of a state that has dramatically reduced its imprisonment rate over the past 20 years in a nearly-continuous downward trend. Even without solid evidence of a causal linkage, this is a brightly-colored flag that further inquiry is warranted.")

[14] Michel Tonry, Doing Justice, Preventing Crime 160–62 (2020); Edward J. Latessa & Brian Lovins, The Role of Offender Risk Assessment" A Policy Make Guide, 5 Victims & Offenders 203, 212 (2010) ("even with large data sets and advanced analytical techniques, the best models are usually able to predict recidivism with about 70% accuracy—provided it is completed by trained staff").

[15] Tonry, supra note 14, at 177. ("Predictive sentencing is ... incompatible with mainstream retributive punishment theories.")

reconsidered. In what follows, I suggest reasons why desert-based sentencing may be just as prone to error and unfairness as risk-based sentencing.

5.1.1 *The Accuracy of Desert*

One reason for doing away with or significantly minimizing risk as a consideration in the criminal justice system is concern about inaccuracy. But the alternative—sentences based solely on desert—is likely no better, for a number of reasons.

First, of course, despite hundreds of years of deliberation, we still have not reached a consensus about relative blameworthiness in a large number of important, commonly occurring criminal scenarios, and thus have not settled on a hierarchy of crime. Should negligent conduct be criminalized and, if so, should negligence be judged on an objective or individualized standard? Is felony murder as culpable as intentional killing? Is a reckless killer always less blameworthy than a premediated killer? When, if ever, should an accomplice receive the same sentence as the principal, and is knowing facilitation the same as purposeful aiding and abetting?[16] Should a person who engages in the same act repeatedly (e.g., acquiring multiple pornographic pictures) be punished for each? Perhaps most relevant to sentencing, should criminal history be considered in assessing desert and, if so, should the length of time between offenses be relevant?[17] The debates are endless, as those of us who have taught or taken criminal law classes know. Yet years of punishment can hang on how they are resolved.[18]

Second, even if we can agree on these points, to the extent punishment depends on evaluations of internal mental states, such as premeditation,

16 For materials exploring these and other debates, see Paul H. Robinson, Case Studies and Controversies (3d ed. 2012), in particular, 855–71 (negligence as a basis for liability); 902–09 (felony murder); 986–92 (complicity); William J. Stuntz & Joseph L. Hoffmann, Defining Crimes (2d ed., 2014), in particular, 212–15 (premeditated v. reckless killing); 887–91 (multiple counts in pornography cases).

17 See, e.g., Jesper Ryberg, Julian V. Roberts & Jan W. de Keijser, Sentencing Multiple Crimes (2018).

18 Alice Ristroph makes similar points:

> Harm is meaningful only up to a point; we might agree that murders and rapes cause harm, but the harm of many other offenses is a matter of continuing dispute. Culpability or blameworthiness is still more inchoate, and sentencing theorists tend to focus on whether certain factors are relevant to culpability instead of explaining what culpability is. Even when one strives to be charitable, it is difficult to escape the conclusion that desert theory takes a widely held but imprecise intuition that wrongdoers should be punished and attempts, without much success, to impose onto this intuition philosophical rigor.

Alice Ristroph, How (Not) to Think Like a Punisher, 61 Fla. L. Rev. 727, 739 (2009).

knowledge, and recklessness, obtaining accurate information about the relevant facts is extremely difficult. Even defendants who are honest have trouble recounting their mental state at the time of the offense. Ultimately, evidence about past mental states—which is crucial to grading most serious offenses—is simply narrative, not objective fact.[19]

Third, even if we can reach consensus on blameworthiness concepts and even if the true mental state of the defendant can be discerned, jurors might not be able to accurately label that mental state. A number of recent studies indicate that laypeople, even when given clear descriptions of the relevant mens rea terms, have trouble differentiating between purpose and negligence, much less recklessness and knowledge.[20] Yet significant sentencing differentials can rest on such determinations.

Finally, and most importantly, even if we nail down the relative gravity of a person's blameworthiness and discern his or her precise mens rea, devising a sentence that "accurately" reflects desert is, to put it bluntly, an exercise in futility, given the absence of a clear outcome measure. Does a thief who stole $1,000 deserve two years, two months, or two days? Does an aggravated murder deserve the death penalty/life without parole (as a number of jurisdictions in the U.S. have declared), fifteen years (the practical maximum in much of Europe), or five years as von Hirsch once suggested?[21] Any of these answers, and many more, could be "correct." In a study I conducted with Lauren Brinkley-Rubinstein, subjects were asked to look at twelve crime scenarios describing only the actus reus and mens rea for the crime, and then to indicate appropriate punishment on a thirteen-point scale.[22] Not surprisingly, agreement on the proper punishment was virtually nonexistent.[23] And the range of sentences was also broad, even when the extreme dispositions beyond two

19 See, e.g., Andrew E. Taslitz, A Feminist Approach to Social Scientific Evidence: Foundations, 5 Mich. J. Gender & L. 1, 19–26 (1998) (arguing that we can never know "objective truth about past mental states in the same way we can know whether an event occurred," and that memories of mental states "at least partly a created narrative").

20 Francis X. Shen et al., Sorting Guilty Minds, 84 N.Y.U. L. Rev. 1306, 1347–48 (2011) (subjects "able to recognize negligent behaviors only 48% of the time"); Robert A. Beatty & Mark R. Fondacaro, The Misjudgment of Criminal Responsibility, 36 Behav. Sci. & L. 457, 466 (2018) (on average, 35 percent of participants given a scenario depicting a negligent mens rea and 75 percent of those given a reckless mens rea scenario stated that purpose had been established).

21 Andrew von Hirsch, Doing Justice 139 (1976) (arguing for a five-year maximum sentence for all but the worst murders).

22 Christopher Slobogin & Lauren Brinkley-Rubinstein, Putting Desert in Its Place, 65 Stan. L. Rev. 77, 94–96 (2013).

23 See id., tbl. 2 (reporting, for the "Control Group," standard deviations ranging from 3.109 to 7.373).

standard deviations were thrown out.[24] Further, in only the least and most serious crime scenarios did more than 25 percent of the sample choose the same punishment.[25]

Thus, while consensus on the ordinal ranking of crimes might be possible, the maximum "anchor" point for the most serious crime and the proper spacing between offenses is open to serious dispute.[26] Perhaps even more disturbing, research indicates that those anchor points are highly manipulable even when judges are making the decisions.[27] For these reasons, and as demonstrated in more detail throughout the following discussion, any system of graded crimes that can be linked to narrow sentence ranges is likely to be based on fiat, not some independent standard of accuracy.

Compare this state of affairs to the validity of risk assessments. Because research on such assessments have a concrete outcome measure—whether a person predicted to reoffend in fact recidivated—risk assessment can at least be associated with explicit true and false positive rates. In contrast, generating true and false positive rates with respect to desert is impossible, because there is no definitive stance on what a positive finding is. Indeed, from the scientific perspective, talk about the "accuracy" of a culpability finding does not make sense.

A cynic might conclude that it is this absence of an outcome measure that explains many people's preference for culpability-based sentencing: we can tell ourselves we are right and not be contradicted by any objective referent. In contrast, risk-based sentencing is shunned because it flaunts in our face how often we are wrong. In fact, however, the "error rate" associated with desert-based sentences is likely to be both high and impossible to know. If risk-based assessment is rejected, it should not be on the ground that it is less accurate than the alternative.

5.1.2 *Desert and Disparity*

A retributive theorist might respond that even if the rationales for desert-based sentences are unfalsifiable, they are fairer, both objectively and in appearance,

24 Id. (reporting, e.g., ranges from zero to four years for theft of a pie and from one day to the death penalty for a killing by pit bulls whose owner allowed them to escape).

25 Id.

26 Cf. Andrew von Hirsch & Andrew Ashworth, Proportionate Sentencing: Exploring the Principles 141–43 (2012).

27 Birte Englich et al., Playing Dice with Criminal Sentences: The Influence of Irrelevant Anchors on Experts' Judicial Decision Making, 32 Personality & Soc. Psychol. Bull. 188, 197–198 (2006). ("Experienced criminal judges who have worked on many related cases and have made many related sentencing decisions were still influenced by a sentencing demand that was determined by throwing a set of dice.")

than sentences based on risk assessments. Desert-based sentencing is fairer, its proponents claim, because it minimizes divergent sentences between similarly situated offenders (a claim that is discussed here) and because it honors human autonomy by grounding punishment on culpable choices (a claim taken up in the next section).

There is no doubt that a major goal of offense-based determinate sentencing is to avoid disparity between offenders.[28] As a practical matter, however, it has failed miserably. First, of course, sentences for the same crime can vary radically from state to state and between the states and the federal government. Second, as many have pointed out, prosecutors' charging decisions and judicial sentencing decisions in determinate regimes manipulate the relevant criteria in ways that have routinely produced disparate racial and other unjustifiable impacts.[29]

But even if these causes of inconsistency could be eliminated, the indecipherability of desert once again undermines the goal of consistency. Because desert is infinitely nuanced, even when focused exclusively on culpable conduct and mental state,[30] sentencing commissions and sentencers understandably have a very difficult time distinguishing between different versions of the same crime. Indeed, as one federal district court judge noted, "[e]ven if sentencing guidelines could possibly capture and weight all sentencing factors, the guidelines would be so complex that it would be 'less likely that the Guidelines will result in consistent outcomes in practice.'"[31]

Take armed robbery. An armed robber can be young or old, a leader or a follower, the one with the gun or the getaway car driver, a person who really needs the money or one who robs for fun. Disagreement as to whether, or the extent to which, these types of variables should be reflected in sentencing

[28] Michael M. O'Hear, The Original Intent of Uniformity in Federal Sentencing, 74 U. Cin. L. Rev. 749, 773, 791–93 (2006) (stating that Congress adopted uniformity as a dominant goal of the federal system because of concerns about public and offender perceptions of disparity).

[29] Amy Baron-Evans & Kate Stith, Sentencing Law: Rhetoric and Reality, 160 U. Pa. L. Rev. 1631, 1689 (2012) ("Research [in determinate sentencing states] has revealed unexplained racial disparities resulting from the exercise of these forms of discretion, and … much of the gap in average sentence length can be traced to charging decisions, particularly decisions to bring charges carrying mandatory minimums"); Melissa Hamilton, Sentencing Disparities, 7 Brit. J. Amer. Leg. Stud. 1, 9, 37–38 (2017) (finding that upward departures under the federal sentencing guidelines vary significantly between judges).

[30] Of course, desert becomes infinitely more amorphous if it is conceptualized as more than this. Cf. Paul H. Robinson & Sean Jacowitz, Extralegal Punishment Factors: A Study of Forgiveness, Hardship, Good Deeds, Apology, Remorse and Other Such Discretionary Factors in Assessing Criminal Punishment, 65 Vand. L. Rev. 737 (2012).

[31] Mark Bennett, A Judge's Attempt at Sentencing Inconsistency after *Booker*: Judge (Ret.) Mark W. Bennett's Guidelines for Sentencing, 47 Cardozo L. Rev. 243, 270 (2019).

guidelines is very likely. This disagreement, in turn, can result in the perception on the part of both offenders and the public that the "deserved" sentences have been mis-calibrated.[32] In contrast, different RAIs tend to arrive at similar results when differentiating high risk and low risk offenders.[33]

More fundamentally, disparity is in the eye of beholder.[34] For reasons noted in the last chapter (in Section 4.2), any effort to ensure consistency across offenses on desert grounds is likely to result in inconsistency across risk or treatability levels, and vice versa. The justification for insisting on one form of consistency over the other reduces to whether one prefers desert or risk as the basis of disposition. While some might be most concerned about ensuring all armed robbers receive the same sentence, others might be more bothered if robbers who have demonstrated an ability to participate in civil society continue to be confined as long as those who are incorrigible. Indeed, the latter concern appears to have been endorsed by the Supreme Court in its recent decisions ordering individualized resentencing of offenders given mandatory life sentences for offenses committed while juveniles, based on their "ability to reform."[35]

In the end, the type of consistency one prefers is likely to be driven by the importance one ascribes to blameworthiness as a basis for punishment.

5.1.3 *Desert and Blameworthiness*

The bulk of antipathy toward risk-based sentencing probably stems not from concerns about inaccuracy or disparity but rather a belief that it undermines

32 Little research supports the notion that either offenders or the public routinely notice disparity in sentences, but even if they do, the "public is more likely to disrespect" pre-established, numerically oriented sentences based on the nature of the offense like those found in determinate guidelines regimes. Lynn Adelman & Jon Deitrick, Marvin Frankel's Mistake and the Need to Rethink Federal Sentencing Guidelines, 13 Berk. J. Crim. L. 239, 250 (2008). While sentences based on RAIs are also "numerical," the hypothesized legitimacy concern in that setting is alleviated if, as I argued in Chapter 4, offenders are permitted to introduce evidence of protective factors.

33 Daryl G. Kroner, Jeremy F. Mills & John F. Reddon, A Coffee Can, Factor Analysis, and Prediction of Antisocial Behavior: The Structure of Criminal Risk, 28 Int'l J. L. & Psychiatry 360 (2005) (finding few differences in results between four RAIs).

34 Christopher Slobogin, The Civilization of the Criminal Law, 58 Vand. L. Rev. 121, 154–55 (2005).

35 See Montgomery v. Louisiana, 136 S.Ct. 718, 736 (2016) (in describing the appropriate disposition in cases violating Miller v. Alabama, 567 U.S. 460 (2012), stating "[t]hose prisoners who have shown an inability to reform will continue to serve life sentences. The opportunity for release will be afforded to those who demonstrate the truth of *Miller*'s central intuition—that children who commit even heinous crimes are capable of change"); see also, Graham v. Florida, 560 U.S. 48, 75 (2010) (holding that juvenile offenders must be given the opportunity to obtain release upon a showing of "maturity and rehabilitation").

the complex of values having to do with autonomy and dignity which have been noted throughout this book; for those who prioritize this concern, the previous chapter's response to the retributive injustice claim is not likely to persuade.[36] Again, however, these worries about risk-based sentencing diminish when honestly compared to analogous concerns about desert-based sentencing. While RAIs may be based in part on factors that are not closely related to desert, culpability-based sentencing may not take sufficient account of desert either. Sentencing guidelines that are meant to improve consistency create, in effect, "culpability algorithms" that can be just as rigid as RAIs, with the analogous advantages and disadvantages that rigidity creates.

The moral dilemmas that plague desert-based sentencing are evident to anyone who has sat through a sentencing proceeding. Most people who commit crime are poor, unemployed, come from a broken family, have a personality disorder, or live in bad neighborhoods, and many commonly exhibit more than one of these traits. Under any sensitive appraisal of blameworthiness, these types of factors should make a person less deserving of punishment. As a number of scholars have argued, criminal conduct committed by those with "rotten social backgrounds" is not the product of unfettered choice but is, at least in part, situationally or biologically constrained.[37] Yet the "whole life" view of moral desert ultimately has very few defenders among retributivists.[38] Even mitigation schemes several steps short of that view have been very cautious,[39] predominately for practical reasons (not the least of

36 Dawinder Sidhu, Moneyball Sentencing, 56 B.C. L. Rev. 671, 674 (2015) ("[R]isk-assessment tools have no legitimate basis in any recognized penological theories"); Bernard Harcourt, Against Prediction: Profiling, Policing and Punishing in an Actuarial Age 188 (2007) (stating that RAIs have "no root, nor any relation to the jurisprudential theories of just punishment").

37 See 2 Ala. C.R. & C.L. Rev. 1 et seq. (2011) (featuring Richard Delgado and Andrew Taslitz arguing for a broad "rotten social background" excuse, Stephen Morse and Paul Robinson arguing against it, and Erik Luna and Angela Harris straddling the fence).

38 See, e.g., Jesper Ryberg, The Ethics of Proportionate Punishment: A Critical Investigation 18–19 (2004) (noting the difficulties inherent in this concept); Stephen Morse, Severe Environmental Deprivation (AKA RSB): A Tragedy, Not a Defense, 2 Ala. C.R. & C.L. Rev 147, 148 (2011) ("criminal law defenses to responsibility are crucial to the just adjudication of guilt and innocence, but they are not an appropriate means to remedy undoubted social, biological, and psychological problems"); Paul Robinson, Are We Responsible for Who We Are? The Challenge for Criminal Law Theory in the Defenses of Coercive Indoctrination and "Rotten Social Background," 2 Ala. C.R. & C.L. Rev 147, 155 (2011) (expressing the same view, but also expressing a willingness to recognize a narrow new defense if "a defendant who would not have committed the offense in question were he the 'old self' [can show] he acted only because of new beliefs and values, forcibly imposed on him, for which he ought not be held accountable").

39 See, e.g., von Hirsch & Ashworth, supra note 26, at 62–74 (laying out a scheme of limited mitigation based on social deprivation, but doubting whether such a scheme "can ultimately be defensible or workable—at least in places where social deprivation is extensive").

which is that it tends to be most lenient toward those who are most dangerous). As a result, absent proof of significant mental illness or justification based on how a "reasonable" person would react, the law assumes that offenders are fully culpable for any harmful conduct they carry out with sufficient mens rea.[40]

One does not have to be a determinist to question this stance. For instance, Chad Flanders has asked, in dissecting Rawls' position on this issue, why criminal justice is retributive (as Rawls suggested) rather than distributive (as Rawls asserted in virtually every other context).[41] It is not my objective, however, to wade into this age-old debate. The only point made here is that the desert alternative to sentencing should not automatically triumph because it is assumed to have few difficulties arriving at "fair" results respectful of the human condition. Instead, as the rest of this chapter assumes, desert goals and risk considerations should be married in a way that advance both, in a system that I call preventive justice.

5.2 PREVENTIVE JUSTICE AND LIMITING RETRIBUTIVISM

In brief, a preventive justice regime adopts sentence ranges consistent with the offender's desert and then relies on expert parole boards to determine the nature and duration of sentence within this range, based on consideration of individual prevention goals (i.e., incapacitation, specific deterrence and rehabilitation) as measured through risk assessment instruments. A system that adopts relatively wide sentence ranges derived from retributive principles, in combination with short minimum sentences that are enhanced under limited circumstances by statistically driven risk assessment and management, can alleviate many of the inherent tensions between desert and prevention, between deontology and political reality, and between the desire for community input and the allure of expertise. If done properly, it should also significantly reduce prison populations.

Preventive justice, defined in this way, is a form of what is often called limiting retributivism. The concept is usually associated with Norval Morris,

40 See, e.g., Fed. Sen. Guidelines, 5H1.12. ("Lack of guidance as a youth and similar circumstances indicating a disadvantaged upbringing are not relevant grounds in determining whether a departure is warranted.") See also, United States v. Wilson, 355 F.Supp.2d 1259, 1273–81 (2005) (discussing debate within the federal district courts about the extent to which offender characteristics should be relevant to sentencing under the retributively focused federal sentencing guidelines, and rejecting the argument that such information may be a basis of departure from the guidelines range).

41 Chad Flanders, Criminals Behind the Veil: Political Philosophy and Punishment, 31 BYU J. Pub. L. 83, 86 (2016).

who almost a half century ago wrote *The Future of Imprisonment*.[42] In that book, Morris proposed that retributivism should play a "negative" role at sentencing.[43] In other words, a person's desert or blameworthiness should act as a constraint on sentencing, but not as a determinant of a particular sentence. As a practical matter, this meant that desert would determine the range of the sentence for particular crimes, but not the disposition in a particular case. Rather, Morris argued, the specific sentence should depend on other, utilitarian considerations—although, importantly, in contrast to both the sentencing schemes popular at the time and to preventive justice, that sentence was to be set at the front-end, not determined by a parole board at the back end. Sentences would also be guided by what Morris called the "parsimony principle"—the idea, endorsed both before and since by many commentators—that punishment should be no more severe than necessary to carry out the state's punishment purposes.[44] Morris' limiting retributivism has often been called a "hybrid" approach that attempts to reconcile, or at least combine, deontologically driven desert theory with the consequentialist goals of protecting the public and conserving public resources.

Morris' version of limiting retributivism, which was a reaction to the indeterminate sentencing regimes that reigned at the time he wrote, proved to be quite popular. A number of states adopted a version of limiting retributivism beginning in the 1970s.[45] For instance, in 1980, Minnesota created sentencing guidelines consistent with Morris' view.[46] The state's guidelines have eleven categories of sentences, which provide fairly narrow ranges (about 20 months) for lower level felonies, and fairly broad ranges (about 120 months) for higher level felonies. The lower end of the most punitive category approximates the higher end of the next most punitive category, the lower end of the second most punitive category abuts the higher end of the succeeding category, and so on. Most lower-level felonies result in imposition of sentences that are then suspended, at least for first time offenders, and terms for those sent to prison depend on a host of factors, but primarily criminal history.

42 Norval Morris, The Future of Imprisonment (1974).

43 Id. at 73.

44 Id. at 60–62. See also Jeremy Bentham (1789), Theory of Legislation (4th ed., 1882, Trubner & Co.); Richard S. Frase, Just Sentencing: Principles and Procedures for a Workable System 32–33 (2013).

45 Richard S. Frase, Sentencing Guidelines in the States: Lessons for State and Federal Reformers, 6 Fed. Sent. Rep. 123, 123 (1993) (noting seventeen states that had adopted "presumptive sentencing rules").

46 Minn. Sentencing Comm'n, Minnesota Sentencing Guidelines and Commentary 7 (2019), available at https://mn.gov/msgc-stat/documents/Guidelines/2019/MinnSentencingGuidelinesCommentary.pdf.

Numerous states have similar sentencing guidelines, although many adopted ranges that were much smaller than Minnesota's.[47] The revisions to the sentencing provisions of the Model Penal Code (MPC), adopted in 2017, likewise call for numerous sentencing categories defined by proportionate culpability.[48] While the MPC would permit risk assessments to influence the sentence if they are based on "sufficiently reliable" tools, that input would be considered by the judge, whose sentence would be determinate and set at the front-end, not subject to change by a parole board.[49]

Like these other limiting retributivist schemes, the type of preventive justice I propose would have sentencing categories based on proportionate culpability. But it differs in three ways. First, given the nebulousness of the blameworthiness concept, the ranges would be fewer and broader than in many versions of limiting retributivism. Second, sentence length within the range would be determined by a parole board at the back-end, not by a judge at the front-end. Third, the focus of the parole board would be solely risk and needs assessment. Retributive (and general deterrence) concerns would be solely legislative matters, integrated into the statutes governing sentencing ranges. They would not inform sentences in individual cases.

The model for preventive justice comes from the sentencing provisions in the *original* Model Penal Code, promulgated in 1962. That version of the MPC mandated only three broad felony sentencing ranges—for first degree felonies, one year up to life in prison (or up to twenty years, depending on which version of the Code was adopted); one to ten years for second degree felonies; and one to five years for third degree felonies[50]—and in each case the one year minimum could involve an alternative to prison. The parole board determined ultimate sentence length, based primarily on individual prevention considerations. The primary difference between the original MPC's approach and preventive justice is that, in the latter regime, risk assessment instruments would modernize the parole board determination. Another difference, although not as crucial, is that, to give retributive goals sufficient due, more sentencing categories would exist.

The various differences between preventive justice, other forms of limiting retributivism, and the original MPC can be fleshed out by looking more closely at three issues: the determination of sentencing ranges; the principles

47 See Richard S. Frase, State Sentencing Guidelines: Diversity, Consensus and Unresolved Policy Issues, 105 Colum. L. Rev. 1190 (2005).

48 American Law Institute, Model Penal Code § 6.11 (2017).

49 Id. at §9.08.

50 American Law Institute, Model Penal code § 6.06 (1962).

—constitutional and otherwise—that would govern preventive justice; and the nature of the parole board in a preventive justice regime.

5.2.1 *The Determination of Sentence Ranges*

The first goal in any limiting retributivism regime, whether or not mixed with risk assessment, is to set the sentence range for each type of crime. At one end of the spectrum are scholars like Andrew von Hirsch and Andrew Ashworth, both retributivists, who believe that "parity" in sentencing is crucial. They thus call for very narrow sentence ranges based entirely on "the degree of harmfulness of the conduct and the extent of the actor's culpability."[51] Although they would allow "limited variations . . . say, in the range of 5–10 per cent" to permit non-prison alternatives and "back-up sanctions" for offenders who violate probation or parole conditions, they argue that preventive aims should never be grounds for deviation.[52] At the other end of the spectrum is Morris, who apparently found acceptable very wide sentence ranges, akin to those associated with indeterminate regimes. At least in his early writings, Morris held to the position that blameworthiness is such a capacious construct that a given crime could be associated with a large variety of sanctions that are, as he put it, "not undeserved."[53] In-between are writers like Richard Frase, who endorses something akin to Minnesota's system of moderately broad ranges. Frase thinks Morris was too casual in his attitude toward desert, but he also rejects the narrow ranges proposed by von Hirsch and Ashworth, not only because, like me, he is willing to differentiate between high and low risk offenders but because he believes broader ranges are necessary to encourage offender cooperation and to provide leeway in meeting correctional priorities.[54]

The wide ranges preferred by Morris make the most sense. For all the reasons canvassed earlier, any other approach ignores the hollowness of assigning specific punishments to specific crimes. Von Hirsch and Ashworth admit as much, conceding that "[t]here seems to be no crime for which one can readily perceive a specific quantum of punishment as the uniquely deserved one."[55] Nonetheless, they claim that precision is still possible because consensus can at least be reached about the ordinal ranking of crimes. Thus, once the maximum anchor point (for instance, life without parole) has been set, punishments can be assigned according to their ranking, with the

51 von Hirsch & Ashworth, supra note 26, at 144.

52 Id. at 162.

53 Norval Morris, Madness and the Criminal Law 151 (1982).

54 Richard S. Frase, Just Sentencing: Principles and Procedures for a Workable System 30 (2013).

55 von Hirsch & Ashworth, supra note 26, at 142.

anchor point providing the upper limit on punishment for the most serious crime and lesser punishments assigned to lesser crimes.[56] The problem with this approach is that consensus about desert is simply not possible. While there is widespread agreement with respect to the ordinal rankings of the most common crimes such as homicide, rape, robbery and theft, outside of those core crimes consensus over ordinal ranking disappears.[57] More importantly, disagreement over the all-important maximum anchor point can be significant; for instance, as the research reported earlier made clear, some might favor the death penalty for murder, while others might prefer a maximum sentence of fifteen years for such a crime. Finally, the "spacing" between crimes on the ordinal scale can also be a matter of serious dispute.

Von Hirsch and Ashworth suggest that the ordinal ranking and spacing questions can be addressed through analyzing the impact of a given crime on the victim's "standard of living," a concept they develop at some length.[58] But, as they acknowledge, "the impact of a crime on the living standard is itself very much a matter of factual and normative judgement" and in any event "is designed mainly to address crimes directly affecting natural persons [e.g., homicide, sex, and property crimes], rather than crimes involving collective interests."[59] More importantly, the standard of living metric addresses only the actus reus of the crime. Von Hirsch and Ashworth suggest that the mental state component, which can be an extremely significant factor in determining desert for many crimes, instead "can be gauged with the aid of clues from substantive criminal law doctrine."[60] But, again as canvassed above, the parameters of an offender's subjective blameworthiness are highly debatable, and the ability to discern and correctly label the relevant facts is far from perfect.

While these difficulties do not mean we should not try to reach conclusions about these matters, they do suggest that any answers arrived at have a wide margin of error, which should be reflected in sentencing ranges. In fact, as indicated above, actual limiting retributivist sentencing schemes like Minnesota's do have relatively wide ranges, especially for more serious crimes. If community views are taken into account, even these ranges are probably too constrained. My research found that, even when people are given relatively simple scenarios providing facts relevant only to actus reus and mens rea, and

56 Id.
57 Paul H. Robinson & Robert Kurzban, Concordance and Conflict in Criminal Justice, 91 Minn. L. Rev. 1829, 1890–92 (2007).
58 von Hirsch & Ashworth, supra note 26, at 143–46.
59 Id. at 146.
60 Id. at 144.

even when the respondents who give outlier responses are weeded out, the punishment chosen varies widely; for instance, sentences differed by as much as four years for minor crimes and from fifteen years to the death penalty for the most serious offenses.[61]

The difficulty of determining, in any nonarbitrary way, the anchoring and spacing thresholds based on desert argues against the von Hirsch and Ashworth scheme and in favor of the significant differentials between minima and maxima that the original MPC proposed. However, a bit more nuance is advisable if retributivist instincts are to be given adequate weight. First, recall that minimum felony sentences in the original MPC were all one year, regardless of how serious the crime was, and that even a one year sentence could be served outside of prison. That outcome is probably too flexible if one takes ordinal desert and the goal of differentiating the worst from the least crimes seriously, and it is drastic enough that it could significantly undermine the general deterrent impact of specific sentences, to the extent there is any. Additionally, as Paul Robinson argues from a consequentialist perspective, a punishment system that departs too far from community sentiment may well lose legitimacy and produce a populace willing to take the law into its own hands or more prone to become non-compliant in other ways.[62] Although I have argued that Robinson overstates the need for adhering strictly to societal views on punishment,[63] a default sentence of one year for a crime like aggravated murder might well trigger the type of delegitimization he describes.[64]

Taking these considerations into account, the preventive justice version of a limiting retributivist regime might adopt ranges for felonies like the following: 10 to 30 years for very serious crimes (such as, and perhaps only for, aggravated murder), followed by four additional tiers of felonies, with ranges of three to ten

61 Slobogin & Brinkley-Rubinstein, supra note 22, at 95.

62 See Paul H. Robinson & John Darley, The Utility of Desert, 91 Northwestern Law Review 453, 498 (1997) ("We conclude that a desert distribution of liability happens to be the distribution that has the greatest utility, in the sense of avoiding crime. Thus, utility theorists ought to support liabilities assigned according to such a desert-based system"); Paul H. Robinson, Geoffrey P. Goodwin & Michael D. Reisig, The Disutility of Desert, 85 N.Y.U. L. Rev. 1940 (2010) (same).

63 Slobogin & Brinkley-Rubinstein, supra note 22, at 96–110 (describing research debunking Robinson's assertion).

64 Id. at 118 (concluding, based on empirical findings, that "[w]here serious crimes such as murder are involved, desert appears to play a much more dominant role for a majority of people"). See also Dena Gromet & John Darley, Restoration and Retribution: How Including Retributive Components Affects the Acceptability of Restorative Justice Procedures, 19 Social Justice 395 (2006) (finding that as crimes increase in seriousness, people are more likely to require a retributive component).

years (for lesser forms of intentional killing, rape and armed robbery), one to five years (for crimes like aggravated assault), one to three years (for crimes like burglary), and up to one year (for, e.g., the typical low-level drug sale crime). Along the lines of von Hirsch's suggestion mentioned in the previous chapter, the minima and maxima might be discounted for youth and for other concrete mitigating circumstances (such as providing substantial assistance to the authorities). They might also be extended for offenders who have committed multiple crimes or when other concrete aggravating circumstances exist, *if* that extension is justified solely on blameworthiness grounds[65] (with respect to risk, previous crimes should be considered only through an RAI). Further, the relevant time periods need not be served in prison; perhaps for all but the first category, alternatives to prison should be an option.

Undoubtedly, many readers will quibble (or perhaps more than quibble) over these ranges and examples, which should bring home the fact that desert is highly malleable. Obviously, legislatures or sentencing commissions that find these choices either too harsh or too lenient could modify them accordingly.

While adjustments to the minima and the addition of two categories to the original MPC's three categories should alleviate the most significant concerns about disproportionality, they would not address von Hirsch and Ashworth's concern about disparate sentences. But, again, this objection assumes both that the desert of two different offenders can be rigorously measured and that desert is the relevant metric for gauging parity. If instead it is taken as a given that calibrating desert for a specific crime is an abstruse exercise (recall, for instance, the many possible variations of "armed robbery" and the people who commit it) and that the whole point of limiting retributivism is to recognize that other criminal justice considerations besides desert may legitimately be considered in fashioning sentences, this concern is appreciably diminished.

That is not to say that parity is not an important goal. For instance, consistent with Chapter 4's discussion of algorithmic fairness, offenders with similar risk levels should be treated similarly, regardless of other characteristics. More generally, the existence of wide sentence ranges and specific sentences based on non-desert considerations should not lead to the conclusion that sentencing can be "lawless," the term Judge Frankel famously affixed to indeterminate regimes.[66]

65 On whether sentence enhancements based on prior crimes can be justified on retributive grounds, see Julian Roberts, Revisiting Prior Record Enhancement Provisions in State Sentencing Guidelines, 16 Federal Sentencing Reporter 177 (2014).

66 Marvin E. Frankel, Criminal Sentences: Law Without Order 3–11 (1972) (in criticizing indeterminate sentencing, stating, inter alia, that "legislatures have not done the most rudimentary job of enacting meaningful sentencing 'laws'," and that as a result sentencing

Several principles, some of them arguably of constitutional status, should govern a preventive justice version of limiting retributivism.

5.2.2 *Governing Principles of Preventive Justice*

The first principle of a preventive justice version of limiting retributivism involves the desert component rather than the prevention component, and it would be straightforward: to satisfy the retributive goal, the minimum sentence required by desert must be served. For most misdemeanors and many lower level felonies (the final three of the five categories proposed above), this sentence might often consist of non-incarcerative restrictions in the community, such as community service and restitution; here, attention should be paid to the fact that some types of community restrictions can have as much "punitive bite" as short prison sentences.[67] Frase argues, as did Henry Hart before him,[68] that the censure associated with a criminal conviction and these types of dispositions can satisfy desert demands at the lower end of the criminal scale.[69] Several other commentators, including von Hirsch and Ashworth, have recognized that retributive goals can be achieved through non-incarcerative alternatives.[70]

However, for more serious crimes (associated with the first two categories described above), probably no community-based condition would satisfy desert, in which case the presumptive sentence would be incarceration for the minimum period of the relevant sentencing range. Frase argues in favor of the practice in many states of making the default sentence the middle of the range, so that judges can depart upward or downward and still stay within desert-based bounds.[71] But if, as we are assuming, any sentence within the range satisfies desert, the parsimony principle—which writers like Morris, Tonry, and Frase himself all endorse (as does the revised Model Penal Code)[72]—dictates that the minimum sentence is the place to start. Building

judges and parole officials exercised broad discretion and wielded enormous sentencing power "effectively subject to no law at all").

67 Robert E. Harlow, John M. Darley & Paul H. Robinson, The Severity of Intermediate Penal Sanctions: A Psychophysical Scaling Approach to Obtaining Community Perceptions, 11 J. Quantitative Criminol. 71 (1995).

68 Henry Hart, The Aims of the Criminal Law, 23 Law and Contemporary Problems 401, 427 (1958).

69 Frase, supra note 54, at 31.

70 von Hirsch & Ashworth, supra note 26, at 156–59.

71 Frase, supra note 54, at 52.

72 American Law Institute, supra note 48, § 1.02(2) (providing that sentences may be "no more severe than necessary").

on the idea that culpability is a hopelessly vague concept, Jacob Bronsther has also concluded that "retributivism can only justify the least harmful 'not undeserved' sentence."[73]

The parsimony principle, reinforced by constitutional doctrine, would also govern the role of risk assessment and risk management. Almost fifty years ago, the Supreme Court decided *Jackson v. Indiana*,[74] involving a challenge to the prolonged detention of an individual who had been found incompetent to stand trial and was unlikely ever to be restored to competence. In concluding that Jackson's detention was unconstitutional, the Court declared that the due process clause requires that the "nature and duration of commitment bear some reasonable relationship to its purpose."[75] This pronouncement, repeated in several subsequent Supreme Court decisions,[76] has at least three implications for any sentence based on a prevention rationale of the type at issue here.

First, *Jackson* can be read to require, consistent with the parsimony principle, that any government deprivation of liberty in the name of prevention must be the least drastic means of achieving the state's preventive aim.[77] That would mean, for instance, that once the desert minimum has been met, there should be a presumption of release, rebuttable only by proof that the person poses a significant risk of reoffending, a proposition some lower courts have adopted.[78] Similarly, even if the individual is incarcerated and is considered high risk when the minimum expires, community-based programs should be the presumptive disposition unless they cannot adequately protect the

[73] Jacob Bronsther, Vague Comparisons and Proportional Sentencing, 25 Legal Theory 26 (2019), available at https://ssrn.com/abstract=3029672.

[74] 406 U.S. 715 (1972).

[75] Id. at 738.

[76] Youngberg v. Romeo, 457 U.S. 307, 324 (1982) (citing *Jackson*, holding that "the State is under a duty to provide respondent with such training as an appropriate professional would consider reasonable to ensure his safety and to facilitate his ability to function free from bodily restraints"); Foucha v. Louisiana, 504 U.S. 71, 79 (1992) (citing *Jackson*, holding that an insanity acquittee may not be committed as dangerous without a showing of mental illness); Seling v. Young, 531 U.S. 250, 265 (2001) (citing *Jackson*, indicating that committed individuals may have a claim for release if they are not receiving treatment).

[77] Slobogin, Prevention as the Primary Goal of Sentencing, supra note 5, at 1138–39 (arguing that, if the government's objective is to prevent harm, "confinement may occur only if necessary to achieve prevention of harm and may continue only if it remains necessary to achieve that aim").

[78] See Carrillo v. Fabian, 701 N.W.2d 763, 771–72 (Minn. 2005) (postponing release beyond the initial parole determination is "a significant departure from the basic conditions of the inmate's sentence"; "under the Due Process Clause of the United States Constitution, [a prisoner] . . . has a protected liberty interest in his [presumptive] . . . release date that triggers a right to procedural due process before that date can be extended").

public.[79] While imprisonment might substantially reduce risk, it may not be any more effective at doing so than placement in a substance abuse treatment program in the community, a vocational training program in a halfway house, or a job-release program coupled with an ankle monitor. *Jackson's* parsimony principle requires consideration of such options.

Second, *Jackson* means that the government *must* provide rehabilitative services if they will reduce the length of the intervention, because otherwise the confinement is not the least restrictive way of accomplishing the state's aim.[80] In other words, whether or not a state provides such services during the phase of punishment that is designed to meet the desert-based minimum, *Jackson* mandates a right to ameliorative treatment if a sentence is prolonged past the minimum because of a risk assessment. It is unlikely this principle could be transformed into an affirmative duty on the part of the state to create treatment services.[81] But it could create an incentive for the state to provide at least those services that are available, because the state will know release is the only alternative. In *Kansas v. Hendricks*, the Supreme Court held that where incapacitation is the goal, treatment need not occur if it is not "available" or "possible," but suggested that if available treatment is not offered, continued preventive detention would violate due process.[82] In *Seling v. Young*, the Court made the same point.[83] Admittedly, both of these cases involved post-sentence "civil" commitment of sex offenders on dangerousness grounds. But in a preventive justice regime, the portion of a sentence that occurs after the minimum is served is based solely on risk and criminogenic needs. If treatment of needs is reasonably possible, it should be provided in such a regime.

79 The courts have applied this concept vigorously in the analogous context of quarantine. Wendy E. Parmet, Quarantining the Law of Quarantine: Why Quarantine Law Does Not Reflect Contemporary Constitutional Law, 9 Wake Forest J. L. & Pol' 1, 4 (2018) ("At a minimum, [due process requires] that quarantine be imposed only when it is necessary for public health (or is the least-restrictive alternative").

80 Eric S. Janus & Wayne A. Logan, Substantive Due Process and the Involuntary Confinement of Sexually Violent Predators, 35 Connecticut Law Review 319, 358 (2003) ("the *Jackson* line of cases suggests a strong right to treatment, one in which *effective* treatment facilitates real progress toward community re-entry").

81 But see Thomas S. v. Morrow, 601 F.Supp 1055, 1059 (W.D.N.C. 1984) (holding that the Constitution was violated when the state provided only available treatment, not "the appropriate treatment").

82 521 U.S. at 366–367 ("the State has a statutory obligation to provide 'care and treatment for [persons adjudged sexually dangerous] designed to effect recovery'") (quoting Allen v. Illinois, 478 U.S. 364, 369 (1986)).

83 531 U.S. at 265 (stating that, if the purpose is "to incapacitate and treat . . . due process requires that the conditions and duration of confinement under the Act bear some reasonable relation to the purpose for which persons are committed").

Finally, *Jackson's* reasonable relationship requirement means that any risk-based confinement that occurs should be proportionate to the risk, and that the longer the intervention extends, the greater the proof of risk that must be shown (a precept that could be called risk proportionality, analogous to desert proportionality).[84] This principle should mean that individuals considered low risk or at risk of committing only minor crimes should never be detained for preventive purposes. Even individuals considered to be high risk could not be confined for prolonged periods of time without increasingly higher showings of risk (and again, no one could be detained beyond the retributively determined maximum sentence). Thus, as previous chapters have recommended, a high risk of serious crime is necessary to prolong the sentence for any amount of time, and risk would have to be reassessed periodically.

Further, this principle would mean that, regardless of whether an offender is diverted to the community from the get-go or is released on parole after serving the minimum sentence in prison, subsequent confinement should occur only if an individual's risk category changes in the wrong direction. In some jurisdictions, almost half of all prison admissions are for probation or parole violations that often consist of very minor infractions, such as disorderly conduct or shoplifting, having nothing to do with serious risk.[85] In a preventive justice regime, those types of detentions would be impermissible in the absence of a second conviction warranting a prison term.

Morris was reticent about allowing risk assessment to influence sentences because of the legitimate concern that assessing a person's risk while in prison may not reflect his or her risk outside of it.[86] But risk assessment done correctly looks at pre-prison information as well as at participation and completion of programs while in prison. Moreover, individuals who are not high risk or who appear to be manageable in the community despite their high risk should be

84 Christopher Slobogin, Minding Justice: Law that Deprive People with Mental Disability of Life and Liberty 143–50 (Harvard University Press, 2006).

85 See Human Rights Watch/ACLU, Revoked (July 31, 2020), available at https://www.hrw.org/report/2020/07/31/revoked/how-probation-and-parole-feed-mass-incarceration-united-states (study of three states finding this to be the case in Pennsylvania, and noting that "most people locked up for supervision violations were not convicted of new offenses—rather, they were incarcerated for breaking the rules of their supervision, such as for using drugs or alcohol, failing to report address changes, or not following the rules of supervision-mandated programs. Of those who were incarcerated for new offenses, in our focus states, many were for conduct like possessing drugs; public order offenses such as disorderly conduct or resisting arrest; misdemeanor assaultive conduct; or shoplifting").

86 Morris, supra note 42, at 35–36.

evaluated outside the prison setting; in particular, conditional release programs can facilitate efforts to assess risk within the community.[87]

Unlike desert, risk is not a static variable. Setting a determinate, unchangeable sentence, whether at the front-end or at the expiration of the minimum sentence, is inconsistent with a risk-oriented regime. Within the desert-based maximum, the outer boundary of a sentence in a preventive justice regime would be determined by periodic assessments of an offender's risk, risk which, because of the parsimony principle, would need to be increasingly more serious to authorize prolonging the intervention.

5.3 PAROLE AS A CONSTITUTIONAL RIGHT

From the foregoing, it should be clear that the parole board is crucial in a preventive justice regime. Those familiar with the traditional parole board might find this position disturbing. Although, as noted at the beginning of this chapter, parole release probably compares favorably to determinate sentencing in terms of reducing prison terms, the way in which the modern parole process operates still leaves much to be desired. As Steven Chanenson put it, "Parole release has historically been an unstructured and wildly discretionary power, subject to the same kinds of irrationalities and abuses that afflict old-style, fully discretionary judicial sentencing on the front end."[88]

However, if parole boards are conceived of as part of the risk assessment and management team, they would look and act quite differently than the parole boards Chanenson describes. Not only would they rely on modern risk assessment and abide by a presumption against confinement once the minimum sentence has been served, but they would also be composed primarily of experts in risk-needs assessment, rather than laypeople and correctional

[87] Conditional release programs have been a mainstay of preventive detention for people found not guilty by reason of insanity for decades. See, e.g., Jeffrey Rogers et al., After Oregon's Insanity Defense: A Comparison of Conditional Release and Hospitalization, 5 Int'l J. L. & Psychiat. 391 (1982).

[88] Steven L. Chanenson, Guidance from Above and Beyond, 58 Stan. L. Rev. 175, 187 (2005). See also Kristen Bell, Legal and Empirical Analysis of Parole Decisions, 54 Harv. Civ. Rts. & Civ. Liberties Rev. 454, 459 (2019) (describing as "one of the most longstanding critiques of parole boards: that their decision-making can be arbitrary and capricious in practice"); Kevin R. Reitz, Questioning the Conventional Wisdom of Parole Release Authority, in The Future of Imprisonment 199, 228 (Michael Tonry, ed., 2004) (noting that parole boards have a history of poor process and patronage appointments); Kenneth Culp Davis, Discretionary Justice 126–33 (1976) (calling the federal parole board the most disappointing agency the author had ever encountered).

officials.[89] Just as importantly, rather than the wide-ranging power typically granted such boards, which are usually permitted to consider retributive and general deterrence objectives as well as risk,[90] the parole board in a preventive justice regime would focus entirely on individual prevention goals.

A potential obstacle to making the parole board the centerpiece of a sentencing system is the Supreme Court's stance, dating from the 1980s, that there is no constitutionally recognized right to a parole hearing.[91] Nor, as Chapter 4 pointed out, is there a right to counsel, witnesses, or cross-examination at any hearing that takes place. Thus, the danger is that a state will adopt a preventive justice regime, but fail to provide the primary mechanism for making it work—an expert, formal parole decision-making process.

In the past twenty-five years, however, a number of Supreme Court decisions have provided a basis for changing this situation, both substantively and procedurally. In *Graham v. Florida*,[92] the Court held unconstitutional a mandatory life without parole sentence for juveniles who commit homicide, and in *Miller v. Alabama*,[93] it extended that ruling to bar all mandatory life without parole sentences for juveniles. The Court's rationale for these decisions turned in large part on its assessment of the ways in which mandatory life sentences are inconsistent with the goals of punishment, two of which—incapacitation and rehabilitation–virtually require parole hearings. As the *Graham* Court explained:

89 See Stefan J. Bing, Note, Reconsidering State Parole Board Membership Requirements in Light of Model Penal Code Sentencing Revisions, 100 Ky. L. J. 871, 888 (2012) (arguing that, given the movement toward evidence-based sentences, parole boards, should include "social scientists in the fields of sociology, psychology, or statistics"); Edward D. Rhine, Joan Petersilia & Kevin R. Reitz, The Future of Parole Release, 46 Crime & Justice 279, 282 (2017) (arguing the same, although contrary to the proposal here, limiting the parole board to a single decision at the end of the minimum sentence, and capping a sentence enhancement to an amount equal to 25–30 percent of the maximum allowable sentence for the offense, the upper end of the relevant range, or fifteen years, whichever comes first).

90 David Ball, Heinous, Atrocious, and Cruel: *Apprendi*, Indeterminate Sentencing, and the Meaning of Punishment, 109 Colum. L. Rev. 893, 903–04 (2009) (stating that "[n]one of the due process cases limits the parole board's authority to its core institutional competence—measuring an offender's threat to public safety—and parole boards can therefore find facts that sound in both retribution and dangerousness," and finding that, in California, parole boards routinely do so).

91 Hewitt v. Helms, 459 U.S. 460, 467–68 (1983) ("[T]here is no constitutional or inherent right to parole and the Constitution itself does not guarantee good-time credit for satisfactory behavior while in prison despite the undoubted impact of such credits on the freedom of inmates"); Conn. Bd. of Pardons v. Dumschat, 452 U.S. 458, 464 (1981) (observing that there is no constitutional entitlement to parole).

92 560 U.S. 48 (2010).

93 567 U.S. 460 (2012).

> Even if the State's judgment that Graham was incorrigible were later corroborated by prison misbehavior or failure to mature, *the sentence was still disproportionate because that judgment was made at the outset.* A life without parole sentence improperly denies the juvenile offender a chance to demonstrate growth and maturity. Incapacitation cannot override all other considerations, lest the Eighth Amendment's rule against disproportionate sentences be a nullity.
>
> [Nor can a] sentence of life imprisonment without parole . . . be justified by the goal of rehabilitation. The penalty forswears altogether the rehabilitative ideal. By denying the defendant the right to reenter the community, the State makes an irrevocable judgment about that person's value and place in society. *This judgment is not appropriate in light of a juvenile nonhomicide offender's capacity for change* and limited moral culpability.[94]

The Court concluded: "A State need not guarantee the offender eventual release, but if it imposes a sentence of life it must provide him or her with some realistic opportunity to obtain release before the end of that term."[95]

Of course, *Graham* and *Miller* made clear they were limiting their reach to mandatory life without parole sentences for juveniles. They were not addressing other types of mandatory sentences, nor were they dealing with adult sentencing. But, in a preventive justice regime, once an offender has served the minimum demanded by retributive and deterrence objectives, the Court's concern about the irreconcilability of irrevocable sentences with the incapacitative and rehabilitative goals of punishment logically affects adult sentences as well. As Richard Bierschbach argues,

> *Graham* recognized the significance of parole—and, implicitly, back-end sentencing generally—to the constitutional regulation of punishment. . . . If taken seriously, *Graham's* view of parole could result in more textured, considered, and just sentences, ones that seek not only to deter and condemn but also to further restoration, reconciliation, and other soft but important values the Court saw as being bound up in parole.[96]

Parole review should also be relatively frequent, both for those offenders who are not released at the end of the minimum term and for those who are

94 Id. at 73–74 (emphasis added).

95 Id. at 82.

96 Richard Bierschbach, Proportionality and Parole, 160 U. Pa. L. Rev. 1745, 1788 (2012). See also Flores v. Stanford, 2019 WL 4572703 (S.D.N.H., 2019) (holding that a plausible Eighth Amendment violation has been alleged if parole board members "have denied, and continue to deny, juvenile lifers release to parole supervision based *only* on the crime committed or juvenile criminal history" . . . "*despite* clear evidence of rehabilitation and maturity") (emphasis in original).

subject to supervision after release. In *Garner v. Jones*,[97] the Supreme Court held that a prolonged hiatus between parole hearings violates the Ex Post Facto Clause if it "create[s] a significant risk of increased punishment" relative to the sentence contemplated at the time of sentencing.[98] If a judge sentences an offender to an indefinite term that presumptively ends when the minimum is reached, as proposed here, a failure of the parole board to conduct frequent periodic reviews after that point could violate that rule. That notion is bolstered by the Supreme Court's decision in *Kansas v. Hendricks*.[99] In upholding the constitutionality of post-sentence commitment of sexually violent offenders—commitments based entirely on the offender's risk, just as those in a preventive regime would be after the minimum sentence is served—*Hendricks* indicated that "constitutional provisions for care and treatment" require release when the offender is no longer dangerous, and noted that the statute in question effectuated that rule by entitling those committed to "*annual* review to determine whether continued detention was warranted."[100]

Even if all of this is conceded, parole boards still might not provide much in the way of review if the procedures remain as anemic as those described in the previous chapter. Recall that, if the prescriptions advanced there are followed, most fit and validity questions about RAIs should be settled jurisdiction-wide, so that case-by-case litigation on those points is not necessary. And if the reasoning in Chapter 2 is followed, a failure to show a high risk of violent crime should require release. Nonetheless, procedural injustice is still likely unless offenders are afforded a more robust adversarial process than currently exists, one that meaningfully enables them to challenge inaccurate information or improper adjustments to the RAI.

Once again, Supreme Court case law—this time much older—might provide a wedge, given the fact that, in a preventive justice regime, the offender is entitled to release at the completion of the minimum sentence unless the board determines he or she poses a high risk of reoffending. Under these circumstances, the parole determination is more akin to the determination made at a parole *revocation* hearing than an initial parole proceeding.[101] In *Morrissey v. Brewer*,[102] the Court required much more process at such

97 529 U.S. 244, 251 (2000).

98 Id. at 255 (stating that a prisoner must show that a rule prolonging time in prison without a parole hearing "created a significant risk of increasing his punishment").

99 521 U.S. 346 (1997).

100 Id. at 353 (emphasis added).

101 Jacob Schuman has also argued that, to the extent the parole board grants "supervised release" rather than outright parole, more process is required. Jacob Schuman, Supervised Release is Not Parole, 53 Loyola L.A. L. Rev. 587 (2020).

102 408 U.S. 471 (1972).

proceedings, including the rights to notice, be present, proffer witnesses and documentary evidence, confront and cross-examine adverse witnesses, and "a written statement by the factfinders as to the evidence relied on and reasons for revoking parole."[103] And in a later case, the Court held that individuals subject to parole and probation revocation proceedings also have a right to counsel, when "a disputed issue can fairly be represented only by a trained advocate."[104] That will almost always be true at the initial parole hearing when the results of the first post-conviction RAI are considered, and in many cases at subsequent hearings as well, especially if the claim is that *Jackson*'s dictates about ensuring the least restrictive available intervention are being violated.[105]

The resources for this more formal parole process could come from a decline in appeals of judicially imposed sentences. Such a decline is highly likely in a preventive justice regime because, whether the result of a guilty plea or the judge's decision after a trial, the sentence will be vulnerable only in the unlikely event the judge picks the wrong sentencing range. Thus, resources that today are devoted to sentence appeals—which can be numerous, especially in determinate sentencing systems[106]—can be transferred to parole hearings and appeals of parole board decisions in a preventive justice regime. Appellate courts presumably would defer to board decisions in most cases, especially if the board relies on an RAI approved by the relevant jurisdiction-wide authority. But they could reverse a board's decision when it is arbitrary and capricious because it clearly violates fit, validity, or fairness criteria or the preventive justice principles outlined above. The result should be a much-improved parole hearing process.

In short, preventive justice and its reliance on RAIs should trigger more oversight of a post-conviction process that has long been ignored.[107] It might

[103] Id. at 489.

[104] Gagnon v. Scarpelli, 411 U.S. 778, 788 (1973).

[105] See Flores v. Stanford, 2019 WL 4572703 *11 (S.D.N.H., 2019) (holding that a due process claim is stated when "[p]arole Board commissioners commonly do not even read such offenders' files before conducting parole interviews or making parole determinations; make parole determinations based at least in part on a risk assessment algorithm the workings of which no defendant knows or understands; predetermine parole outcomes before conducting parole interviews; and pay no attention to other commissioners' questions and offenders' answers during interviews").

[106] Wayne LaFave et al., 6 Criminal Procedure 738 (3d ed. 2007) (noting that appeals of sentences in indeterminate regimes were rare, but that "[w]ith the advent of presumptive sentencing and guideline sentencing, the landscape of appellate sentencing review in this country was altered dramatically").

[107] Laura I. Appleman, Retributive Justice and Hidden Sentencing, 68 Ohio St. L. J. 1307, 1307 (2007). ("Largely concealed from the public eye, components of hidden sentencing such as

also help bring out of the shadows a *pre*-conviction process that has long resisted regulation.

5.4 PREVENTIVE JUSTICE AND PLEA BARGAINING

The foregoing discussion proceeded on the assumption that determinate, retributively oriented sentences are primarily the product of judicial decision-making. In fact, however, that is usually not the case. As Justice Kennedy stated in *Lafler v. Cooper*, "criminal justice today is for the most part a system of pleas, not a system of trials,"[108] pleas that often produce a disposition agreed upon by the parties and presented as a fait accompli to the judge, who more often than not signs off on it. Whether justifiable or not, the dominance of plea bargaining and guilty pleas is understandable. The huge increase in criminal cases since the 1960s,[109] combined with the expense, in both time and money, of full-blown jury trials, has made plea bargaining the primary engine of American criminal justice,[110] the mechanism for resolving over 95 percent of all criminal cases.[111]

Prosecutors wield an enormous amount of power in the plea bargaining process. It is well documented that the trial penalty can be three to four times the plea bargain deal (in *Lafler*, for instance, the plea offer-trial differential was more than 350 percent),[112] and it rarely falls below a 15 percent increase.[113]

probation, parole, and post-release supervision have been ignored by both scholars and policy-makers.")

108 566 U.S. 156, 170 (2012).

109 In 1960, the FBI reported 2,019,600 index crimes; by 1972 the number was 5,891,924. FBI, U.S. Dep't of Justice, Crime in the United States 1972: Uniform Crime Reports 61 tbl.1 (1973).

110 Writing over thirty years ago when trials were simpler than they are now, Albert Alschuler wrote, "[r]eluctant to reconsider our expensive trial procedures, we press most defendants to forgo even the more expeditious form of [bench] trial that defendants once were freely afforded as a matter of right." Albert A. Alschuler, Implementing the Criminal Defendant's Right to Trial: Alternatives to the Plea Bargaining System, 50 U. Chi. L. Rev. 931, 971–72 (1983).

111 Stephanos Bibas, Regulating the Plea-Bargaining Market: From Caveat Emptor to Consumer Protection, 99 Cal. L. Rev. 1117, 1138 (2011). ("[T]oday, 95 percent of criminal convictions result from guilty pleas and only 5 percent result from trials. Plea bargaining is no longer a negligible exception to the norm of trials; it is the norm.")

112 Lafler was charged with assault with intent to kill and three other offenses. The prosecutor offered to dismiss two of the charges and recommend a sentence of 51 to 85 months to the judge; when Lafler refused the deal he was tried on all counts, convicted and sentenced to 185 to 360 months. 132 S.Ct. at 1383.

113 Nancy J. King et al., When Process Affects Punishment: Differences in Sentences after Guilty Plea, Bench Trial, and Jury Trial in Five Guidelines States, 105 Colum. L. Rev. 959, 992 (2005) (finding increases in sentences for those who go to trial ranging "from 13% to 461% in Washington, from 58% to 349% in Maryland, and from 23% to 95% in Pennsylvania").

Even in a regime, such as the federal sentencing guidelines, that stipulates a narrow retributive range for a particular crime, the formal discount for a guilty plea is substantial (25–35 percent), and presumably well beyond what even a flexible retributivist would permit.[114]

The Supreme Court has seen nothing wrong with this situation. Representative is *Bordenkircher v. Hayes*.[115] There the prosecution told Paul Hayes, charged with his third offense (uttering a forged check), that if he did not plead guilty and accept a five-year sentence he faced trial under a three-strikes statute that required life in prison upon conviction; Hayes refused the deal, was convicted and was sentenced to life.[116] The Court upheld the life sentence. Although recognizing that the "breadth of discretion that our country's legal system vests in prosecuting attorneys carries with it the potential for individual and institutional abuse," due process was not violated in this case because the prosecutor "no more than openly presented the defendant with the unpleasant alternatives of forgoing trial or facing charges on which he was plainly subject to prosecution."[117] While true, the latter statement ignores the fact that the two alternatives in the *Hayes* case—five years versus a life sentence—bore no relationship to one another, under any theory of punishment (retributive, deterrent, or incapacitative).

Usually, of course, defendants like Hayes take the deal, sometimes because it provides more certainty, but most often because it is simply too good to turn down given the alternative. As federal district court judge Jed Rakoff noted in 2012, "the average sentence for federal narcotics defendants who entered into any kind of plea bargain was five years and four months, while the average sentence for defendants who went to trial was sixteen years."[118] Research indicates that sometimes the differential is even significant enough to induce guilty pleas from people who are entirely innocent, because they are so fearful of the sentence that would be imposed after conviction at trial.[119]

114 Stephanos Bibas, Plea Bargaining Outside the Shadow of Trial, 117 Harv. L. Rev. 2463, 2488 (2004). Bibas notes that informal discounts are often far greater, especially in connection with charge bargaining. Id. at 2536.

115 434 U.S. 357 (1978).

116 Id. at 665–66.

117 Id. at 365.

118 Jed Rakoff, Why Innocent People Plead Guilty, N.Y. Rev. Books, Nov. 20, 2014.

119 See Lucian E. Dervan & Vanessa A. Edkins, The Innocent Defendant's Dilemma: An Innovative Empirical Study of Plea Bargaining's Innocence Problem, 103 J. Crim. L. & Criminology 1, 34, 36 (2013) (detailing a laboratory study finding that over 50 percent of the "innocent" subjects pleaded guilty and accepted minimal punishment to avoid more aversive treatment); Alexandra Natapoff, Misdemeanors, 85 S. Cal. L. Rev. 1313, 1313 (2012) ("[I]nnocent misdemeanants routinely plead guilty to get out of jail because they cannot afford bail"); D. Michael Risinger, Tragic Consequences of Deadly Dilemmas: A Response to

Front-end sentencing, of the type that occurs in determinate and limiting retributivist regimes like Norval Morris's, exacerbates this situation. In these types of systems, the sentence is largely controlled by the charge, which is completely controlled by the prosecutor. While judges retain formal authority to set sentence, that authority is constrained by the narrow range associated with the charges agreed upon by the parties. Given the fact that criminal conduct can often fit within several different crime categories, or can be split into multiple counts, this charging authority gives the prosecutor tremendous leverage over defendants, particularly when mandatory minima are attached to the charges.[120] As Angela Davis summarizes, "the prosecutor's control over charging and plea bargaining decisions gives her the power to control the entire criminal justice system."[121]

A preventive justice system could have a significant, felicitous impact on this situation. Many of the advantages of plea bargaining could be maintained, while its negative effects could be minimized. That is because when sentencing is controlled at the back-end, by a parole board, the specific charge becomes largely irrelevant; risk becomes the focus once the minimum sentence is served.

At first glance, the preventive justice paradigm might appear to be *too* successful at reducing prosecutorial leverage. If, as occurs in such a regime, the length and nature of sentences are largely determined by back-end decisionmakers, prosecutors would seem to have little of substance to offer defendants prior to trial, and plea bargaining would be hard to sustain. In his mammoth study on plea bargaining in the nineteenth and twentieth centuries, George Fisher documented this dynamic.[122] Based on his examination of practice in Massachusetts, California and New York, Fisher concluded that "[t]he demise of the indeterminate sentence, one of the most promising of the late nineteenth century's progressive brainchildren, bears the mark of plea bargaining's malice."[123] Because indeterminate sentencing robs both prosecutors and judges of the power to control sentence lengths, it "hobbled the plea-

Allen and Laudan, 40 Seton Hall L. Rev. 991, 996 (2010) (estimating an "absolute floor" of 4.5 percent wrongful convictions resulting from guilty pleas in serious felony cases).

120 See, e.g., Cynthia Hujar Orr, Mandatory Minimum Sentencing Provisions under Federal Law 8 (2010). ("[E]ven if a defendant has minimal culpability or a strong defense, faced with a mandatory minimum sentence of ten or more years, a defendant will almost always forego his right to a trial.")

121 Angela Davis, The Prosecutor's Duty to End Mass Incarceration, 44 Hofstra L. Rev. 1063, 1071 (2016).

122 George Fisher, Plea Bargaining's Triumph, 109 Yale L. J. 857 (2000).

123 Id. at 860.

bargaining regime," and thus was resisted (and eventually upended) by both groups.[124]

But Fisher's study also reveals that some forms of this resistance allowed indeterminate sentences to co-exist with plea bargaining. For instance, in states where indeterminate sentence provisions applied only if the defendant went to state prison, prosecutors and defendants agreed to non-prison dispositions, either in less secure institutions or under probationary conditions.[125] Prosecutors also prevailed upon parole authorities to release pleading defendants when the minimum sentence expired, if they had "behaved" while in prison or successfully completed treatment.[126]

These adjustments signal a way in which plea bargaining could work within a preventive justice regime. Attorneys would commission their own risk assessments as part of the pretrial process.[127] In those cases involving very serious crimes or very high risk offenders the prosecutor might not be willing to bargain at all. But in other cases the prosecutor might offer the defendant probation, a partially suspended sentence, a minimum security setting, or the minimum prison term for a reduced charge, contingent upon the defendant admitting criminal conduct, waiving the right to jury, and completing a designated risk management program. The risk management program might include substance abuse treatment, vocational training, anger management, and a host of other rehabilitative programs, either within or outside of prison.[128] If the defendant accepts the offer, and the judge signs off on the agreement, then the parole board would be bound by the arrangement. If the program is not completed successfully, then the terms of the agreement would

124 Id.

125 Id. at 1048–49; 1055–56 (describing Fisher's study of nineteenth and early twentieth century practice in Massachusetts' indeterminate sentencing regime, in which the percentage of state prison sentences decreased as a result of plea bargaining, and a study in California in the early 1970s, during the heyday of indeterminate sentencing in that state, which indicated that "the most important axis along which plea bargaining took place became the distinction between a state-prison term and no state-prison term").

126 Id. at 1054, 1056 (describing practice in Illinois and California in which "some judges and prosecutors appealed to parole authorities to stand by promises made in the course of plea negotiations that the defendant would walk free on a certain date").

127 If the assessment assumed that the defendant has committed the crime charged, that assumption would not be admissible at trial if the parties did not reach agreement. See Fed.R.Evid. 410 (prohibiting introduction at trial of statements made during plea bargaining).

128 As noted in Section 2.6, in general, programs that are therapeutic rather than punitive, aim at high-risk offenders, and take place in the community are the most effective at reducing risk. Brandon C. Welsh et al., Promoting Change, Changing Lives: Effective Prevention and Intervention to Reduce Serious Offending, in From Juvenile Delinquency to Adult Crime: Criminal Careers, Justice Policy, and Prevention 245 (Rolf Loeber & David P. Farrington, eds., 2012).

establish the consequence: a different program, revocation of probation and imprisonment, more onerous prison conditions, or extension of the prison sentence, with ultimate control of the individual's disposition once again in the hands of the parole board, informed by the results of an RAI.

Fisher's research indicates that this type of agreement can work, because prosecutors are able to make a concrete promise, up-front, despite a sentencing structure featuring a back-end decision-maker. Practice today confirms that observation. The agreements reached in a preventive justice regime would probably not be that different from those obtained today in the run-of-the-mill misdemeanor or lower level felony case, where sentence is often suspended and probationary conditions are imposed.[129] They would be even closer in form to those that occur on a routine basis in today's drug courts, where either sentencing or prosecution is suspended if the defendant agrees to undergo substance abuse treatment and succeeds at it.[130] The added advantage is that offenders have a heightened incentive to complete such programs.

While this plea bargaining regime thus has analogues in current practice, it also differs from today's bargaining system because it takes place in the shadow of an indeterminate sentencing system where defendants who do not bargain have their ultimate disposition determined by a parole board. In such a regime, many defendants will be most interested in trading for dispositional certainty and a particular dispositional environment, and only secondarily for a reduction in sentence length. Indeed, the *duration* of an offender's sentence might be roughly the same regardless of whether a bargain occurs; in both bargained and non-bargained cases a risk assessment (by the parties and the parole board, respectively) will play the predominant role.[131] Because of this possible durational similarity between a bargained sentence and a parole board sentence, plea bargaining in a preventive justice regime would be less one-sided. The prosecutor would not be able to threaten long post-trial sentences of the type involved in *Hayes* and in Judge Rakoff's drug cases,

[129] Michael M. O'Hear, Plea Bargaining and Procedural Justice, 42 Ga. L. Rev. 409, 464 (2008). ("In misdemeanor and other low-level cases, the defendant is apt to receive a sentence of straight probation or a relatively brief period of closer supervision.")

[130] Ryan S. King & Jill Pasquerilla, Drug Courts: A Review of the Evidence 3 (2009), available at http://www.sentencingproject.org/doc/dpdrugcourts.pdf (describing the two models of drug courts as "deferred prosecution and diversion"—where successful completion of the program avoids prosecution—and "post-adjudication"—where defendants plead guilty but avoid sentence and perhaps have their conviction expunged if they successfully complete the program).

[131] According to Fisher, the usual practice under indeterminate sentencing regimes in the early twentieth century was to release prisoners at the completion of the minimum term. Fisher, supra note 122, at 1050.

because there would be no such sentences. At most, the prosecutor would only be able to suggest that a failure to accept an offer will expose the defendant to a particular maximum sentence, full imposition of which will depend on an uncertain parole process and, in cases where serious needs are identified, the offender him or herself.

The prosecutor will still have control over charging, and thus some control over the minimum sentence. This power is unlikely to be significant under the sentencing ranges proposed earlier, where the lowest three categories all have a minimum of one year. Of course, a legislature might opt for more categories, with greater gaps between minima. If the history of federal sentencing is any guide, prosecutors interested in more bargaining power will lobby for precisely that type of regime; as Shon Hopwood has demonstrated, federal prosecutors "often advocate for policies that make it easier . . . to charge and incarcerate people—as if that is the only worthy goal of the federal criminal justice system. And all too often federal policymakers—whether members of Congress, the White House, or the U.S. Sentencing Commission—have listened."[132] But if those policymakers stand by a parole-driven system of the type described here, such changes should be largely cosmetic. While every minimum sentence must be served in a limiting retributivist system, it need not be served in prison, when, based on a risk-needs assessment, a judge at the front-end concludes otherwise. And defendants will know that even if they reject a plea based on a lower charge than the prosecutor will insist on at trial, any post-trial sentence imposed will be driven by a risk assessment after the minimum on the higher charge is served. Thus, even aggressive politicking will not provide appreciably greater leverage for prosecutors dealing with lower risk defendants.

Under these circumstances, innocent people will be less likely to plead guilty and guilty people will be less likely to accept unduly harsh offers. Further, given the prosecution's relatively reduced power, negotiations are likely to be more meaningful than the take-it-or-leave it phenomenon that characterizes pretrial bargaining today. It is also likely that there will be fewer plea agreements overall even with guilty defendants. But if Fisher's findings are correct about how plea bargaining worked 100 years ago in the shadow of indeterminancy, deals will still be common.[133] While some guilty defendants may be willing to gamble on the parole board, others who are risk averse will want the certainty of the plea agreement rather than the uncertainty of the

[132] Shon Hopwood, The Misplaced Trust in the DOJ's Expertise on Criminal Justice Policy, 118 Mich. L. Rev. 1181, 1184 (2020).

[133] Fisher, supra note 122, at 1056–57 (summarizing reasons plea bargaining and indeterminate sentences coexisted).

indeterminate sentence, especially if less of the sentence is spent in prison.[134] Defendants may also want to plead guilty to settle their case quickly, avoid publicity, reduce pretrial detention (although such detention should be rare if RAIs are used), or minimize the collateral consequences of conviction on more serious charges.[135]

Plea bargaining recognizes that, in the typical case, the principal decision will be about disposition rather than guilt. If that is so, it makes sense to shift criminal justice power from lawyers to experts, especially if the disposition is aimed at achieving preventive goals like rehabilitation and specific deterrence. Preventive justice not only can coexist with plea bargaining but should enhance its ability to arrive at efficient, accurate results.

5.5 CONCLUSION: PREVENTIVE JUSTICE IN PRACTICE

Sentencers today are required to consider an amalgam of factors—principally, culpability, general deterrence, and the individual prevention goals of specific deterrence, rehabilitation, and incapacitation that can be informed by a risk-needs assessment. Preventive justice separates the individual prevention goals from other considerations. No longer, for instance, would prosecutors or judges have to balance the mitigating impact of youth or mental difficulties against the possibility that they contribute to an offender's dangerousness. Judges would not need to decide what to do when an offense calls for a long sentence on deterrence grounds, but a short sentence on culpability or risk grounds. These types of calculations are difficult, if not impossible, for judges to carry out with any degree of "accuracy"; the inherent conflict between sentencing goals has long been recognized.[136] Instead, retributive and deterrence considerations would determine the legislatively authorized sentence ranges, and the judge's only jobs would be to select the appropriate range and decide whether the minimum will be served in or out of prison, informed in the typical case by the parties through the plea bargaining process and the results of an RAI. Then, the parole board, relying on risk-needs assessment using RAIs, would control what happens after the minimum sentence is

134 Further, a reduction in the amount of plea bargaining could enhance efficiency. Darryl K. Brown, The Perverse Effects of Efficiency in the Criminal Process, 100 Va. L. Rev. 183, 186 (2014) ("[p]lea bargaining ... can perversely increase demand for criminal prosecutions" because it facilitates them).

135 See Thea Johnson, Fictional Pleas, 94 Ind. L. J. 855 (2019) (describing "fictional pleas" to lesser charges in an effort to avoid collateral consequences).

136 See Roscoe Pound, Criminal Justice and the American City, in Criminal Justice in Cleveland 576 (Roscoe Pound & Felix Frankfurter, eds., 1922) (noting the "fundamental conflict with respect to aims and purposes" of punishment theory).

served. This division of responsibility makes sense: legislatures are best equipped to make general evaluations of culpability and deterrence; lawyers, juries and judges are best situated to evaluate culpability in individual cases; and parole boards have the most expertise about risk.

A couple of concrete examples of how preventive justice would work may be useful. Take first Paul Hayes, the individual in *Bordenkircher v. Hayes* who went to trial on an uttering charge and received life in prison under a habitual offender statute. Such a statute could still exist in a preventive justice system, if members of the legislature or sentencing commission are able, with a straight face, to conclude that any combination of three felonies makes a person sufficiently blameworthy to deserve a sentence exceeded only by the death penalty, and if lawmakers also conclude that it is permissible, from a desert point of view, to enhance a sentence based on convictions for which the individual has already served his sentence. As it is today, however, habitual offender statutes are usually as much incapacitative as retributive in motivation;[137] to the extent they are the former, they would be improper in a preventive justice regime, because a defendant's risk is based on individualized RAI assessments, not blanket conclusions that anyone who commits three felonies will be high risk the rest of his or her life.

Suppose that, consistent with these points, the legislature has enacted a habitual offender statute that, unlike the statute in *Hayes*, more reasonably merely triples (solely on retributive grounds) the minimum and maximum for felony offenders with two or more previous felonies. Under the five-tier scheme described in this chapter, Hayes' most recent crime of forgery would probably fit in the fourth sentencing category, with a range of one year to three years. Because of his two prior convictions—the first for detaining a female (a lesser included offense of rape) when he was seventeen years old, for which he served five years in a reformatory, and the second for robbery, for which he received probation for five years—Hayes would thus be subject to a three-year minimum and a nine-year maximum.

If this statute existed in a determinate sentencing regime, the prosecutor could threaten Hayes with prosecution under the habitual offender statute and a maximum sentence of nine years after conviction, unless he pleads guilty to a lesser penalty. In contrast, in a preventive justice regime, Hayes and the

137 See Rhys Hester et al., Prior Record Enhancements at Sentencing: Unsettled Justifications and Unsettling Consequences 209, 223 (2018). ("Character theories can eventually lead to the conclusion that the offender is such an outlaw that he has forfeited any right to have his punishment limited by retributive, human rights, or other deontological principles. Such an open-ended forfeiture concept may indeed be the core rationale of three-strikes and repeat and career offender statutes, which almost all retributive scholars oppose.")

prosecutor would both know that, even if Hayes is convicted as an habitual offender and the judge selects imprisonment, there is a possibility of release after three years, depending on the risk-needs assessment of the parole board. Faced with those facts, and perhaps also with the results from an RAI submitted by the defendant or commissioned by the state, the bargaining position of the prosecutor would be much weaker, and might result in a more lenient disposition–for instance, a year in prison followed by two years of probation during which Hayes would have to make restitution for the forgery and complete vocational training. If Hayes agreed and the prosecutor recommended the deal to the judge, that is likely to be Hayes' sentence. If the parties cannot agree, and Hayes is convicted at trial as an habitual offender, the judge would sentence him to three to nine years, with the ultimate penalty after three years to be decided by the parole board, meeting annually.

The case of Eric Loomis, referenced several times in this book, is more complicated. Loomis was charged with five offenses: (1) first-degree recklessly endangering safety; (2) attempting to flee or elude a traffic officer; (3) operating a motor vehicle without the owner's consent; (4) possession of a firearm by a felon; (5) possession of a short-barreled shotgun or rifle.[138] He agreed to plead guilty to the second and third charges. The maximum penalty for those crimes, if the sentences were served consecutively, was seventeen years and six months. The judge, after receiving the COMPAS score, which rated Loomis "high risk," sentenced him to six years of imprisonment and five years of extended supervision after release.[139]

Under the scheme outlined in this chapter, the maximum for the two charges to which Loomis pleaded guilty would be much lower. But assume that all five charges are in play. Similar to what would occur under the current system, those charges allow the prosecutor to threaten Loomis with fairly high minimum and maximum sentences, assuming the relevant statutes, the jurisdiction's sentencing guidelines, and the double jeopardy clause permit the sentences for all five crimes to be served consecutively.[140] The difference in a preventive justice regime is that, at the end of his minimum sentence, whatever it is, Loomis could be considered lower risk than he currently is and thus earn release. That possibility should temper any tendency on the part of the prosecutor toward a harsh offer.

138 881 N.W2d at 754.

139 Id. at 756.

140 For a discussion of how these three legal sources interact (and why the relevant law governing this interaction should be changed), see Michael L. Seigel & Christopher Slobogin, Prosecuting Martha: Federal Prosecutorial Power and the Need for a Law of Counts, 109 Penn St. L. Rev. 1107 (2005).

In both of these cases, the job of the judge at sentencing would be to confirm that the defendant has committed the crime charged and to impose the statutory sentence or sentences, based either on the plea deal, his or her reassessment of that deal, or a jury's verdict. The judge need not agonize over how desert, risk, deterrence and other considerations interact, because the convicted offender will always serve the minimum associated with the charge of conviction (in prison or in the community, depending primarily on the offender's risk designation), and will only serve beyond that period if the parole board determines it is necessary based on its risk-needs assessment. This scheme immensely simplifies the sentencing decision, which many judges today believe is the "most trying," the "most difficult," and the most "emotional[ly] taxing aspect of their job."[141] Separating the culpability and risk determinations also eliminates the danger that use of RAIs will make risk more "salient" to the judge than other punishment concerns, and thus also avoids the possibility, suggested in some research, that high risk scores will harm poor defendants more than wealthier ones when they draw judges who are otherwise willing to be more lenient to those in straitened circumstances.[142]

This version of limiting retributivism is similar to the indeterminate sentencing of yore, a system that was quite popular in this country through the mid-twentieth century.[143] The essential rationale for it was put forth by Herbert Wechsler, who wrote in his 1961 defense of such a system:

> Even when aided by a competent presentence study and report, the court is poorly equipped at the time of sentence to make solid and decisive judgments on the period required for the process of correction to realize its optimum potentiality or for the risk of further criminality to reach a level where release of the offender appears reasonably safe. The organs of correction, on the other hand, are best equipped to make decisions of this order and to make them

141 See Mike Scarcella, The Hardest Thing about Being a Judge? Feb. 19, 2020, available at https://www.law.com/nationallawjournal/2020/02/19/the-hardest-thing-about-being-a-judge-what-courts-say-about-sentencing/?slreturn=20200422140025.

142 See Jennifer L. Skeem, Nicholas Scurich & John Monahan, Impact of Risk Assessment on Judges' Fairness in Sentencing Relatively Poor Defendants, 44 L. & Hum. Beh. 51 (2020) ("When risk assessment information was added . . . judges were more likely to sentence the relatively poor defendant to incarceration than his more affluent counterpart").

143 See Douglas A. Berman, Re-Balancing Fitness, Fairness and Finality for Sentences, 4 Wake Forest J. L. & Pol'y 151, 157 (2014). ("As the rehabilitation ideal grew in prominence throughout the 1900s, trial judges . . . were afforded nearly unfettered discretion to impose upon criminal defendants just about any prison term selected from within wide statutory ranges, and parole officials exercised similar discretion concerning actual release dates.")

> later on in time, in light of observation and experience within the institution.[144]

Beginning in the late 1960s, enthusiasm for indeterminate sentencing withered, and it is fair to say that there are many fewer adherents of it today. However, if desert is given its due through sentencing ranges, if parole boards are professionalized and their decisions subject to review, and if those boards use RAIs that are developed properly and properly used, indeterminate sentencing should be given another chance. The preventive justice version of limiting retributivism, in which sentences are constrained by broad conceptions of desert and are otherwise based on scientifically vetted assessments of risk and on periodic reviews of how well risk has been managed, can incorporate attractive elements of both retributive and consequential theories of punishment and at the same time put a dent in the modern prosecutor's inordinate power.

144 Herbert Wechsler, Sentencing, Correction and the Model Penal Code, 109 U.Penn. L. Rev. 465, 476 (1961).

6

Moving Forward

The Need for Experimentation

For cultural reasons that distinguish us from much of the rest of the world, our prisons and jails are teeming with more prisoners per capita than any other country, at incredible expense nationwide. Most of these prisoners will not commit serious crimes if they are released, especially if their criminogenic needs can be identified and accommodated. The vast majority of those in pretrial detention and about 40 percent of those who are imprisoned after conviction are charged or convicted of nonviolent offenses,[1] the majority of whom pose a low risk of violent offending upon release. And among offenders who have committed violent crimes, one study, using a conservative definition, found that over 30 percent posed only a low risk of any type of reoffending,[2] and another study found that this group posed only a slightly higher risk of violent reoffending than offenders convicted of nonviolent crimes.[3] While many of these offenders may deserve substantial punishment

1 Ram Subramanian et al., Incarceration's Front Door: The Misuse of Jails in America 5 (Vera Inst. of Justice, 2015), available at https://www.vera.org/downloads/publications/incarcerations-front-door-report_02.pdf ("nearly 75 percent of the population of both sentenced offenders and pretrial detainees are in jail for nonviolent traffic, property, drug, or public order offenses."); E. Ann Carson, U.S. Dep't. of Justice, NCJ 253516 Prisoners in 2018, at 21 tbl.13 (2020), available at https://www.bjs.gov/content/pub/pdf/p18.pdf (indicating that 55.7 percent of state prisoners are incarcerated for violent crime, ranging from murder—14.3 percent—to aggravated or simple assault—10.8 percent).

2 Michael O'Hear, Early Release for Prisoners Convicted of Violent Crimes: Can Anyone Escape the Incapacitation-Retribution Catch-22?, 52 Conn. L. Rev. 10 (2020) (so finding, assuming a person is "low risk" if they are over sixty, have no prior conviction, or have not committed an offense in the past fifteen years).

3 J. J. Prescott & Sonia Starr, Understanding Violent Crime Recidivism, 95 Notre Dame L. Rev. 1643, 1697–98 (2020) ("Our synthesis of the recidivism literature and our new empirical analysis suggest that this population [offenders serving sentences for violent crimes], especially individuals with prior homicide convictions who are older at release, are unlikely to reoffend, although they are somewhat more likely to commit new violent crimes relative to those released after serving time for nonviolent offenses."); John Anderson, Recidivism of Paroled

on retributive grounds, these numbers suggest that life terms and long mandatory minimum sentences are unnecessary to protect the public even from those who have committed the more heinous offenses.

Risk and needs assessment instruments are crucial tools for pinpointing the hundreds of thousands of arrestees and offenders who can, with relative safety, be diverted to community programs or be released with no restrictions. Without the quantitative clarity and authority of these instruments, governments will have neither the wherewithal nor the will to make serious inroads on our incarcerated populations. Given retributive urges, decriminalization will at most affect the lowest level misdemeanors. For the same reason, significant reductions in sentences for more serious crimes are unlikely to be countenanced by the American public, unless those reductions take place on an individualized basis and can be shown to be of lower risk offenders. And without concrete proof that particular offenders are low risk, our elected and politically appointed decision-makers are, understandably, unlikely to opt against confinement. In short, if the goal is to make significant inroads on the incarcerated population in the United States, risk assessment technology may be the only realistic method of doing so.

Risk assessment instruments will never provide predictive proof beyond a reasonable doubt, and they will always rely on risk factors that correlate with immutable characteristics. But they can be more accurate and objective than any other method of evaluating the potential for reoffending, and they can be structured in a way that violates neither the letter nor the spirit of the Equal Protection Clause. Viewed properly, they do not mechanistically threaten the free will premise of our system, but rather can significantly improve our ability to identify those who will choose, in the exercise of their autonomy, to commit crime in the future.

Of course, this potential can only be achieved if risk assessment instruments are properly constructed and provide the type of information the legal system needs. The bulk of this book has been devoted to developing a jurisprudence of risk that can guide both empiricists and legal decision-makers in developing and using these instruments. In each setting in which risk is an issue, the law

Murderers as a Factor in the Utility of Life Imprisonment, 31 Current Issues in Crim. Just. 255 (2019)(finding, among those imprisoned for homicide, that very few commit another homicide and only a small percentage commit another violent offense); Report of the Independent Review Commitment Pursuant to the Requirements of Title I of the First Step Act 2 (Dec. 21, 2020) (review of PATTERN risk results concluding that "there appears to be no significant difference in the collective recidivism risk files" of those eligible for early release—i.e., those charged with less serious crimes—and those who were not eligible—i.e., those charged with more serious crimes.)

needs to clarify the *fit* issues that risk tools are expected to address. More specifically, policymakers must identify much more precisely than they have to date what likelihood, of what outcome, during what period of time, justifies incarceration as opposed to some lesser intervention (as well as, ideally, specify what those effective alternative interventions are). Government also needs to monitor the *validity* and *fairness* of instruments that purport to answer these questions by evaluating their calibration, discriminant, external, and current validity, and by paying particular attention to whether the instrument's static risk factors (which are most likely to correlate with race, gender or socioeconomic status) provide an appreciable degree of incremental validity. Steps must also be taken to ensure that application of these tools in individual cases is carried out *reliably*; a particularly important aspect of the reliability determination emphasized in this book is ensuring that any adjustments to the results of a valid tool occur only when they derive from research-based factors that are not already incorporated in that tool.

The fit inquiry is a normative one that is best addressed by legislatures, sentencing commissions, and appellate courts. The validity and fairness inquiries are ultimately the responsibility of the courts, but are probably best undertaken initially by a government agency such as a sentencing commission, aided by independent peer reviewers that have the expertise to evaluate empirical claims. The reliability inquiry should be carried out in each case by the relevant legal decision-maker (judge, parole board or correctional official), ideally aided by counsel when judges or parole boards are involved.

All of these evaluations require transparency with respect to the content of risk assessment tools. Trade secret claims by private developers cannot be countenanced; at the least, the agencies and courts evaluating validity should have access to pertinent data *in camera*. Risk algorithms that are based entirely on machine learning can create analogous opacity problems that must be avoided, even if accuracy is thereby sacrificed. Unless such algorithms can eliminate false positives and false negatives entirely (which will not happen in any version of the foreseeable future), defendants whose liberty is at stake, and governments that have a duty to treat its subjects with dignity, should have the ability to challenge the basis of a prediction and how it was reached.

If created and used consistently with these recommendations, risk assessment instruments should have a significant impact on both the pretrial and post-conviction processes. They would have an even greater impact if their results are treated presumptively, that is, given dispositive effect unless adjustments are made under the narrow circumstances described above. And, in the sentencing context, they should have greater impact still if they are used within a system of preventive justice that relies on risk to calibrate the nature and length of sentences within a retributive framework.[4]

As with any set of recommendations, these proposals can be co-opted or manipulated in bad faith, and improperly implemented by those acting in good faith. The inertia and engrained interests of the criminal justice system have often proven immune to reform efforts of the past. In his book *The Failed Promise of Sentencing Reform*,[5] Michael O'Hear paints a depressing picture about the reform efforts that have aimed at lowering incarceration rates over the past two decades. After documenting those failures, he points to both structural and ideological reasons why they recur. In brief, he concludes, when legal actors are given discretion—which is the usual way reformers try to undo the effects of set bail schedules, mandatory minima, truth-in-sentencing, and the like—they tend to maintain the status quo, because "the underlying political dynamics that caused the imprisonment boom have in some important respects remained unchanged."[6]

Most relevant to this book, O'Hear documents that when permitted to ignore RAIs, or to determine for themselves what RAI results mean, judges and correctional officials will take advantage of that discretion to avoid substantially changing their behavior.[7] One of the most blatant recent examples of this dynamic occurred in connection with the PATTERN, the federal sentencing RAI; in the summer, 2020, the Bureau of Prisons—under the direction of the Department of Justice and while the public was distracted by the coronavirus—secretly changed the PATTERN's cut-off scores, with the result that the number of prisoners considered minimum risk has probably been reduced by a factor of ten.[8] Similar examples abound. Presumptive

4 Ben Grunwald has developed a statistical model that can help calculate the impact of various adjustments to our sentencing policies. Ben Grunwald, How to Reduce the Prison Population by X% (2021). Under his model, assuming the reforms proposed in Chapter 5 are applied to current and future offenders so that both admissions and time served are lowered significantly, the prison population in the United States could be reduced by somewhere in the vicinity of 70 percent in five years. Email communication from Ben Grunwald, Feb. 24, 2021.

5 Michael O'Hear, The Failed Promise of Sentencing Reform (2017).

6 Id. at xvii (also noting that repeal of mandatory minima and tough-on-crime laws "do not *require* judges to show great leniency, and that often judges have continued to impose more or less the same sentences they had before reforms took effect.") (emphasis in original).

7 Id. at 80 (noting that North Carolina's justice reinvestment package had virtually no impact on prison populations, in large part because "it left officials with ample discretion to disregard or underuse the new tools").

8 Ian MacDougall, Bill Barr Promised to Release Prisoners Threatened by Coronavirus—Even as the Feds Secretly Made it Harder for Them to Get Out, Propublica, May 26, available at https://www.propublica.org/article/bill-barr-promised-to-release-prisoners-threatened-by-coronavirus-even-as-the-feds-secretly-made-it-harder-for-them-to-get-out.

parole efforts akin to those proposed in Chapter 5, while very successful in increasing early release in some states (and quadrupling early releases in New Jersey), died on the vine in other states because of fear-mongering by law enforcement groups.[9] Community-treatment programs and drug courts meant to be alternatives to prison have, in some jurisdictions, expanded incarcerated populations, because "violations" become a back door to jail, triggered by officials who "have proven loathe to surrender their ultimate source of power over the offenders in their charge."[10] Likewise, attempts at deeper changes, such as reallocation of money away from state prisons and toward "justice reinvestment" initiatives in high-crime neighborhoods, raise the hackles of very powerful law enforcement and correctional groups that have considerable credibility with the public.[11]

Perhaps most importantly, O'Hear suggests, members of the public will continue to listen to tough-on-crime rhetoric until their tendencies to believe in the incorrigibility of criminals, the correlation of crime with race, and the low moral worth of offenders (compared to their victims) can somehow be tempered.[12] On this assumption, O'Hear places his hope in education of the public about the low likelihood of harm from crime compared to other types of injuries, and on humanizing stories about offenders who are often perceived as the "other."[13] He also points to the possibility that larger changes in society, such as reduced economic insecurity and the diversification of the population, could mitigate the punitiveness of American society.[14]

One should not dismiss these suggestions, especially in an era when the Black Lives Matter, Defund the Police, and Abolish Prison movements are taken increasingly seriously. Nor should society ever give up on improving the debilitating social conditions that fuel crime. But changing strongly held beliefs and values among the majority of the population is a long-term project that requires the commitment of the media and politicians, and neither economic security nor integrated populations, even if they do eventually

[9] O'Hear, supra note 5, at 68–69.

[10] Id. at 200–01.

[11] Id. at 202–03 and 211 (describing California's realignment policy in positive terms but noting that it was the result of litigation that went to the Supreme Court, and concluding, with respect to the likelihood of a referendum or statute requiring a similar result, that "[t]he odds would seem very long indeed in the absence of some fundamental rethinking about crime and punishment in U.S. society").

[12] Id. at 204–05 (describing the public's punitive attitudes and concluding that, at most, the public is willing to go along with reform only with respect to nonviolent offenders and only if it saves money).

[13] Id. at 217–22.

[14] Id. at 217.

occur, dissipates fear of crime and criminals.[15] In the meantime, we should experiment with a yet-to-be-tried reform that directly confronts those fears, and that simultaneously helps identify, in a quantifiable way, the societal defects that must be corrected to have a lasting impact on crime and imprisonment rates.[16]

As recounted throughout the foregoing chapters, many jurisdictions are already using risk and needs assessment instruments. But very few vet those instruments through a peer review process, give their results presumptive effect in either the pretrial or post-conviction settings, or train judges, lawyers and correctional officials in their use. Until a few pioneering jurisdictions give RAIs a fair shot, we cannot know whether the hypotheses that this book advances about their benefits will be borne out. If the integration of well-constructed and presumptively applied risk assessment instruments into the pretrial and post-conviction setting does not significantly reduce incarcerated populations, recidivism rates, and prison costs, it is probably not worth pursuing on a nationwide basis. But the bet here is that, without such experimentation, the American carceral system will be stuck where it is now for some time to come.

15 See, e.g., James Forman, Locking Up Our Own: Crime and Punishment in Black America (2017) (documenting the tough-on-crime rhetoric and actions of the predominately black community in Washington, DC).

16 Sandra Mayson, Bias In, Bias Out, 128 Yale L. J. 2218, 2285–86 (2019) (noting risk algorithms can be used as a "diagnostic tool" that can "identify[] sites and causes of racial disparity in criminal justice" and "help[] to illuminate the causal pathways of crime and arrest risk.").

Index

Printed by Integrated Books International,
United States of America